Out of Order

Affirmative Action
and the Crisis of Doctrinaire Liberalism

Out of Order

Affirmative Action
and the Crisis of Doctrinaire Liberalism

Nicholas Capaldi

Prometheus Books
Buffalo, New York

Library of Congress Card Catalog No. 84-43181
ISBN: 9780879752798

For Sidney Hook

Contents

Acknowledgments

The original research for this book was done during the 1978-79 academic year while I had the honor of being both a national fellow and an NEH fellow at the Hoover Institution, Stanford, California. I wish to thank the director of the Hoover Institution, W. Glenn Campbell, the associate director, Dennis L. Bark, and the head of the domestic studies program, Thomas Moore. Among the many staff members at Hoover who went out of their way to make my stay a memorable and productive one I wish to thank Milorad Drachkovitch, George Marotta, James March, Giovanni Sartori, Robert Conquest, John Bunzel, Roger Sherman, Alvin Rabushka, Lewis Gann, Robert Hessen, and Janet Dutra. Other visitors that year who aided as well included Paul Seabury and Joseph Shattan.

I am most especially indebted to the Earhart Foundation, for a summer grant which made possible the time to complete the writing of the manuscript and for its continued encouragement in helping to get the book published.

Additional financial support was provided by the CUNY Research Foundation, for which I wish to thank both the foundation as well as Albert Levenson and James N. Jordan of Queens College who supported my application.

Among the early supporters of my project I owe special thanks to Leonard Sussman of Freedom House; Jude Dougherty, Dean of the School of Philosophy, Catholic University; and Miro Todorovich of University Centers for Rational Alternatives.

A number of individuals have by their own writings, discussions, and example served as an inspiration for my work. They include Sidney Hook, John Bunzel, Paul Seabury, Thomas Sowell, and Barry Gross. Others who have provided suggestions, criticism, and moral support include James Buchanan, Tibor Machan, Nino Langiulli, Tony Flew, Hilail Gildin, Philip Lawler of *Policy Review,* and U.S. Senator Orrin Hatch. I should also acknowledge the unfailing support of my publisher and friend, Paul Kurtz.

Three individuals read early drafts of the manuscript and offered me the benefit of their insight and skill: Lewis Gann, Gene Sachs, and Henry Regnery. Needless to say, none of these many individuals to whom I owe a great debt is in any way responsible for my format, conclusions, or obstinacy.

Affirmative Action, the University, and the Crisis of Doctrinaire Liberalism

> Despair is the price one pays for setting oneself an impossible aim. It is, one is told, the unforgivable sin, but it is a sin the corrupt or evil man never practices. He always has hope. He never reaches the freezing-point of knowing absolute failure. Only the man of good will carries always in his heart this capacity for damnation.—Graham Greene, *The Heart of the Matter*

The policy of affirmative action has disturbed the national conscience for almost two decades. Instead of solving the problem of equal opportunity for which it was presumably designed, it has instead created a new moral dilemma in the form of reverse discrimination. The problems remain unresolved, and we have less of a consensus now than we used to on how even to define those problems.

What we shall pursue is a sustained, comprehensive, and definitive examination of affirmative action, encompassing the historical, legal, political, sociological, economic, and moral dimensions of the issue. But beneath the maelstrom of statistics and court decisions, we shall discover a fundamental debate about the structure of the social world, the nature of man, and a conflict of values.

The focus is on affirmative action in higher education. The choice of focus is not parochial but intrinsic to the problem itself. It is not an accident that most of the controversy over affirmative action has centered on higher education. The Bakke case was just the most dramatic example of this controversy. Affirmative action as a public policy was first applied on a massive and national scale to institutions of higher learning. In retrospect it is easy to see why. To begin with, higher education in America has traditionally been viewed as the symbol of equal opportunity. At the same time, the university has become, in the eyes of many, the primary institution to which we look for help in both defining social problems and seeking solutions to them.

For the university, the result was continuous turmoil. The peculiar bitterness of the controversy reflected a double conflict. One conflict was between the university and those on the outside who sought to impose affirmative action on it. The other conflict was inside the university between those who resisted and those who supported the imposition of affirmative action. Many of those supporters were the social scientists who had formulated and advanced affirmative action as a national priority. What was at issue was not just a debate about public policy but the special relation of the university to public policy formation and implementation.

Here we have come to the crux of the matter and to the central theme of this book. The following chapters will show that affirmative action was the inevitable consequence of the social philosophy known as doctrinaire liberalism, that doctrinaire liberalism is the entrenched philosophy of academic social science, and that affirmative action very nearly destroyed the university as a viable, independent institution—and it would have if that policy had remained unchecked. Since doctrinaire liberalism attaches a special role to education, and since the conflicting demands made upon the university as a whole revealed the inability of doctrinaire liberalism to generate coherent policies, especially in an area crucial to itself, that social philosophy has undergone a crisis of confidence.

The heart of doctrinaire liberalism is the belief that man is the victim of circumstances greater than himself—social, political, and psychological. The masses cannot comprehend these great impersonal forces that guide their destiny. Understanding is necessarily limited to a vanguard of enlightened men and women who can free mankind by obtaining control of the state machinery and using their new-found power for the purpose of breaking the chains that have always fettered mankind. If government intervention, regulation, and control of all existing institutions is necessary in order to liberate the oppressed, then surely the university will be no exception. Indeed, the university is one of the keys to the success of the program. It is but a short step from this to preferential hiring and curriculum control.

In order to challenge doctrinaire liberalism, one must question the belief that the masses are victims of circumstances beyond their control or understanding and that this dictates government intervention in order to liberate them. In fact, it is not just one belief but is embedded in a complex series of assertions, some of which are only implicit. In order to expose the falseness of this *set* of beliefs, we must locate that set within an even wider web of other beliefs and show how the entire fantasy has been spun.

Doctrinaire liberals choose to stress oppression because it seems to dictate the need for state intervention. Therefore, one of the requirements for qualifying as oppressed is that there be some way in which the state can intervene on your behalf. In addition, the oppression must be so obvious and of such long standing that no one would dare either to question it or, more especially, to analyze it. In short, it must have such moral force sufficient to cut off all discussion except about the means to overcome it.

In this book we take blacks as the paradigm case of all oppressed groups. We do so for a number of reasons. Doctrinaire liberals would claim that the most unambiguous case of oppression is the case of blacks. Since this is their strongest suit, any refutation of doctrinaire liberalism here would have grave repercussions. Second, blacks as a case are the most readily apparent to the average reader. Third, this focus will serve to keep the arguments more tightly knit. Other cases can be considered parenthetically. Finally, it is to be noted that blacks enjoy a curious superior moral stature among university intellectuals. One of the worst forms of moral opprobrium in academe is the epithet "racist."

The question we address in this book is not whether blacks have been victimized by discrimination. The question we shall ask is whether affirmative action is based upon a valid definition of the nature and extent of discrimination and whether it is both an adequate and suitable policy for dealing with discrimination. What are the symptoms of the problem or problems with which we are dealing? Is more than one diagnosis possible, and, if so, which are the most plausible? And even if we were to agree on the diagnosis, are we not obliged to raise the question of whether the cure is not worse than the disease?

The issues involved are so emotional, and the stakes for some individuals so high, that we should not be surprised to discover how difficult it is for many to untangle all of the strands involved. Hardly ever will we find serious attempts to distinguish prejudice from discrimination, to define "prejudice," to define "discrimination," to spell out what "equal opportunity" means. All of these concepts require much more careful scrutiny that they have received.

One of the most appalling dimensions confronted in a study of this kind is the simplistic level at which the issues have been engaged by social scientists. Here more than anywhere else one must recognize the extent to which academic social science has allowed itself to be captured by doctrinaire liberalism. The illusion is that society is like a machine. We built it, we know how it works, and we can fix it. There are "right buttons" to push, even if we cannot always find them. We have come to think that when social science finally matures as a science our knowledge and control of the social machine will be comparable to knowledge and control of the physical universe. Meanwhile, it seems to many that we are only just on the way and must make do with the provisional truths that we have. The latter, of course, can be flawed and may not always work out. That is, we may push the wrong buttons. Yet, the seemingly modest belief that there are wrong buttons masks a colossal hubris about there being right buttons.

The task, as I see it, is to unearth our present dominant social philosophy, to recognize it as such, to recognize the extent to which it colors our judgments and evaluations, to understand its history, to note its peculiar development in our society, and gradually to unfold the distortions to which it is subject.

ORGANIZATION OF THE BOOK

This book is divided into three parts. Part 1 deals with the policy of affirmative action. Part 2 deals with the university and its relation to affirmative action. Part 3 is an analysis of the social philosophy of doctrinaire liberalism and its relation to both affirmative action and the university.

Part 1 consists of chapters one and two. In chapter one, "From Jim Crow to Reverse Discrimination," we provide a historical and sociological account, focused upon blacks and education, of the origins of affirmative action. This chapter will provide the groundwork for explaining *how we have shifted from equality of opportunity and individual merit to the concept of group entitlement and statistical equality of result.*

In chapter two, "Twisting the Law," we provide an analysis of the evolution of the policy of affirmative action from the Civil Rights Act of 1964 through the *Bakke* decision and beyond. The emphasis is upon the policy of affirmative action as formulated, developed, applied, and interpreted from the point of view of the federal bureaucracy, specifically the department of Health, Education, and Welfare and the Equal Employment Opportunity Commission. The conclusion reached is that affirmative action is a total, bureaucratic distortion of the original legislative act and subsequent court decisions. We provide a detailed, point by point comparison of legislative acts and court decisions with the restatement of these in bureaucratic directives and policy statements.

Part 2 consists of chapters three, four, and five. In chapter three, "The Modern American University," we provide a historical account of the development of the American university from its inception to today. We account for its structure and how it developed, give a breakdown of the various factions within the academic community who have provided conflicting views of the purpose or purposes of the university, and explain how each of these factions has emerged since the end of the Civil War. A crucial part of the chapter will concern itself with funding and the shift from private sources to public sources. Finally, I identify a new nexus, dubbed the "bureaucratic-academic complex", those members of the social sciences who, in various ways, link the federal bureaucracy with the academic world. The idea of technological social science (social engineering) emerges as the connecting link between affirmative action, the university, and doctrinaire liberalism.

In chapter four, "Federal Regulation of Higher Education," we show what happens when the policies described in chapter two are applied to an institution such as we have described in chapter three. We trace the unfolding logic of affirmative action policies and the subsequent reaction of university administrators and faculties to such policies. One could dwell on the ironies of this situation if it were not for the serious deterioration of the integrity of the university and for the element of corruption that was introduced.

In chapter five, "Fact and Myth about Affirmative Action in Higher Education," we examine every specific argument that has ever been offered for affirmative action. We examine these arguments individually and collectively, and we attempt to present them in the strongest possible light. The upshot is that these arguments are embarrassingly inadequate, unable to withstand either factual confirmation or logical analysis. The conclusion at which we arrive is that *affirmative action is not a solution to a problem; it is, rather, a policy in search of problems.*

Part 3 consists of chapters six through eight. Chapter six, "The Illogic of Affirmative Action," is the philosophical heart of the book. Instead of treating the arguments for affirmative action in isolation, we treat them as part of a larger, integrated theory. Here it will become clear that affirmative action is not designed to ameliorate longstanding and past due grievances but to create a new social order. Affirmative action makes much more sense when seen as encompassing an organic theory of the state, a collectivist notion of society, and a teleological theory about participation. However, this way of saving affirmative action from incoherence invalidates traditional understandings of discrimination, invokes dubious philosophical positions, and leads us in a sinister direction.

Chapter seven, "The Politics of Affirmative Action," examines affirmative action as a form of state activism. Here we identify the political spectrum in American politics, the end of consensus, and how we have progressed from minimal government to state activism and from state activism on behalf of individual rights to state activism on behalf of group entitlement. We argue that group entitlement is not a response to the demands of constituents or to social developments but the creation of politicians and the bureaucratic-academic complex. The second main point made in this chapter is that state activism in general and affirmative action in particular will *lead to fascism.* We indicate how fascism is a product of doctrinaire liberalism. We draw precise parallels between the corporative state of fascism and a projected future America where representation and control of power are by race, sex, and ethnic background.

If affirmative action is not a solution to a problem but a policy with other roots, just what are those roots? In the concluding chapter, "The Impossible Dream," we provide an explanation of how state activism has become a dominant force. There are two intertwined factors. First, state activism is the logical consequence of the theory of doctrinaire liberalism. Second, it is in doctrinaire liberalism, with its alleged experts on human nature and social "laws," that we find a special role, an elitist role, for academic social science. Under the guise of doing science, what we have been given is indoctrination in a social ideology. We summarize what is wrong with doctrinaire liberalism on both theoretical and practical grounds, show how it undermines and distorts important values in our culture such as individual freedom and responsibility, and how we can begin to reconstruct our tradition.

CHAPTER 1

From Jim Crow
to Reverse Discrimination

> What we want from this court is the striking down of race.—Thurgood Marshall (*Brown* v. *Board of Education*, 1954)

> In order to get beyond racism, we must first take account of race.—Justice Blackmun (*University of California Regents* v. *Bakke*, 1978)

SHORT HISTORY OF OPPRESSION

Modern liberals as a whole argue for state intervention on behalf of oppressed peoples who are unable to liberate themselves because of circumstances beyond their control. There would seem to be no clearer case than that of blacks in America. Brought here against their will, their status as slaves was sanctified by the United States Constitution. Slavery as an institution up until 1865 speaks for itself as a form of oppression. Even from 1865 to 1866, Black Codes limiting the activities of blacks prevailed in the South. Such codes were outlawed during Reconstruction, but "white supremacy" returned after Reconstruction as a result of both social custom and the terrorism of such clandestine groups as the Ku Klux Klan. This supremacy or control was largely effected by preventing blacks from voting. The devices used included not only intimidation but the poll tax and literacy tests. We may note in passing that such taxes and tests reflected the economic and educational deprivation of former slaves.

Toward the end of the nineteenth century, states began passing laws making segregation a permanent feature of life in the South. They were known as Jim Crow laws. Such laws made separate or segregated schools, forms of transportations, facilities such as lavatories, and even

7

amusements mandatory. These laws were extended in the first two decades of the twentieth century to encompass separate hospitals, churches, and even jails. The United States Supreme Court upheld the constitutionality of such laws. Whereas Congress had in 1875 prohibited discrimination in hotels and theaters, in 1883 the Supreme Court declared the 1875 Civil Rights Act unconstitutional. In *Plessy* v. *Ferguson* (1896), now famous because of Justice Harlan's dissenting voice, the court upheld the constitutionality of "separate but equal" accommodations. In 1908, in the case of *Berea College* v. *Kentucky,* the court upheld the right of a state to forbid a college, even a privately supported one, to teach integrated classes.

Organized opposition to Jim Crow laws started as early as 1905, with the Niagara Movement headed by W. E. B. DuBois, and, in 1910, with the founding of the NAACP (National Association for the Advancement of Colored People). Through the 1930s, opponents of Jim Crow laws limited themselves to the contention that specific separate facilities were not, in fact, equal. The great impetus to overcoming such segregation came with the Second World War, largely in response to the newly felt need for national unity. Already building black voters into his coalition, Franklin D. Roosevelt created the Fair Employment Practices Committee in June of 1941. The committee saw to it that antidiscrimination clauses were added to federal contracts. In July of 1948, the year after Jackie Robinson commenced playing for the Dodgers, President Truman formally ended segregation in the armed forces.

On May 17, 1954, the U.S. Supreme Court "reversed itself" and declared that segregation "is inherently unequal." In short, separate cannot be equal. Furthermore, all blacks proscribed from attending public schools with whites were found to have been denied the equal protection clause of the Fourteenth Amendment (dating back to Reconstruction). Again, we pause to note that this landmark decision focused on education. In March of 1956, the Court extended this decision, in the case of *Brown* v. *the Board of Education* (of Topeka, Kansas), to all state-supported institutions of higher learning. Earlier, on May 31, 1955, federal district courts were granted jurisdiction over desegregation lawsuits and encouraged to proceed "with all deliberate speed."

In the wake of the historic *Brown* v. *Board of Education* decision by the Supreme Court, Congress passed the Civil Rights Act of 1957, the first piece of civil rights legislation since Reconstruction. The act prohibits actions interfering with persons voting in federal elections. The attorney general is directed to bring suit on behalf of anyone deprived of his voting rights. Finally, a Civil Rights Commission was set up. The voting rights act was strengthened and extended in successive Civil Rights Acts in 1960, 1964, 1970, and 1975.

The important point to be noted here is that Jim Crow laws and white supremacy in the South were, as we have previously indicated, largely effected by preventing blacks from voting. Blacks are no longer disenfranchised in either the North or the South, and their muscle in the voting booths is felt all the way to the White House. If this is a correct picture, then we can expect to see the gradual disappearance of the vestiges of Jim Crow as blacks are increasingly enfranchised. That is exactly what has happened. The Civil Rights Act of 1964 struck down Jim Crow laws in public accommodations. The Civil Rights Bill of 1968 prohibits discrimination in housing, or at least 80 percent of all housing.

We may now return our narrative to the issue of schooling. The 1954 decision by the Supreme Court did not have smooth sailing. As late as 1963, three states (Mississippi, Alabama, and South Carolina) still had not desegregated even their elementary schools. In South Carolina only Clemson College was desegregated. In 1962, James H. Meredith had need of federal marshals in order to become the first black to attend a publicly supported school in Mississippi (the University of Mississippi). Violence and terror still flared sporadically in the bombing of schools and churches.

Two sets of statistics are especially relevant here. By 1963, 92 percent of all blacks in the South still attended all-black schools. At the same time, of the 240 formerly all-white colleges, 152 now admitted blacks. Relatively speaking, institutions of higher learning were more responsive to the Supreme Court's decision than publicly supported primary and secondary schools. It is conceivable that part of the explanation for this lies in their independent sources of income. With regard to elementary and secondary schools, much more needed to be done. In short, there is a difference between desegregation and integration, a difference to which we shall presently return. These events of 1963 account both for the strength and far-reaching nature of the 1964 Civil Rights Act and for the provision in the 1968 Civil Rights Bill protecting persons who choose to exercise the right to attend a school.

We have so far characterized the oppression of blacks by pointing to Jim Crow laws segregating access to public institutions. We have pointed to the systematic disenfranchisement of blacks. We have asserted a direct connection between the two. We have witnessed the gradual disappearance of Jim Crow and the growth, even the power, of black enfranchisement. Nor are blacks, as a consequence of desegregation, prohibited from attending formerly all-white schools. To the extent that this constitutes liberation, blacks are no longer oppressed.

A curious change was taking place in the discussion of the oppression of blacks, a change that became increasingly clear between 1964 and 1968. To understand this change we may raise the question of why the fight for civil rights focused on schools, although there were many other dimensions to the struggle, including such well-publicized events as

Martin Lurther King's bus boycott in 1955 and freedom rides in 1961. Yet, the schools remained paramount. The question is, Why?

It was widely believed—and still is—that the schools were *the* most important of all institutions to desegregate. This belief seems to have been held for two reasons. First, it was believed that racial stereotypes were reinforced by school segregation and that bringing children together in integrated schools would undermine racial stereotyping and lead eventually to an integrated society. Few contest the first half of the belief; many would find the second half naive. Facts subsequently seem to have borne out the charge of naiveté. Second, it was believed that blacks had suffered economically because they had received an inferior education in previously segregated schools. The poll tax played a peculiarly symbolic role here by epitomizing the assumption that all of these elements, such as not voting and attending a segregated school, were all neatly tied together. The Supreme Court outlawed all poll taxes in 1968. To sum up, the hypothesis seems to have been widely accepted that integrating the schools would, by a ripple effect, solve every problem that had ever been associated with blacks.

Tentatively at least, we may raise the issues of oppression with regard to economics and education. There were some overt and uncontestable features of the economic oppression of blacks. It was all too true that they were the last to be hired and the first to be fired. In response to these overt and direct forms of economic oppression, the Civil Rights Act of 1964 contained provisions prohibiting discrimination by employers and unions. But it has been well argued that economic oppression may be more subtle. Inadequately educated blacks cannot compete fairly, even in a desegregated economy. So, once more we have landed on the pivotal importance of schools.

NEW HYPOTHESIS OF COVERT OPPRESSION

With regard to the issue of education, we may raise the question, What constitutes oppression? The immediate answer is inferior schools.[1] When pressed to identify inferior schools, we are routinely given a peculiar input-output argument. Inferior schools are identified in two ways: first, the products of inferior schooling achieve less when measured against the population as a whole. Second, inferior schools can be identified by input; they lack the overt characteristics of successful schools. Successful schools seem to be schools with elegant plant facilities, usually in all-white neighborhoods, with high funding and a faculty consisting largely of white graduates of well-known universities. The assumption behind this argument is that education is almost exclusively the product of schools and that there is a direct causal nexus between input and output.

If this hypothesis is plausible, then a case has been made for educational oppression, because any causal nexus is beyond the control of the student.

Now, what can be said about this hypothesis? Is it plausible? The most obvious objection centers on output. All of the so-called successful schools also turn out illiterate students and students who fail to go on to either higher education or high-paying careers. Correspondingly, the so-called unsuccessful schools periodically still produce a number, small as it is, of brilliant students. In response to this objection, those who assert the hypothesis of educational oppression reply that the statistical correlation in general proves their point, regardless of the exceptions. For future reference, I shall refer to this as the *trend argument*. A second objection centers on the question of input. For every input that has been singled out as crucial to overcoming educational oppression, there is counter-evidence to show that the alleged crucial input is not at all significant.[2] In response to this objection, we are told that further hidden variables are really at fault. For future reference I shall refer to this as the *hidden variable argument*.

We may sum up the foregoing argument for educational oppression in terms of three theses: (1) student performance is totally the result of circumstances beyond the control of the student; (2) this first point can be established purely by appeal to statistics about output; and (3) the same set of statistics establishes the existence of hidden variables responsible for differences in output.

I think we can see how far we have come from the earlier issues of slavery, Jim Crow, disenfranchisement, and overt economic oppression. All of those issues are matters of fact. The argument for educational oppression is a matter of hypothesis. All of the former examples of oppression have been overcome. In short, black oppression in any traditional, objective sense has been eliminated. Some people still believe that oppression exists, and they have offered an elaborate hypothesis focusing on education.

To understand why, we must dig more deeply into the change in perspective that surfaced between 1964 and 1968. In 1968, the Kerner Commission issued a report in which it concluded that "our nation is moving toward two societies, one black, one white—separate and unequal." To exemplify what the Kerner Commission had in mind, we may note the differences among the following:

1. segregated school
2. all-black school
3. integrated school
4. fully integrated school
5. ideally integrated school

Prior to the 1954 Supreme Court decision, a segregated school$_1$ would be one which by state law was restricted to either whites or blacks. That is now illegal. Curiously, the expression "segregated" is always taken as meaning exclusion of blacks.

With regard to (2), an "all-black school," we must make a distinction in time and place. Prior to 1954 (or 1963 in some states) an all-black school in the South was a segregated school$_1$. In the North an all-black school was never a segregated school$_1$. Since 1963, an all-black school would no longer be a segregated school; rather, it would reflect population, housing patterns, and school district lines. Such an all-black school would now be called *de facto* segregated, as opposed to *de jure* (by law) segregated. This extension of the word "segregated" accustoms people to accept the elaborate hypothesis of educational oppression, which is yet to be proved. It uses a word, a highly loaded word, in place of a serious argument. Instead, I shall call this segregated$_2$. There is no argument yet to establish that segregated$_2$ is the same as segregated$_1$.

An "integrated school" (3) is, technically speaking, a school that is open to all. Technically speaking, all schools are integrated. Again, we shall note the curious transition of language. In popular parlance, an integrated school is a school with at least one black student amongst many white students.

A "fully integrated school" (4) is a school where the percentage of black students to white students is proportional to the percentage of blacks to whites in the population (either local, state, or national—take your pick). But, a "fully integrated school" is not the same as an "ideally integrated school." In fact, once we understand what an "ideally integrated school" is, we shall have to say that an integrated school is a segregated school$_3$ and a fully integrated school is a segregated school$_4$. So what is an ideally integrated school(5)? It is a school (a) that is fully integrated and (b) where the percentage of black honor students (and every conventionally recognized form of achievement) is proportional to their percentage in the population.

The Kerner Commission presupposes such a statistical frame of reference for every institution and facet of our "nation," not only schools but housing and jobs as well. That is, behind the shift in discussions about overcoming the oppression of blacks is some operative ideal of what our "nation" should be. We have moved beyond the realm of facts as they are to what ideally some people would like or expect. I say some people because I do not know how to determine what the "nation" wants. Here the emotive term "nation" again hides or masks what should be a more open and elaborate argument. It follows from the logic of such loaded terms that where one has an "ideal" one can measure our "progress towards that ideal." If we surreptitiously redefine segregation as the absence of integration, and if we surreptitiously redefine "integration" as the ideal suggests, then we have made little progress in overcoming the oppression of blacks.

Not only has the trend argument emerged as the advance man of a social ideology, but its brother, the hidden variable argument, is not far behind. For if I were to produce even blacks who specifically rejected an ideally integrated society as their model, the proponents of the educational oppression hypothesis would claim that such blacks were victims of a subtle form of psychological deprivation. By now we have long ago left the world of fact and entered the world of semantics and political and social ideology.

If we are not to succumb to a total distortion of fact, I think it is high time that we recognize that we are no longer dealing with the oppression of blacks. Rather, we have entered a new dimension of social philosophy. The legal and objective foundations of the oppression of blacks are now behind us. Doctrinaire liberalism can no longer piggyback on the civil rights movement, which has run its course, although we should not be surprised if it continues to masquerade as a continuation of the civil rights movement.

JACKIE ROBINSON AND AFFIRMATIVE ACTION

The shift from the old conception of oppression to the new hypothesis of oppression was exemplified in a recent debate. This shift is not always honestly acknowledged.

Is affirmative action, as currently understood by HEW, a continuation of the same social philosophy that was at work when Jackie Robinson gained admission to professional major league baseball? That is one of the questions raised by the exchange between Sidney Hook and Nathaniel R. Jones on the significance of the *Bakke* ruling.[3]

Hook raised the case of Jackie Robinson in the following way: "In no field of American life was deplorable racial prejudice so widespread as in organized sport. After Jackie Robinson broke the color bar, merit and merit alone became the criterion for the selection of members of our football, basketball, and baseball teams. Who cares what the racial composition of those teams should be? Who speaks of quotas and numerical goals here . . . ? The absence of minorities in considerable numbers in our professional schools today is [due to] . . . educational deprivation on elementary and secondary levels, a deprivation largely reflecting economic conditions. . . . affirmative action programs in the original sense . . . do not call for preferential hiring or selection. They can be administered with the understanding that a single equitable criterion of merit will be applied to all."[4]

Mr. Jones[5] (NAACP) replied as follows: "First, Jackie Robinson and major league baseball do not afford support for Professor Hook's position on affirmative action, nor his clarion call for a return to the 'good old days' of 'excellence'. Branch Rickey's search for a 'first' was the kind of affirmative action, racially sensitive, which today draws so much of the author's wrath. Was there not then the cry from sports writers and baseball functionaries, that highly skilled and qualified white players were passed over in order for Mr. Rickey to experiment with race?"[6]

Like Professor Hook, I find the cases of Jackie Robinson and affirmative action so dissimilar that I believe those differences are worth enumerating. No doubt there were some who booed Jackie Robinson and who booed the pre-Bakke admissions program at the University of California, Davis. But then there are some of us who cheered Jackie Robinson and who booed the pre-Bakke admissions program. I think it is worthwhile to explain why.

It is worth recalling the original situations, since this highlights more than anything else the differences between them. Prior to Branch Rickey's initiative, discrimination based upon race was the official policy of professional sports. It resulted in a total ban on black athletes. At the same time, black athletes set up a rival system, challenged the discriminatory system when allowed, and produced stars who earned the admiration of many nonblacks. In the case of medicine, it should be noted that there are practicing black physicians, that medical schools do accept black applicants, and that at the new medical school at Davis there was not, and could not have been, a previous history of discrimination. Not only is there no overt policy of discrimination, but, as far as I know, no one claims that there is a rival medical system created by black physicians, currently unlicensed, waiting to dazzle us.

There are three senses in which Branch Rickey's recruitment of Jackie Robinson bears an analogy to affirmative action: (1) It was unpopular with many people; (2) it was a "first," just as Davis was the "first" school to have a quota (or at least the first to admit it); (3) Rickey did not wait for blacks to apply; he actively recruited Robinson.

Let us examine each of these analogues. To begin with, being unpopular is hardly a sign of virtue. In a society with as much freedom (and license) as ours, I doubt if anything can muster universal popularity. Everything is unpopular to some individual or group. Not only is unpopularity not a sign of virtue, it is not a sign of truth. Genocide is also unpopular. Ironically, it is the "establishment" that supports hidden-quota affirmative action (just look at the *Bakke* briefs!), whereas in the case of Jackie Robinson the establishment supported discrimination.

The University of California at Davis introduced its quota admissions program apparently on its own initiative, voluntarily, and as a first. It was not compelled to do so by HEW. However, Davis is a school totally supported by public funds from the state of California. Its administrators are and must be acutely sensitive to the fact that continued funding is at the discretion of a board of regents and a governor. There is no escaping the fact that it was ultimately a politically based initiative. Branch Rickey, on the other hand, was not acting under any kind of governmental pressure, direct or indirect. He was engaged in a private profit-making activity subject to the pressures of the marketplace. To this extent, we might more perceptively classify his act as good old-fashioned imaginative capitalist entrepreneurship. This is not meant in any way to demean or dismiss the humanitarian or moral dimension of his act. But Rickey was acting against overt discrimination. Davis was not.

The third analogy is even more revealing. Rickey's sensitivity went beyond pious platitudes about equal opportunity into active efforts at recruitment. At the same time, Rickey's sensitivity extended not only to a desired goal but to the means as well. We are all on the side of the angels, but some of us are also wary about the road to hell. Rickey was acutely sensitive to the problems that any black would have in being the "first," and he was sensitive to the problems nonblacks would have in adjusting to the situation. Rickey made sure that he chose someone who was "first" in more senses than one. Finally, Rickey understood just how counter-productive an ill-conceived experiment could be.

Now let us turn to those factors where the analogy definitely does not hold. Jackie Robinson went through the official "admissions" procedure by which players gain acceptance into the major leagues—that is, by playing minor league baseball at the Montreal farm club of the Brooklyn Dodgers. He was evaluated by his performance against white players, all of whom were playing according to the same rules. Not only did he have to go through the same screening process, but he did so with flying colors. The Dodgers did not bring him up to the major leagues over or instead of a white player who may have had better credentials, such as a higher batting average or fielding percentage or capacity to steal bases. The analogy with Bakke is most strained at this point. It would only be an analogy if the Dodgers also had a half-dozen other infielders with vastly superior records. Recall that Bakke's credentials were embarrassingly superior to those who gained admittance over him. Second, when Jackie Robinson played, the rules of the game remained the same for him as for everyone else. (He did not get four strikes; they did not move first base thirty feet closer to home plate when he came to bat; and they did not move second base thirty feet closer to first base when he got to first base.) No black ever claimed, in the case of Jackie Robinson, that prior discrimination meant that different evaluative criteria should be used in judging him. If someone now suggests a double standard, then they must admit the clear difference between the case of Jackie Robinson and presently interpreted affirmative action.

Jackie Robinson was not endowed by Branch Rickey with a fail-safe policy. If he had hit .190, I doubt that he would have continued playing on a pennant contender. No doubt Robinson would have been the first to admit his failure and not blame it on the "system." He did not advocate that society owed him a position, only that he had a right to earn one. How can anyone compare this to the spectre of HEW, which insists that anything short of numerical parity is discrimination?

The issues involved are too important and complicated to be left here, and I certainly cannot deal with all of them in this context. But I think two other related arguments are worth mentioning. One might point out that the skills necessary for entering medical school cannot be acquired as easily as the skills for athletics. Professor Hook has certainly addressed himself to that issue and suggested that the problem lies else- where. If so, then that is where it should be solved. Alternatively, one might argue that current admissions criteria such as test scores and grade averages are not directly related to one's later professional performance in medicine in the same way that minor league ball is tied to major league ball. As an academic, I can only agree, and that is why I write letters of recommendation. Yet, if I damn the present scale, I can do so only if I subscribe to another scale that I think is better. If someone has other criteria for admission and retention, then I am all for discussing them and perhaps trying them. But I cannot accept criteria that a priori have numerical parity built into them. This is the crucial reason the Bakke case is totally unlike the Jackie Robinson case. This is not the imaginative and creative use of policy to enrich our lives but a hypocritical and cynical political ploy.

Finally, I turn to the concept of "excellence." No doubt, to some it is a "code" word. But I think the history and sociology of the concept are something on which we should agree. There never were any good old days of excellence. Excellence is something we have always had to fight for. Rickey fought for it (not a racially balanced infield); Jackie Robinson fought for it; Professor Hook still fights for it. It is a fight not only against entrenched privilege but against those who would institute a new, more devastating and demeaning form of privilege.[7]

THE SHACKLED RUNNER

Hitherto government intervention had been justified by an appeal to the existence of overt oppression. Starting in 1964, government intervention would be justified by appeal to the hypothesis of covert oppression. I say hypothesis because, rather than presenting us with direct evidence, liberals assert a connection between past facts (slavery, Jim Crow, "segregation," and so on) and present facts such as crime and unemployment. The connection is not itself a fact but a controversial hypothesis. I say covert oppression because it is alleged that blacks are oppressed not by present overt conditions but by the residue or lingering effects of past conditions.

The essence of this argument is to be found in a now famous speech delivered by President Lyndon B. Johnson in 1964. It is referred to as "The Shackled Runner." In it, Johnson asserted that blacks and other "minorities" have engaged in a long-term race but have for long been forced to run bound in chains. The civil rights movement has removed the chains, so that blacks can now run unimpeded. Nevertheless, the formerly bound runners are still far behind, because of the past. In no sense can the race be fair without a realignment that takes the past into account.

The metaphor has been elaborated in a number of ways that reflect in part different perceptions of the social world. For some, the race is like a vast marathon of individual contestants;[8] for some, the race is an inter-generational relay race, perhaps of family teams; for some, the race consists of two teams, one black and one white. We shall have occasion in a later chapter to explain why different versions of liberalism identify the contestants in such diverse ways.[9]

Now, what lies behind the metaphor of the shackled runner? It is a metaphor subjected to much speculation, distortion, and misunderstanding. I believe that it can be best understood as follows. Implicit in the metaphor of the shackled runner is a view of human psychology that contends that there is a basic human nature existing in man independent of all external origins.[10] The social world itself is a product of this basic human nature. In technical jargon, we would say that man is fundamental, while society is derivative, that the natural state of man is pre-social. Stripped to its fundamental and natural state, this nature reveals itself as one of striving or desiring. Hence, the metaphor of the runner.

But while the striving, the running, is independent of all external origins (we try to run, no matter what), it is not independent of external influence. How well, how far, how fast, and in what direction I run are influenced by such things as the conditions of the track, the presence or absence of obstacles, how well I have trained, and how I perceive my relationship to the other runners. All of these influencing factors are, it is being claimed, beyond the control of the runner. They are all environmentally determined. How well I run, then, does not depend upon me but on circumstances beyond my control. Circumstances invariably favor some runners over others, through no fault or virtue of their own. There are a few more steps to the implicit argument, but the upshot is that the function of government is to remove all of the obstacles.

It is argued that what the civil rights movement accomplished was to allow blacks to participate. What is needed now is a movement to make the racing fair, and thus was born affirmative action. Affirmative action programs consist of three parts: first, a *platitude stage* in which it is reaffirmed that the race is to be fair, and a fair race is one in which no one has either special disadvantages or special advantages (equal opportunity); second, a *remedial stage* in which victims of past disadvantages will be given a special help to overcome those disadvantages; third, a *realignment stage,* in which all runners will be reassigned to those positions on the course that they would have had if the race had been fair from the beginning.

Problems arise with stages two and three. With regard to stage two, the criteria of who is to count as disadvantaged by the past are hotly contested. With regard to stage three, it is argued by some that realignment necessarily gives special advantages to some of the runners, and this is in violation of the official platitudes. In short, we have the charge of reverse discrimination.

There is one very obvious answer to the charge of reverse discrimination. Realignment does not give special advantages; rather, it restores the race to what it would have been if there had been fairness right from the beginning. Surely, it will be argued, some runners are only where they are relative to other runners because they have profited, even if unintentionally, from past unfairness.

I would find this response to the charge of reverse discrimination convincing, if—and it is a big if—I were prepared to accept an as yet unstated theory of history and social structure. This view of history and social structure are the other elements of the liberal theory that control the metaphor of the shackled runner.

We may characterize those elements as follows. There is only one race ever in town, affectionately called the "mainstream." Not only is there one race, but every facet of life, every institution, can be understood only by how it relates to that race. In fact, every institution can be placed into a kind of dove-tailing hierarchy of means and ends ultimately culminating in the "race." Even when people say that they do not want to participate, that is itself a reflection of their disadvantaged past. Here again, the hidden variable argument will come to the rescue.

Moreover, the entire history of the world can be understood as moments in that race. Not only is it a race with a history, but the race is definitely headed toward a particular end-state. Hence, at any point in the race we can evaluate whether the runners are on or off course. This can get a little complicated because those who chronicle the race may themselves be off course, which is why revisionist historians must periodically rewrite history. Now, since by our previous psychological theory we were forced to conclude that runners are not responsible for being off course, we can actually calculate the distance between where they are and where they would have been if they had not been hampered. This distance is referred to as the "gap." The aforementioned trend argument is the official track record of the "gap." It takes a great deal of social scientific skill to calculate the trends. The government is simply that branch of society that sees to it that the race is fair by closing the "gap." The government, finally, is so committed to fairness that it can even recognize and admit that some of its own past realignments were unfair, and this calls for further meta-realignments. Meta-realignments are the special province of the Supreme Court.

All liberals subscribe to some version of this theory contained in the metaphor of the runner. All liberals do not necessarily agree on all features of the theory or the metaphor. Which features they accept and which features they reject account for the proliferation of competing versions of liberalism. It is not necessary to go into these versions yet, but one example will help to illustrate this point. There can be different understandings of what the final upshot of the race will be. Moreover, even the question of the knowability of the final outcome may be in dispute. One could argue that we know and always have known the ultimate outcome of the race. One could argue that social scientists have just recently discovered or calculated what the end will be. One could argue that we are still evolving toward that understanding, and while we know some things, we do not, in this transitional period, know the whole picture. Finally, one might hold that we shall not know until we actually arrive at the end. This should illustrate the range of possible interpretations of the same metaphor and ultimately of liberal doctrine itself.

DOCTRINAIRE LIBERALISM: A WORKING DEFINITION

We are now in a position to articulate a working definition of doctrinaire liberalism. This task will be greatly facilitated by the use of some technical terms to which we can refer back.

Liberalism consists of a basic psychological theory and derivative theories of social structure, politics, and history. The theory of liberalism in general and its basic psychological component can be defined as *teleological*. A theory is teleological if it seeks to explain any act, event, or process as the outcome of goal-directed behavior. The goals need not but can be conscious. The most obvious area of teleological explanations is in biology. We say, for example, that an acorn is explained by noting that it has a built-in goal to become an oak tree. It need not necessarily reach its goal, but the only alternative to the built-in end is destruction. An acorn cannot become something other than an oak. In social science we frequently encounter teleological explanations when some social practice is explained as fulfilling some overall social end.

Now, we certainly use teleological language when we explain the individual acts of human beings. We might, for example, explain someone's purchase of an expensive automobile by saying that his ultimate goal is to impress people. But what is peculiar to liberalism is the belief that every human being has a built-in nature to achieve certain ends, that these ends are not matters of choice or of external factors. Like the acorn, we all either fully develop into our true selves or we fail in varying degrees. So our end or goal is fulfillment. Returning to our race metaphor, the goal is to win, but there are winners, not a winner. Theoretically, everybody can be a winner. Unlike acorns, human beings are much more complex, having not just one drive or desire but many. There are or can be a lot of things we want or want to be. But we need not fear any ultimate incoherence, for there is no ultimate conflict among all of the legitimate drives. This is the utopian element in liberal psychology.

All experienced conflict is symptomatic of not following our true nature. Sometimes conflicts are the product of ignorance or misperceptions on our part. Sometimes the experienced conflicts reflect external constraints on our development. Oppression is an example of an external constraint. Again, like acorns, in order to fulfill our drives there are certain external conditions that must be met. Just as the acorn must fall onto fertile ground that is accessible to sunshine and water, so must a human being be provided with an environment that supplies certain necessary conditions. These necessary conditions for the full development of the built-in nature of human beings are known as *needs*.

In liberal psychology, the ends are desires provided from within. The means are provided by the environment. There is no element of real choice. All choices that we appear to make reflect the information available to us and the criteria for employing the information. But these, too, are provided by the environment. Ignorance and misperception are thus forms of oppression or external constraint. This explains the overwhelming importance attributed to a particular conception of education. It explains as well the belief that there is a causal nexus between input and output in education. Attributing all choice to external factors and stressing the overwhelming importance of the external environment, liberal psychology can be termed *environmentalist*.

This leads us into the liberal conception of sociology. For the liberal, society is the individual writ large. That is, the structure of society is a macrocosm of the structure of the individual. Just as each individual is the product of his interacting drives, so society is the product of the interacting individuals who make it up. This mirror imaging of individual and society we can call *psychologism*. It says that all social explanation is reducible in principle to an explanation of individual psychology plus information about the nonhuman environment. Just as there is no ultimate conflict between the legitimate drives within an individual, so there is no necessary ultimate conflict among the members of any and all societies. The utopian element is presupposed here as well. Conflicts that do exist are symptomatic of either ignorance or external constraints. The equilibrium among members within a society is guaranteed by the assumption that no individual can be completely fulfilled and secure in that fulfillment as long as others are not. All social evil is the result of ignorance operating through time to create inefficient institutions that generate a false sense of interest. In addition to psychologism, liberalism subscribes to *historicism,* in this case a theory of social change in which events are interpreted as moving or progressing toward a definite end. Because liberals know the built-in end, they are the final arbiters of whether we are making progress or regressing.

Reason, or rationality, operates here in a number of ways. It helps to discover or articulate our desires. It adjudicates apparent conflicts among the desires of an individual. I do not eat four eclairs, for example, because I do not want the anticipated bellyache. Reason helps through proper education to cultivate an enlightened or long-range view of our interests, culminating in a view of the ultimate social harmony. Just as no one desire, no one legitimate desire, is more important than any other in its right to be fulfilled, so no one person is any more entitled to fulfillment than any other. Egalitarian democracy is the form of government that most nearly reflects this assumption. All persons, like all desires, need a fair hearing. Just as reason adjudicates and weighs the relative merits of each desire, so the legislative process does the same for the assembly of individuals. Politics is truly a science, a technique for articulating the harmonious ends and then engineering the means. Finally, to the extent that particular individuals or particular institutions fail to grow properly and are unable to take self-corrective action on their own behalf, the state may intervene to set them right. This is the justification for *interventionism.*

The remainder of this book is designed to show how pervasive this view of life is, how deeply education is implicated in it, how disastrous it is as a source of policy, and how false it is.

ALTERNATIVE POSITIONS

In the previous section we articulated a working definition of doctrinaire liberalism implicit in the shackled runner metaphor. We are now in a position to use our definition to show how different kinds of liberals reacted to the new hypothesis of covert oppression.

Meritocracy: According to this version of liberalism, there is a common core of genetic attributes that define human nature, but some of these (talents) vary widely with each individual. There are or can be significant differences in natural ability. There is, however, no way of telling in advance what the outcome of a fair competition will be. No position is taken on the actual statistical results or eventual outcome in a nondiscriminatory society. Quite possibly, blacks will occupy 11 percent of the key roles, possibly 2 percent, possibly 29 percent, and so on. There is a consistent adherence to a strong belief in individual excellence and merit, hence the label of meritocracy, an aristocracy of merit. The commitment to individual excellence or merit is itself justified on the grounds that excellence improves growth, productivity, and efficiency. The latter are thought to provide even greater opportunities for *all* members of society.

The problem for meritocrats is that they are deeply disturbed by what a commitment to equal opportunity implies. Since they themselves recognize that it is impossible to enumerate the existence and degree of all the external factors that might influence performance, they agonize over whether all that can legitimately be done has in fact been done. At the same time meritocrats recognize that there are limtis to what the state should do. For the state to help some is also to burden other participants. Reverse discrimination is inconsistent with excellence, especially in the absence of any objective criteria for establishing covert oppression. The meritocrats sincerely believe that policies like affirmative action will be detrimental in the long run even to minorities because of the ultimate undermining of growth and productivity, which depend upon efficiency and excellence.

Elitism: According to this second version, there are differences in individual talent, but such differences are proportional by group to the population as a whole. As stated by one government agency, "Intelligence potential is distributed among Negro infants in the same proportion and pattern as among Icelanders or Chinese, or any other group. . . ." Since blacks are 11 percent of the total U.S. population, then 11 percent of all key roles in every field should be or would be, in a fair competition, held by blacks. All statistical disparities are evidence of a lack of equal opportunity and the persistence of discrimination.

This version is *elitist* in the sense that it believes some individuals are superior to others, but it also believes that superior individuals emerge statistically as the leaders of specific groups. Elitists can and do consistently advocate quotas. Precisely because of their basic assumption of proportionality, they can use proportionality as the acid test of whether there is in fact equal opportunity. *Equality* means proportionality to an elitist, and it is not seen as incompatible with excellence. When the correct proportion is achieved, then and only then will we know for sure that real equal opportunity exists and that covert oppression has been eliminated. The state is now supposed to act not on behalf of individuals and their rights but on behalf of group entitlement. Elitism is espoused not just by blacks but by women's liberation organizations and many others. Elitists have spurred the revival of ethnic identification.

The one question we should raise here is, Why do elitists hold both that talent varies and that it varies proportionately by group? The hypothesis is not implausible, but then neither is it compelling. Certainly there is no scientific consensus on the distribution of talent. Once we admit that talent varies, why commit oneself to any preconception of how it varies? Moreover, if one were to argue that objective disparities of achievement are environmentally caused, then why not entertain the final logical position that all native talent is equal and that performance is totally the result of environmental accidents? This possibility is just as plausible as the one about distribution being proportional to groups.

Given that there is no objective reason whatsoever to hold the view of group proportionality, we are led to speculate on the motives for holding this position. I am going to suggest two. First, there is, I shall maintain, a corrupt, sinister, and cynical political attempt to use this argument about equality to alter permanently the power structure in America to the advantage of the self-appointed elitists among blacks, women, and other ethnic groups. The rhetoric of equality masks domination.

The second group to whom this argument has a strong emotional appeal (I deny that the appeal is rational) are those mostly sincere proponents of the old civil rights movement who had grandiose expectations about what the end of objective discrimination would bring. While there has been marked improvement, the results economically, politically, socially, morally, and even aesthetically have come nowhere near meeting their private expectations or wishes. Rather than reexamining their assumptions about eventual outcome or even reconsidering their simplistic theories about the causes of the failed outcome, they have chosen to stick with the old shibboleths. The belief in group proportionality is just the latest epicycle in their social gospel. It is held with varying degrees of conviction.

Egalitarians: According to the third version, although talents may vary widely, such talent differentials are either irrelevant or secondary. They are irrelevant because all human beings are equal in possessing some common core of attributes, and it is these equal attributes that are crucial. This version has a totally different notion of social goals. According to it, the goal of social institutions is not to foster individual excellence and merit in the meritocratic sense but rather to foster the common core. The heart of the common core is the alleged fundamental need to participate in social life in some meaningful way (i.e., to identify oneself with the social whole). Equality means the common core to an egalitarian. It does not mean equal opportunity, and it does not mean proportionality. The key concepts here are *participation* and the social whole. This third version is collectivist as opposed to the first version, which is individualist, and to the second version, which is proportionalist.

For egalitarians, the hypothesis of covert oppression is taken so seriously that they are consistently committed to a wholesale reorganization of society. This includes not only rectifying past status but also challenging the whole meritocratic notion of what is valuable and excellent and productive. Egalitarians argue that traditional values such as individual merit are either wrong or incorrectly interpreted from the point of view of a vision of an ideal society which they propose as a replacement for our traditionally conceived society. The means for achieving these new goals is state activism on behalf of a new social whole. The state exists to create institutions that foster the common core of participation in a new social whole. While meritocrats permit government intervention to correct identifiable and remediable past injustice to individuals, and while elitists permit government regulation of institutions on behalf of group entitlement, egalitarians advocate total government control of all institutions. We are now talking about totalitarianism.

There is an interesting transition from the second version (elitism) to the third version (egalitarianism). Why, egalitarians will ask, do elitists take a stand one way or the other or worry over imponderables like the distribution of talent? Would it not be more consistent to argue that all natural talent is equal and that all differences of individual achievement are, like all forms of consciousness, environmentally determined? Or, once we admit that individuals differ, why expect these variations to be insignificant in large groups? Why would it matter if some statistically identifiable groups were more successful or less successful? After all, in the end it is only individuals who actually possess or lack a talent.

Here egalitarians can say to elitists that what really concerns people is the prospect of belonging to a group that is perceived as less valuable (if not inferior). But this is a problem, it will be argued, because people do not really see themselves as individuals but rather as members of a group. This provides the opening wedge. If people perceive themselves as members of a group, then the less talented (let us say the bottom 20 percent) will still feel less valuable (or inferior) even within the framework of elitism. A female, for example, who is in the bottom 20 percent of females will not feel better because 51 percent of the top roles are held by females. Our hypothetical female will still feel left out and is more likely to identify with the other "losers" who are the bottom 20 percent of their respectively designated groups. Hence a more egalitarian solution is required.

SUMMARY

The debate over affirmative action can be construed in one of two ways. Either it can be construed in terms of our traditional cultural values such as fairness and the way in which those values have been interpreted by Congress and elaborated by the courts, or it can be construed as part of a debate in which discrimination and equal opportunity have been *redefined* to reflect conflicting views about man, the facts of history, and the structure of the social world.

As the debate now shapes up, we have the following. Meritocrats accuse elitists and egalitarians of reverse discrimination and of undermining individuality in the name of group entitlement. Elitists are suspicious of the makeup of a meritocratic society and secretly fear that meritocrats are racists *manqué* who are too complacent about a society that might ultimately be indistinguishable from the old system. At the same time, elitists think of egalitarians as temporary allies but as an ultimately disposable lunatic fringe. Egalitarians worry about the elitists being coopted, and accuse the meritocrats of adopting a whole host of ad-hoc assumptions that appear indistinguishable from a defense of the status quo. This debate on domestic policy within liberal circles is *the crisis of doctrinaire liberalism.*

CHAPTER 2

Twisting the Law

> And the little trusting reader of newspapers comes into the courtroom with righteousness beating in his breast, with reasonable arguments prepared, and tremblingly lays them out before the dozing masks of his judges, not suspecting that his sentence has already been decided—and that there are *no* means of appeal, *no* time limits or methods to correct the most evil, self-serving decision, though the heart burns with the injustice of it all.
>
> There is simply a wall. And its bricks are laid in a mortar of lies
>
> We have called this chapter "The Law Today." But really it should be called: "There is No Law."
>
> The same perfidious secrecy, the same fog of unrighteousness hangs in the air around us, hangs over our cities more densely than the city smoke itself.
>
> A powerful State towers over its second half-century, embraced in hoops of steel. The hoops are there indeed, but not the law.—Alexander I. Solzhenitsyn, *Gulag Archipelago.*

INTRODUCTION

The moral that many would have us draw from the incident at Watergate is that government power can be abused, especially by unprincipled individuals. But there is another kind of abuse of government power: an abuse practiced by a group, and based upon high principles. Nowhere is such abuse more evident than in the development and application of the policy of affirmative action.

A shorter version of this chapter originally appeared in *Policy Review* (Spring 1980), pp. 39-58.

TALE OF TWO TITLES: LEGISLATIVE INTENT

The Civil Rights Act of 1964, as passed by Congress, contained two important provisions, known as Title VI and Title VII. Title VI prohibits discrimination on the basis of race, sex, or national origin in public accommodations and in federally assisted programs. This includes federally assisted education programs. Title VII prohibits discrimination by employers or unions, whether private or public. It is unlawful for any employer "to fail or refuse to hire or to discharge any individual or otherwise to discriminate . . . because of such individual's race, color, religion, sex, or national origin."[1]

In the most unequivocal fashion, the sponsors of the measure in the Senate made clear that this act was designed to foster equal opportunity (meritocracy), not preference and not racial balance (i.e., not elitism or egalitarianism).

Senator Hubert H. Humphrey: "Title VII does not require an employer to achieve any sort of racial balance in his work force by giving preferential treatment to any individual or group."[2]

Senator Harrison A. Williams: [Title VII] "specifically prohibit[s] the Attorney General, or any agency of the government, from requiring employment to be on the basis of racial or religious quotas. Under [this provision] an employer with only white employees could continue to have only the best qualified persons even if they were all white."[3]

In the ensuing debate, the floor manager in the Senate, Senator Joseph Clark, and Senator Clifford Case both stated: "It must be emphasized that discrimination is prohibited as to any individual. . . . The question in each case is whether that individual was discriminated against." Further, in response to the charge that the bill would ultimately require quotas, Senator Clark replied that, "quotas are themselves discriminatory."[4] Two provisions were added to spell this out:

> 703 (h) . . . it shall not be unlawful employment practice . . . for an employer to give and act upon the results of any professionally developed ability test provided that such test, its administration or action upon the results is not designed, intended or used to discriminate because of race, color, religion, sex or national origin. . . .
>
> 703 (j) Nothing contained in this title shall be interpreted to require any employer . . . to grant preferential treatment to any individual or to any group because of the race, creed, color, religion, sex, or national origin of such individual or group on account of an imbalance which may exist with respect to the total number or percentage of persons of any race, color, religion, sex, or national origin employed by any employer. . . .

Congress did not order the termination of the effects of past discrimination; it outlawed discrimination per se. If anyone still doubts this, then let him listen to the words of Representative Celler, chairman of the House Judiciary Committee and the congressman responsible for introducing the legislation: "It is likewise not true that the Equal Employment Opportunity Commission would have power to rectify existing 'racial or religious imbalance' in employment by requiring the hiring of certain people without regard to their qualifications simply because they are of a given race or religion. Only actual discrimination could be stopped."[5]

THE BUREAUCRATIC IMPERATIVE

According to Article II, section 3, of the U.S. Constitution, the chief executive, namely, the president of the United States, is charged "to take care that the laws be faithfully executed. . . ." Presumably, the president is to be faithful both to the Constitution and to the intent of the specific legislation. As the power of the federal government has grown, a vast bureaucracy has grown up to aid in the administration of the laws. In addition to the potential conflict between a specific piece of legislation and the Constitution, there are two other kinds of conflict. The president may have his own understanding of the legislation in opposition to the congressional understanding. The bureaucracy may have its own understanding of the legislation in opposition to either Congress or even the president. As subsequent events will make clear, not only did all of these conflicts emerge but they were at root conflicts among competing versions of liberalism. Liberalism, you should recall, is not part of either the Constitution or the laws. It is a social ideology that colors people's perceptions of what is and what ought to be the law.

The president's interpretation of the law and his directives to the bureaucracy are found in so-called executive orders. The first such order bearing on our concerns, No. 8802, preceded the Civil Rights Act of 1964. It goes back to 1941 and was issued by Franklin D. Roosevelt, ordering an end to discrimination in defense industries. In 1961, President Kennedy issued Executive Order No. 10925, prohibiting job discrimination among contractors doing business with the federal government. In that executive order he used the expression "affirmative steps" to direct contractors to actively recruit and encourage minority applicants. In response to the Civil Rights Act of 1964, President Lyndon Johnson issued Executive Order No. 11246 in 1965, stressing the need for "affirmative action"[6] with regard to minorities. Executive Order No. 11375 of 1967 extended affirmative action to women. It should now be clear that the expression "affirmative action" is not and never was part of the Civil Rights Act of 1964. Its origin is in the executive branch of government.

The executive policy of affirmative action, however, was not defined by any president. It was defined by the bureaucracy. In May 1968, the Department of Labor issued Order No. 4:

> A necessary prerequisite to the development of a satisfactory affirmative action program is the identification and analysis of problem areas inherent in minority employment and an evaluation of opportunities for utilization of minority group personnel. The contractor's program shall provide in detail for specific steps to guarantee equal employment opportunity keyed to the problems and needs of members of minority groups, including, when there are deficiencies, the development of specific goals and time-tables for the prompt achievement of full and equal employment opportunity. Each contractor shall include in his affirmative action compliance program a table of job classifications. . . . The evaluation of utilization of minority group personnel shall include . . . an analysis of minority group representation in all categories.[7]

This order contains mention of "needs," a key concept in the liberal constellation. It further specifies the meaning of affirmative action in terms of "goals" and "time-tables" in the case of "deficiencies," but the latter had not yet been specified. Further guidelines were issued on February 5, 1970. Affirmative action was further defined as "a set of specific and result-oriented procedures to which a contractor commits himself to apply every good faith." Finally, the guidelines issued on December 4, 1971, spelled out the ultimate logic of affirmative action—quotas. It all turned on the term *underutilization.*[8]

> 'underutilization' is defined as having fewer minorities or women in a particular job classification than would reasonably be expected by their availability. . . .

In short, anything less than an ideally integrated workforce (equivalent in meaning to the ideally integrated school we discussed in the previous chapter) would bring down the wrath of the government. The basic assumption is that the law intended to create an ideally integrated society.

HOW THE BUREAUCRACY SEES ITSELF

From time to time various units of the federal bureaucracy concerned with administering the Civil Rights Act of 1964 issued statements in an attempt to explain their position. One such document was issued by the U.S. Commission on Civil Rights.[9] Its introduction begins with a statement of the problem. The problem, it seems, is the existence of a *gap* between blacks and whites, a gap reflected in statistics about income, income trends, and the proportional representation of blacks to whites in positions of high status.

For most of the past decades, the ratio of black to white family income has remained fairly constant while the dollar gap between the two groups continues to grow. . . . the dollar gap between the two groups has increased from $3,000 to $5,000.

As the status and rewards of particular types of employment increase, minority participation tends to decline. This is particularly true in the professions where blacks, who are 11 percent of the population, constitute only 2.2 percent of all physicians, 3.4 percent of the lawyers and judges in the country, and hold only 1 percent of the engineering jobs.[10]

Why is this gap a problem? The answer is found in the conclusion. There it is stated that the operative *ideal* is an ideally integrated society:

The aspiration of the American people is for a "color-blind" society, one that "neither knows nor tolerates classes among citizens."[11]

The quoted portion are the words of Justice Harlan from his dissent in the *Plessy* v. *Ferguson* case (1896). What is peculiar is the interpretation given to a classless society. Apparently, according to EEOC (Equal Employment Opportunity Commission), Harlan's classless society would be one where no invidious comparisons could be made or found statistically. Moreover, a classless society is one where "all people will have an equal opportunity to *develop their full potential* and to share in the effort and the rewards that such development brings."[12] [Italics added.]

Given the foregoing ideal, and given the statistical disparity, it is encumbent upon EEOC to show the connection. This it does by arguing that the "disparities" are caused by "the persistence of discriminatory practices." This would not be enough to make EEOC's case because discriminatory practices have been outlawed. So a few sentences later the real culprit is identified as "discriminatory practices and their effects."

Here we have arrived at the crux of the matter. The Equal Employment Opportunity Commission has moved from the issue of overt oppression to covert oppression. It has accepted the hypothesis of economic and educational oppression and identified them as the lingering effects of overt oppression. It then goes on to define *affirmative action* as the policy designed to overcome covert oppression:

[Affirmative action is] . . . any measure, beyond simple termination of a discriminatory practice, adopted to correct or compensate for past or present discrimination or to prevent discrimination from recurring in the future.[13]

Affirmative action, then, is to fulfill the ideal by moving into stages two and three, compensation and realignment. Realignment is specifically embraced by EEOC, which quotes a federal court judge:

> Affirmative action is essential . . . to place eligible minority members in the
> position which the minority would have enjoyed if it had not been the
> victim of discrimination.[14]

The teleological and historicist perspective of EEOC is now perfectly clear. The obvious question is whether those elements of the liberal social ideology are the specific directives of either the legislative act or of the U.S. Constitution. We shall ignore for the moment what any president may have intended.

It should be rather clear from the previous section on legislative intent that the Civil Rights Act of 1964 addresses itself to overt oppression, not covert oppression; that it is concerned with identifiable cases of past acts of discrimination with regard to specific individuals, not groups; that it specifically rejects the concept of realignment. How is EEOC going to justify its distortion of the act of Congress? It will do so by appealing to the acts of the judicial branch of government.

Here again the teleological and historicist elements of liberal social ideology appear. According to EEOC, we are witnessing "the evolution of equal employment law."[15] Evolution by itself simply means change through time, but for EEOC the development is in a special direction, and that is what makes it teleological. That direction is alleged to be implicit in the Civil Rights Act of 1964. Of course we know that it is definitely not explicit. "What was not fully apparent in 1964 was the magnitude of the effort that would be required to create *genuine equality of opportunity* and the specific measures needed to accomplish the task."[16] [Italics added.] I take it that equal opportunity is "genuine" when it achieves the ideally integrated society. Finally, it appears to be EEOC's notion that law evolves in the courts and in the bureaucracy.

No one would seriously question the contention that in Anglo-Saxon jurisprudence the common law evolves. That, in fact, is its great strength and source of vitality. But evolution is not to be confused with progress. Hitherto the evolution was understandable only from a conservative point of view. This is something in the American tradition that liberals choose to ignore. This law is a vast reservoir of precedents and not a neat logical or metaphysical system of first principles about universal human nature from which we deduce applications. We are witnessing the attempt to superimpose upon our conservative practice a liberal teleological theory. When liberals talk about judicial discretion, what they really mean is not adjusting the inherited wisdom of the past to the present but rather viewing the past and present as progress toward some utopian future. Even when liberals recognize the importance of legislative intent, they reserve the right to interpret it as well from the point of view of the future![17]

The first important case to have come up was the product of the so-called Philadelphia Plan. The construction trades unions in Philadelphia were all-white, resulting in large part from father-son practices in the union. The Department of Labor, in 1969, ordered an end to that practice and instituted goals and timetables in minority recruitment. This was the first major application of Order No. 4 of 1968. The Contractors Association of Eastern Pennsylvania took the case to court and appealed Order No. 4 on the grounds that Title VII bans discrimination and that the "goals and timetables" of Order No. 4 are discriminatory quotas. In 1971, in federal court, the Third Circuit Court of Appeals, the secretary of labor was upheld. The contractors then took the case to the Supreme Court, but the Supreme Court refused to hear it. In the federal court, Judge John Gibbons seemed to endorse the notion that realignment was implicit in Title VII:

> Clearly the Philadelphia Plan is color-conscious. . . . [In order to reject it we] would have to attribute to Congress the intention to freeze the status quo and to foreclose remedial action [to] overcome existing evils.[18]

EEOC cites this case and others from the federal courts to establish that "goals and timetables [have] been repeatedly upheld by the courts."[19] Two other 1971 cases were also important in the eyes of EEOC, explaining the force of the 1971 guidelines and the use of the concept of underutilization. In the case of *Swann* v. *Charlotte-Mecklenburg Board of Education*, the U.S. Supreme Court concluded that local communities could voluntarily, that is, on their own initiative, assign students by race for educational purposes even where no prior de jure segregation existed. EEOC concluded from this that the Supreme Court was upholding realignment:

> The Supreme Court has given broad scope to the States in taking voluntary action to promote equality, even when the action is race conscious and is not explicitly designed to remedy a constitutional wrong.[20]

The watershed case in EEOC's tale of the evolution of equal employment law is supposed to be the 1971 case of *Griggs* v. *Duke Power Company*, wherein the Supreme Court interpreted Title VII as forbidding the use of aptitude tests and the requirement of the North Carolina power company that employees have a high school diploma, even if there were no intent to use these as discriminatory.[21] Minorities failed the test disproportionately, presumably because of previous educational deprivation. EEOC interprets this decision not only as an endorsement of the statistical trend argument but as an endorsement of realignment. It is in their eyes an endorsement of realignment because the Supreme Court is allegedly rejecting any practice with adverse impact on minorities.

There is one important qualification in the decision, and it is one admitted by EEOC. The Supreme Court does not literally bar tests or other criteria if those tests and criteria are demonstrably and directly related to job performance. Fair enough. But behind this seemingly major concession are two ploys:

Ploy I: Are we talking about minimum standard performance or best possible performance? If the former, almost everyone can have almost every job. Moreover, other government regulations make it next to impossible or impractical to dismiss the less or least able employees.

Ploy II: Any definition of a performance that has adverse impact can be attacked as discriminatory. Part of the strategy here is to make it costly for employers to prove that their tests are job-related. Moreover, in December of 1977, EEOC issued *Interpretation Regulation Guidelines for Remedial and/or Affirmative Action Appropriate under Title VII of the CRA*.[22] Focusing on race and sex, and excluding mention of religion or national origin, Item 4 promises to protect employers from reverse discrimination suits, and Item 5 makes clear that EEOC reserves the right to use its bureaucratic discretion to decide if enough has been done.

These two ploys explain why from EEOC's point of view the test of discrimination is no longer *intent* to disciminate but having an *adverse impact* on minorities. This is known as institutional discrimination as opposed to intentional discrimination. The neat thing about this concept is that it provides the missing link to past overt oppression, since institutional discrimination allegedly reflects the cumulative effects of past acts of intentional discrimination.

For EEOC these cases can be interpreted as accomplishing the following. First, affirmative action can deal with alleged covert oppression; second, affirmative action need not confine itself either to the past or to individuals but can deal with groups; third, affirmative action can seek to engineer realignment. These points are buttressed by an appeal to the Justice Department and to one other court case. The Justice Department has declared:

> The consequences of discrimination are too complex to dissect case-by-case. . . . and a [school or employer] dealing with imponderables of this sort ought not to be confined to the choice of either ignoring the problem or attempting the Sisyphean task of discerning its importance on an individual basis.[23]

In short, EEOC may safely ignore individuals and concentrate on groups. The connection between groups and realignment is achieved by appeal to the Supreme Court statement that (*and here I quote EEOC's quote of the court record*):

. . . absent discrimination, it is to be expected that work forces will be "more or less representative of the population in the community from which employees are hired."[24]

We have now completed our survey of how the bureaucracy has taken Titles VI and VII, as well as executive orders on affirmative action and the actions of various courts and other bureaucratic agencies, and interpreted and implemented them solely from within the perspective of liberal social ideology. What are we to make of it? I want to argue, and I hope to show in the next section, that this is a complete distortion of the law as well as the Constitution. For the moment, I would characterize the operations of the bureaucracy as akin to a group of lawyers who have commandeered fire engines and rushed to a number of buildings. These buildings have been selected because an ethereal smoke is coming out of each. I say ethereal because not everyone can see the smoke and the alarms haven't gone off. The lawyers then proceed to pour kerosene onto the buildings. When asked why, they respond, "Where there's smoke there must be fire." When asked why the use of kerosene, they say that it is the best they can do, for they have no water.

THE ROLE OF THE JUDICIARY

Article III, section 1, of the U.S. Constitution establishes that "the judicial power of the United States shall be vested in one Supreme Court, and in such inferior courts as the Congress may from time to time ordain and establish." Section VI states that "this constitution, and the laws of the United States which shall be made in pursuance thereof . . . . shall be the supreme law of the land. . . . anything to the contrary notwithstanding." A crucial element in the interpretation of the law is the concept of *judicial review*, the power of the Supreme Court to determine when laws are consistent with the Consititution. Judicicial review is not specified in the Constitution itself but was the result of judicial construction or interpretation. Chief Justice John Marshall, in the case of *Marbury* v. *Madison*, ruled that without judicial review a written constitution would be powerless to limit the abuses of government power.[25]

The power of judicial review of the U.S. Supreme Court is exercised with restraints imposed by that court upon itself. *First*, the Court operates with the assumption that the legislature did not "intend" to violate the Constitution. Hence, the burden of proof must rest with the party that sues. In fact, the Court prefers not to rule on issues of constitutionality if any statute can be interpreted in a manner that will save appearances. *Second*, in order to avoid frivolous suits and constant disruption, the suing party must have a direct and substantial interest in the matter at stake. *Third*, in the name of the separation of powers, the Court recognizes that some questions are political and therefore nonjusticiable. Among these are the responsibilities of the president to see to the faithful execution of the laws. However, this does not mean that the president has carte blanche. For in 1935 the Supreme Court invalidated the National Industrial Recovery Act because it allowed the chief executive to make laws; and in 1952 it invalidated Truman's seizure of the steel mills because the action required an act of Congress. These restraints, especially the third, provided the space within which EEOC carried out its distortion.

One other technicality about the operations of the U.S. Supreme Court is worthy of note. If the Court decides to review a case from a lower court or courts, it issues a writ of *certiorari*. The petition to grant such a writ must have the support of at least four justices. We have already indicated at least three reasons for the Court's not acting on a case or issue. Failure to gain the support of at least four justices is another. Even more important for our purposes is the fact that the Court will not always issue a writ of *certiorari* and routinely does not provide an explanation for its failure to do so. To provide an explanation would in effect be to rule on every case. Without this self-imposed restraint, the principle of the separation of powers would be violated by the Court itself.

It is this restraint that is subject to the most misunderstanding and potential abuse. Failing to issue a writ of *certiorari*, does not signify that the Court approves of the decision of the lower court. We have indicated a number of reasons why the Court might refuse to issue a writ. Moreover, the ruling of the lower court remains effective, but only within the geographic limits of that circuit court. It is not national law. It is even possible that the majority of the Supreme Court may consider a lower court ruling in error, and still not issue a writ. That is why the law of the land and the dictates of the U.S. Constitution may be determined only by looking to the actual and specific decisions of the U.S. Supreme Court— and not in what it refuses to decide.

We are now in a position to expose EEOC's systematic distortion of judicial action. The key is in the definition of affirmative action as under-utilization determined by statistical survey, and the introduction of goals and timetables to overcome the discriminaton as implicitly measured by the underutilization. These concepts emerged clearly in 1971. In 1971 the Supreme Court refused to overrule or review the decision of the Third Circuit Court in the Philadelphia Plan. EEOC took the denial of a writ of *certiorari* to mean that the lower court's decision in that specific case could be extended as law to all cases. The denial of *certiorari* is specifically claimed by EEOC to be an endorsement of the policy "to grant preferential treatment simply because of racial imbalances that exist in the work force."[27] The statement by EEOC moves back and forth about cases and persistently uses the expression the "courts" almost indiscrim-

inately for federal courts and the Supreme Court. But no decision by the
federal courts is the same as a decision by the Supreme Court.

The next distorted case was the *Swann* decision in 1971. EEOC
assumed the Supreme Court to be making realignment the law of the
land. On the contrary, if we read the dictum of Chief Justice Warren
Burger we see the specific rejection of such a concept:

> . . . a prescribed ratio of Negro to white students reflecting the proportion
> for the district as a whole. To do this as an educational policy is within the
> broad discretionary powers of school authorities; absent a finding of consti-
> tutional violation, however, that would not be within the authority of a
> federal court.
>
> . . . mathematical ratios was within the equitable remedial discretion of the
> District Court.[28]

There is a difference between what is permissible voluntarily and what
the courts can order in the absence of specific proof of discrimination. A
remedy presupposes a finding of prior discrimination. Reading this back
into the Philadelphia Plan, we note that previous discrimination was a
factor. Reading this forward to *DeFunis* and *Bakke*, we note that such
assignments as the Court allows excludes no individual but merely concerns assignment to a specific school. *DeFunis* and *Bakke* involved
exclusions.

The other 1971 case used by EEOC to establish realignment was
Griggs. Rather than endorsing realignment, the Supreme Court went out
of its way to disclaim it and, in addition, to uphold the merit principle. In
this case the merit principle recognizes not just whether people are qualified but who is better qualified.

> Congress did not intend . . . to guarantee a job to every person regardless
> of qualifications. . . . [Title VII] does not command that any person be
> hired simply because he was formerly the subject of discrimination, or
> because he is a member of a minority group. Discriminatory preference for
> any group, minority or majority, is precisely and only what Congress has
> proscribed. . . . Congress has not commanded that the less qualified be
> preferred over the better qualified simply because of minority origins. Far
> from disparaging job qualifications as such, Congress has made such quali-
> fications the controlling factor, so that race, religion, nationality, and sex
> become irrelevant.[29]

It does not seem to me that the decision of the Supreme Court
could be any clearer. The most that EEOC could validly infer from
Griggs was that employers would have to validate or justify any job
requirements. Having to tread lightly, EEOC resorted to convincing employers to institute voluntary goals and timetables. This raised in its turn

the question of the constitutionality of self-imposed quota systems. I use the expression "quota system" in this context because any employer who had validated criteria would not need any specific numerical target. We should recall that we are discussing cases where there is no history or evidence of previous discrimination. We should also keep in mind what "voluntary" means in this context.

The first challenge to this "voluntarily" imposed quota system came in university admissions, not in the job market. Marco DeFunis had been denied admission to the University of Washington Law School, which had a separate admissions procedure and different evaluation criteria for minority applicants. DeFunis raised the constitutional issue by appealing to the Fourteenth Amendment, not Title VI or VII, claiming that he had been denied equal protection of the laws. A lower court upheld DeFunis, and the judge, Lloyd Shorett, instructed the University of Washington Law School to admit DeFunis. The university complied but also appealed the case to the Washington Supreme Court. The latter court reversed the lower court decision. The case was then appealed to the U.S. Supreme Court, although DeFunis continued to attend the law school. Oral argument was held before the Court on February 26, 1974, but in late April a majority of the Court declared the case moot. That is, it decided not to review the case. The question is why, and what did that mean? The reason is simple enough. Since the Court had assurance that DeFunis would be graduating from the law school, the Court could claim that there was no longer a party with a direct and substantial interest.

Many other interested parties were disappointed by the refusal of the Court to review the issues involved. Many people tried to make much of the failure to decide, just as others tried to capitalize on the fact that four justices (Douglas, Marshall, White, and Brennan) dissented on mooting the case. The latter wished the Court to arrive at some decision. So what did the decision not to decide mean?

Let us confine ourselves to what is purely objective. First, DeFunis had successfully challenged the University of Washington Law School. Second, one may reasonably infer that mooting was as technically based as it appeared to be. One of the mooters, Blackmun, later voted for realignment in *Bakke*. Among the other mooters there was support for Bakke. Among the dissenters to mooting, Douglas was opposed to realignment, whereas Marshall was in favor. In retrospect from the *Bakke* case, we can see that three of the mooters (Stewart, Rehnquist, and Burger) would consistently maintain that the issues involved could be resolved by reference to the statutes alone without appeal to the U.S. Constitution. Third, EEOC had originally issued a brief in support of the University of Washington and against DeFunis, but Solicitor General Robert Bork (under Nixon) had requested the Court not to accept the brief. The Court complied.

EEOC could take small comfort in the DeFunis result. Its response consisted of two points: first, to cloud the issue, and second, to insist that special minority admittees were qualified. The purpose was to salvage some vestige of realignment by obscuring the difference between minimally qualified and best qualified. This is consistent with the ploys used in connection with the *Griggs* case.

> While courts have differed in their view of the constitutionality of affirmative admissions programs, none has found reason to dispute the representation of the professional schools that the minority students admitted were qualified.[30]

Under the circumstances EEOC is forced to adopt a more defensive posture, which means arguing that affirmative action is the overcoming of past discrimination and that such discrimination is inferable from the statistics. Increasingly, statistics must be used because, with the passage of time and the objective working out of the Civil Rights Act of 1964, overt cases of discrimination are harder and harder to find. That is why EEOC keeps invoking the Justice Department:

> But as the Justice Department has noted, it would be an extraordinarily difficult task to require professional schools to substitute for their present programs a case-by-case examination of the impact of discrimination on each minority applicant.[31]

No doubt universities will be heartened by the solicitous concern shown for them by EEOC. Moreover, I shall not dwell on the obvious hypocrisy and contradiction of this stance on admissions with the merciless demand that universities validate their hiring criteria. The important point is that the Justice Department is just another government bureaucracy and *not* the Supreme Court. The Justice Department neither makes the law not determines it. We may also question whether the task is difficult ("Sisyphean"), or is it just impossible to make the case? In order to make the case, one would have to prove that statistical underachievement is a direct result of previously segregated schools and public facilities. This, as we have repeatedly pointed out, is *a hypothesis and not a fact*. And the one thing that advocates of realignment want to avoid is an open challenge to their hypotheses or even to have them exposed as hypotheses.

The other obvious difficulty that EEOC faces is the explicit mention in Titles VI and VII of individuals and not groups. Their endeavor to overcome this obstacle leads to the greatest distortion. Repeatedly EEOC makes use of the 1977 case *International Brotherhood of Teamsters* v. *United States* to claim that the Supreme Court accepts the statistical argument as proof of discrimination. When we examine the actual case record we find, yes, that statistics are allowed; but the qualifications on the use of statistics are never mentioned by EEOC. Let us note them:

> The Government bolstered its statistical evidence with the testimony of individuals who recounted over 40 specific instances of discrimination. . . . individuals who testified about their personal experiences with the company brought the cold numbers convincingly to life. . . . We caution only that statistics . . . like any other kind of evidence . . . may be rebutted. In short, their usefulness depends upon all the surrounding facts and circumstances.

> . . . statistical evidence was not offered or used to support an erroneous theory that Title VII requires an employer's work force to be racially balanced. . . . 703 (j) makes clear that Title VII imposes no requirement that a work force mirror the general population. . . .

> . . . figures for the general population might not actually reflect the pool of qualified job applicants. . . .[32]

We stress that the U.S. Supreme Court has made clear—in that part of its judgment that EEOC fails to quote—that Title VII will not justify realignment. If this were not enough, we may cite an instance where EEOC does quote the exact words of the Court and then offers an interpretation of those words that is consistent with EEOC's own cherished support of realignment but is a ludicrous distortion of the Court's own view. First, the Court:

> . . . *absent explanation*, it is *ordinarily* to be expected that nondiscriminatory hiring practices will in time result in a work force more or less representative of the racial and ethnic composition of the population in the community from which employees are hired. [Italics added.]

Now, EEOC:

> . . . the most appropriate guide may be found in the Supreme Court's suggestion that absent discrimination, it is to be expected that work forces will be "more or less representative of the population in the community from which employees are hired."[33]

Not only is there a very strong difference between an "expectation" and "ordinarily to be expected," for the latter implies all sorts of qualifications, but the Court spoke about what might be the case in the absence of explanation, not in the absence of discrimination. There surely are all kinds of possible explanations for the lack of statistical parity. There are in fact many alternative hypotheses, perhaps some with more plausibility than the covert oppression hypothesis so dear to liberals.

THE BAKKE CASE

In a case very similar to *De Funis*, Alan Bakke sued the Medical School of the University of California at Davis on the grounds that his rejection was an instance of reverse discrimination. Davis had set aside 16 seats out of each class of 100, specifically for minorities. Bakke argued that this violated Title VI of the 1964 Civil Rights Act. He did not raise the constitutional issue but merely referred to specific statutes.

In July of 1978, the Supreme Court ruled five to four in Bakke's favor. By the narrowest of margins, the Supreme Court had ruled in no uncertain terms that the Civil Rights Act of 1964 did not condone the interpretation of affirmative action given by EEOC, HEW, and myriad other government bureaucracies.

Some of the details are worth noting. Although a majority ruled in Bakke's favor, not all members of the majority did so with the same explanation. Four of the justices (Burger, Stewart, Rehnquist, and Stevens) ruled on the narrow grounds that Section 601 of the Civil Rights Act of 1964 prohibits reverse discrimination. In their eyes, the statutory grounds were unusually clear. In effect, this bears out what we have so far said about Title VI and Title VII. For these men, the mere technicalities of the statutes are totally at odds with the liberal reading.

The fifth justice who supported Bakke, Lewis Powell, went even further and decided on fundamental constitutional grounds that the Medical School of the University of California at Davis had violated Bakke's rights under the Fourteenth Amendment and had denied him the equal protection of the laws.

Powell then joined the dissenting minority (Marshall, Brennan, White, and Blackmun) and formed a second but different majority who ruled that a university could continue to take race into account in admissions decisions, even at the graduate level. This decision reversed the California Supreme Court, which had not only upheld Bakke but had forbidden the university to use its discretion on admissions.

Perhaps the most remarkable thing to emerge from this split was the attempt on the part of the liberal elements in the media to present Powell's moves as a compromise and to minimize the extent to which the Court's decision undercut affirmative action. Even a cursory reading of the opinions of the justices will show just how untenable such a feat of legal gymnastics is.

The basic facts are:

1. Powell's support of Bakke was more sweeping than that of the

other justices because he anchored his support in the Constitution.

2. Powell's reasons for the second decision about taking race into account is totally at odds with the reasons given by the "minority four" and provides no support whatsoever for a liberal reading.

3. A careful reading of Powell's decision will reveal that it is both a point by point rebuttal of the Brennan interpretation (who spoke for the "minority four") and an uncompromising and explicit rejection of re-alignment and the hypotheses on which it is based.

To begin with, Powell reiterated that the law and previous Supreme Court decisions were directed toward overt instances of oppression:

Petitioner [U. of California] contends that on several occasions this court has approved preferential classifications without applying the most exacting scrutiny. Most of the cases upon which petitioner relies are drawn from three areas: school desegregation, employment discrimination, and sex discrimination. Each of the cases cited presented a situation materially different from the facts of this case.

The school desegregation cases are inapposite. Each involved remedies for clearly determined constitutional violations. E.g., *Swann* v. *Charlotte-Mecklenburg* . . . the scope of the remedies was not permitted to exceed the extent of the violations. . . .

The employment discrimination cases also do not advance the petitioner's cause. For example, in *Franks* v. *Bowman Transportation Co.* . . . (1975), we approved a retroactive award of seniority to a class of Negro truck drivers who had been the victims of discrimination—not just by society at large, but by the respondent in that case. . . . But we have never approved preferential classifications in the absence of proven constitutional or statutory violations. . . .

Petitioner also cites *Lau* v. *Nichols* . . . (1974). . . . Lau, properly is viewed as a case in which the remedy for an administrative finding of discrimination encompassed measures to improve the previously disadvantaged group's ability to participate, without excluding individuals belonging to any other group from enjoyment of the relevant opportunity—meaningful participation in the electoral process.

. . . When a classification denies an individual opportunites or benefits enjoyed by others solely because of his race or ethnic background, it must be regarded as suspect.

Moreover, the overt instances of oppression can only be against individuals and specific groups of individuals:

We have never approved a classification that aids persons perceived as members of relatively victimized groups at the expense of other innocent individuals in the absence of judicial, legislative, or administrative findings of constitutional or statutory violations. See, e.g., *Teamsters* v. *United States* . . . (1977).

Powell then goes on to reject the hypothesis of covert oppression as an unsubstantiated hypothesis. Here Powell makes clear his differences with the "minority four" in words that come close to accusing them of distorting the Constitution:

. . . I disagree with much that is said in their opinion.

They would require as a justification for a program such as petitioner's, only two findings: (i) that there has been some form of discrimination against the preferred minority groups "by society at large" . . . and (ii) that "there is reason to believe" that the disparate impact sought to be rectified by the program is the "product" of such discrimination. . . .

The breadth of this hypothesis is unprecedented in our constitutional system. The first step is easily taken. . . . The second step, however, involves a speculative leap: but for this discrimination by society at large, Bakke "would have failed to qualify for admission" because Negro applicants . . . would have made better scores. *Not one word in the record supports this conclusion*. . . . [Italics added.]

On the basis of the foregoing, Powell concludes that anything like realignment into an ideally integrated society is constitutionally unacceptable:

. . . the plurality offers no standards for courts to use in applying such a presumption of causation to other racial or ethnic classifications. . . . it would seem difficult to determine that any of the dozens of minority groups that have suffered "societal discrimination" cannot also claim it, in any area of social intercourse. . . .

There is no principled basis for deciding which groups would merit "heightened judicial solitcitude" and which would not. . . . The kind of variable sociological and political analysis necessary to produce such rankings simply does not lie within the judicial competence—even if they otherwise were politically feasible and socially desirable.

Moreover, there are serious problems of justice connected with the idea of preference itself. First, it may not always be clear that a so-called preference is in fact benign. . . . Second, preferential programs may only reinforce common stereotypes holding that certain groups are unable to achieve success without special protection based on a factor having no relationship to individual worth. See *DeFunis* . . . (Douglas, J.,dissenting). Third, there is a measure of inequity in forcing innocent persons in respondent's position to bear the burdens of redressing grievances not of their making.

By hitching the meaning of the Equal Protection Clause to these transitory considerations, we would be holding, as a constitutional principle, that judicial scrutiny of classifications touching on racial and ethnic background may vary with the ebb and flow of political forces. Disparate constitutional tolerance of such classifications may well serve to exacerbate racial and ethnic antagonisms rather than alleviate them. . . . Also, the mutability of a constitutional principle, based upon shifting political and social judgments, undermines the chances for consistent application of the Constitution from one generation to the next, a critical feature of its coherent interpretation.

Anything short of this, in Powell's view, is a sacrifice of principle to expediency. To drive home this point in the most dramatic fashion, Powell quotes in ironic fashion the words of Archibald Cox (of Watergate fame—a man of principle, no doubt) and the attorney for the anti-Bakke camp:

In expounding the Constitution, the Court's role is to discern "principles sufficiently absolute to give them roots throughout the community and continuity over significant periods of time, and to lift them above the level of the pragmatic political judgments of a particular time and place."

There are two other elements in Powell's position worth stressing. The first is the meaning of the Court's decision for the federal bureaucracy, and the second is its relevance for education. With regard to the bureaucracy, Powell makes clear that the University of California at Davis Medical School did not carefully formulate its quotas, but, rather, uncritically accepted them from HEW and EEOC—and that the latter were acting unconstitutionally in formulating them in the first place.

. . . isolated segments of our vast governmental structure are not competent to make those decisions at least in the absence of legislative mandates and legislatively determined criteria.

In addition, recalling the old Anglo-Saxon legal principle that people are innocent until proven guilty, Powell dwells on the meaning of EEOC's magical phrase "good faith":

In short, good faith would be presumed in the absence of a showing to the contrary in the manner permitted by our cases.

Addressing the issue of education, Powell affirms the separation of university and state. It is not the business of the university to run society, nor is it the business of the government to run education:

> Petitioner [U. of California] does not purport to have made, and is in no position to make such findings. Its broad mission is education, not the formulation of any legislative policy or the adjudication of particular claims of illegality.

> . . . It is the business of a university to provide that atmosphere which is most conducive to speculation, experiment and creation. It is an atmosphere in which there prevail "the four essential freedoms" of a university— to determine for itself on academic grounds who may teach, what may be taught, how it shall be taught, and who may be admitted to study. (Frankfurter, *Sweezy* v. *New Hampshire*, 1957).

We stress Powell's notion of who runs the university and for what purposes. Moreover, Powell places his finger on a much missed subtle point critical to both education and to government intervention. Diversity, like creativity, is not subject to rules. A standardized and uniform conception of diversity is self-contradictory.

> Petitioner's special admission program, focused solely on ethnic diversity, would hinder rather than further attainment of genuine diversity.

Finally, Powell praises the Harvard Plan (finding the unpolished diamond), which, while taking race into account, is different from any quota system precisely because the plan does "not insulate the individual from comparison with all other candidates for available seats."[34]

THE BUREAUCRATIC REACTION

U.S. Attorney General Griffin Bell: "This is the first time the Supreme Court has upheld affirmative action, and it has done it in about as strong a way as possible."[35]

HEW Secretary Joseph Califano: ". . . strongly supports this nation's continuing effort to live up to its historic promise—to bring minorities and other disadvantaged groups into the mainstream of American society through admissions policies that recognize the importance of diverse, integrated educational institutions."[36]

EEOC head Eleanor Holmes Norton: "My reading of the decision is that we are not compelled to do anything differently from the way we've done things in the past, and we are not going to."[37] The following was reported in the *Los Angeles Times*:

Mrs. Norton said the EEOC had found "several indications" in the opinion by Justice Lewis Powell "that we may continue to set numerical targets" for the hiring of women and members of minorities. . . ."virtually everything we do falls under the rubric of congressionally authorized actions," which Justice Powell's opinion appeared to uphold.[38]

The *Bakke* decision and the opinion of Justice Powell represent not the vindication of affirmative action but the explicit restriction of it to stage one (platitudes) and noncontroversial instances of stage two (remediation). In no uncertain terms it rejects realignment. Are we to conclude from this that the aforementioned spokesmen and spokeswoman for the bureaucracy are simply putting the best face on what otherwise must have been a bitter disappointment for them?

There is another scenario possible. The *Bakke* decision represents a mere, temporary setback for those liberals who seek realignment. To begin with, one vote would have completely changed the course of America. The "minority four" of Brennan, White, Blackmun, and Marshall explicitly accepted the concept of realignment. When one recalls that Burger, Powell, Rehnquist, and Stevens were appointed by Nixon and Ford, all since 1969, it is easy to imagine that had Hubert H. Humphrey won election in 1968, the Court would have been completely different. The Court is not a monolithic entity; rather, it consists of a changing set of nine members, Moreover, the Constitution is in the final analysis what a majority of the Court says that it is. There is yet hope for the future. After all, *Brown* v. *Board of Education* in 1954 reversed *Plessy* v. *Ferguson* (1896). A future Court may reverse *Bakke*. When you believe in teleology, history is ultimately on your side.

For those who had hoped to compare the *Bakke* case to the *Brown* case of 1954, there is a peculiar irony. Thurgood Marshall was the first black Supreme Court justice, but he did not join the Court until 1967. The *Brown* case was decided by nine white men, and no proponent of civil rights or affirmative action ever questioned the wisdom of that decision. Now that the Supreme Court is racially balanced (there are nine justices, and blacks make up 11 percent of the United States population), the decision is not to their liking. Is there a lesson to be learned from all this?

In the meantime, it is business as usual. The bureaucracy reports to and is responsible to the president. If need be, the bureaucracy can defy, ignore, or circumvent even the president. If the president is at all inclined to activist intervention, then he can become a captive of his subordinates and agencies. The chief executive has merely to look at the figures and claim credit for solving our problems. The figures might tell him that women and minorities are increasingly being employed and earning more. That proves that the problem of discrimination is being solved. Of course, this might exacerbate the problem of inflation, but then that problem will be the excuse for even greater intervention into the economy.

At the same time, the bureaucracy can carry out the unpleasant aspects of the job without having to take responsibility for what it does. It is merely following orders. It behaves like the police force told to produce suspects and get convictions. The surest convictions require a confession, and such confessions are implicit when employers agree to goals and timetables. The bureaucracy can even engage in benign torture, such as holding up contracts and funds. Making a good faith effort is a kickback, sometimes outright extortion. More often than not it is an added cost passed on to the consumer.

The original government brief on Bakke was prepared by Wade McCree, solicitor general, and Drew Days, assitant attorney general for civil rights. Both were blacks who had made it on their own. They originally supported Bakke's admission, declared Davis's program unconstitutional, and gave tentative support to the use of race in admissions. When their brief was leaked, tremendous opposition from domestic advisor S. Eizenstadt, Califano, the Black Caucus headed by Representative P. Mitchell, U.N. Ambassador Andrew Young, and Secretary of Housing and Urban Development Patricia Roberts Harris forced a retreat.

Two attempts have been made in Congress to clip the wings of bureaucratic abuse. In 1976, the House passed an amendment to an education bill that specifically prohibited the HEW secretary from requiring "the imposition of quotas, goals, or any other numerical requirements on the student admission practice of an institution of higher education . . . receiving Federal funds." The Senate balked and a compromise measure was adopted, one that specifically addressed the benign torture of holding up money:

> It shall be unlawful for the Secretary to defer or limit any Federal financial assistance on the basis of any failure to comply with the imposition of quotas (or any numerical requirements which have the effect of imposing quotas) on the student admission practices of an institution of higher education. . . .[39]

In 1977, the House had tried once more with an even stronger provision:

> None of the funds appropriated in this Act may be obligated or expended in connection with the issuance, implementation, or enforcement of any rule, regulation, standard, guideline, recommendation, or order issued by the Secretary of Health, Education, and Welfare which for purposes of compliance with any ratio, quota, or other numerical requirement related to race, creed, color, national origin, or sex requires any individual or entity to take any action with respect to (1) the hiring or promotion policies or

practices of such individual or entity, or (2) the admissions policies and practices of such an individual or entity.[40]

On this bill, the Senate not only balked but refused even to compromise.

What, then, is the message from Congress? Congress has two houses, one of which, at that time, (the House of Representatives) was opposed to realignment, and one of which (the Senate) condoned it. This division provided another space for bureaucratic misrepresentation. The real moral of this story is that it is easier to make a law than it is to either unmake it or prevent its abuse. In an interventionist government, the hardest vote is a "no" vote.

In retrospect, it is clear that Congress should have defined "discrimination." Some attention was called to this matter but it came from sources deemed beyond the pale.[41] No doubt some members of Congress thought that the concept was clear enough, especially in light of the statements made by those who initiated the legislation. The intent of the law is clear enough, but the actual consequences of enforcement are another matter. The consensus achieved in 1964 was only a shadow hiding from each member the very different visions of what would emerge. To be sure, most of the bill's supporters were liberal, but liberalism is a formula into which each can plug his private vision. I think that it was not deemed necessary in 1964 and 1965 to define "discrimination," because at that time liberals had little idea of the inherent conflicts in their shared ideology. The significance of affirmative action is that for the first time we have been confronted with the shattered remnants of a once unified ideology.

Although Congress may have been of many minds about the outcome of the law, not the law itself, the forces installed in the bureaucracy were not so divided. For them, nothing short of the ideally integrated society was acceptable. In effect, goals, timetables, underutilization, and quotas became not solutions to a problem but solutions in search of a problem. In order to justify quotas, now the hallmark of a fair race, the bureaucrats were eager to uncover "discrimination" in places where sane men would never have dreamed of finding it.[42]

RECENT HISTORY

The *Bakke* battle may be over, but the war is not. Liberals continue to seek out interpretations of Supreme Court and even lower court action that will show in some arcane way that *Bakke* is not final. One candidate sometimes proffered is the *Weber* decision of 1979.

Brian Weber unsuccessfully sued Kaiser to overturn an agreement between Kaiser and its union to use a racial quota rather than seniority in choosing participants, already employed, for a training program. Weber retained his job but failed to be selected for the special program. The Supreme Court argued that Title VII does not require preference but permits it in some specially qualified cases.

The *Weber* decision does not constitute a reversal of *Bakke*. It does not in any way permit EEOC to impose quotas and it does not legitimate realignment. Technically, the case concerns the voluntary self-imposition of quotas by mutual agreement of private business and unions. We should also note in passing that Justices Powell and Stevens withdrew from the case, and Justice Potter Stewart joined the "minority four." The wording of the decision was careful enough to avoid compromising Justice Stewart's position on *Bakke*. The *Weber* case did not deal with new jobs; the agreement was temporary; there was no commitment to maintaining racial balance; and there was no decision on defining what is permissible affirmative action. It should also be noted that the original five to four split in the Court resurfaced in the 1980 decision that faculty at private universities are not employees, but part of management.

More important for our focus is to glimpse briefly what has happened in the federal bureaucracy since Ronald Reagan took office, for this will bear out that the real trenches run through the corridors of the federal bureaucracy. By late 1981, different branches of the bureaucracy were following different and conflicting policies totally dependent upon the extent to which Reagan had been able to put his people into office. The Justice Department is on record as opposing affirmative action as well as busing; the Labor Department claims to favor goals and timetables but also wants to relieve federal contractors of excessive paperwork requirements; EEOC, under J. Clay Smith, Jr. (a Carter appointee) continues to march to the old tune. In fact, Smith had to be reprimanded in a September 22, 1981, letter from the Justice Department in which he was reminded that there is *no statutory authority for goals and timetables.*

The bureaucratic conflict came to a real head when, in November of 1981, President Reagan removed Arthur S. Flemming as chairman of the U.S. Commission on Civil Rights. Curiously, no member of that commission had resigned when Reagan took office. Subsequently, Reagan appointed Clarence Pendelton to replace Flemming. Pendelton is on record as being opposed to both busing and affirmative action as remedies. In 1983, the committee was restructured.

What conclusions do I draw? The policies of the bureaucracy depend upon who is appointed. President Reagan has slowly but surely moved to terminate the bureaucratic misuse of the doctrine of affirmative action. Both the 1981 furor with Smith and the 1983 furor with the Civil Rights Commission came at exactly the same time as Reagan was proposing new nominations for the agencies. Finally, Senator Orrin Hatch has moved to curtail once and for all the abuse of bureaucratic power by proposing a constitutional amendment outlawing quotas.

I would speculate that the future of this issue may be determined by the composition of the Supreme Court. President Reagan is in a strategic position to make appointments such as Justice O'Connor. On the other side, we are increasingly hearing about the burdensome workload of the Court, and this may be a signal that the liberals are preparing once more to pack the Court in order to offset Reagan appointees. But recently Chief Justice Burger proposed a lower buffer court rather than increasing the size of the Supreme Court.

I am convinced that the policy of affirmative action is the product of a kind of historical hallucination, as witnessed by the fact that some people think the policy was intended to overcome the results of slavery. Discrimination has been replaced by "slavery" in their view of the intent of the law. I have tried in this book to provide a form of therapy for this misperception. If the historical review fails to accomplish a truer perception, it is because egalitarians, as we shall see, are driven by political fanaticism, not by any objective grievance that could be understood or dealt with within the historical framework of the social life we all share.

CHAPTER **3**

The Modern American University

> I could be more respectful of most of the current repud-
> iations of the university conceived as center for the dis-
> passionate study of nature, society, and man if it were
> not for the fact that in these there is more than repud-
> iation of the university: there is also repudiation of the
> ideal of dispassionate reason. I do not see how civilization
> can very long survive that.—Robert Nisbet, *The Degra-
> dation of the Academic Dogma*

ORIGINS

We are witnessing the slow strangulation of the modern American university. The major question raised by this ongoing event is whether it is a
case of suicide or murder, for the curious paradox is that the university is
both the perpetrator and the victim.

We who are apt to take for granted the success and prestige of the
modern American university might do well to recall its history. Although
universities are medieval European institutions in their origins, and colleges existed even in colonial America, the modern American university
as we know it is largely a product of the post–Civil War period.[1] Its
prestige is even more recent. Indeed, in the latter half of the nineteenth
century students could go directly from high school into law and medicine. The number of lawyers and doctors who had college degrees actually
declined during this period. Even as late as 1889, Andrew Carnegie could
excoriate that "as far as business affairs are concerned. . . college education as it exists is fatal to success in that domain."[2] At the same time,
Carnegie's remark is symptomatic of the important event in the last half
of the nineteenth century that was to create the modern American university. Advanced education became a necessary condition for sustaining
and advancing the industrial revolution. This is true of the whole of the

51

industrial world. As a result, business became the patron of universities and readily employed their graduates. The post–Civil War advance of industrialization thus accounts for the increased growth and later the prestige of the modern American university, but it does not account for either the existence or the internal structure of universities.

FACTIONS

The diversity of factions comprising the modern university reflects the historical fact that the American educational tradition has always been marked by wide diversity. Institutions of higher learning were the product of a variety of sources: local communities, religious affiliation, or private benefactors. Against this background we can now note the four competing conceptions of what a university is supposed to be, each with its own well-organized and articulate supporters within the university community.

Perhaps the oldest faction reflects the religious origin of universities, when it existed to train clergymen. This faction advocated "discipline and piety" as the main focus of a university education. Its main stronghold was the small college. Significantly, it saw itself in opposition to science for allegedly encouraging atheistic materialism. In an increasingly secular world, it drifted into the third faction, to be discussed below, liberal culture.

In this context, we should recall that many of the people who emigrated to America because of religious conflicts were themselves religious fanatics. The Protestant Reformation, with intellectual roots in neo-Platonic Augustinianism, encouraged the view that knowledge of right and wrong were matters of intuitive, or a priori, insight originating from divine grace. In the context of modernity, the Reformation subscribed to the view that standards were internal and that the individual externalized them in his action rather than conformed to external standards. All of this, as Luther and Calvin discovered, encouraged a certain amount of free-lance lunacy. It was this sort of thing that led Enlightenment thinkers to see religion as socially disruptive. Nevertheless, there remains in America a strong residue of this element in the form of individuals who actively obey their private conscience. William Lloyd Garrison was not the only kind of abolitionist. So was John Brown. The American radical tradition feeds on this element even when it is purely secular, and young people respond to this appeal.

The second faction can be described as *utilitarian*: the university exists as a means to social ends defined externally to the university itself. Whatever their private beliefs, this was certainly a view of the university that could be sold to private donors by the administration. It is a view that naturally stressed vocationalism. It was an anti-elitist view with strong ties to democracy and equality. An example of equality is that for many years Michigan had no chapter of Phi Beta Kappa. Another version of this view was the Wisconsin Idea, the development of extension classes to bring the university to all communities and the use of the college graduate as civil servant to aid both in social and technical planning.

This last point becomes increasingly influential on public affairs. First, each graduate by being knowledgeable would be a "force for civic virtue" in the fight against corruption; second, the university would train future leaders; third, science and scholarship could aid in the solution of social problems. This view is largely associated with President Andrew Dickson White of Cornell. Recall that the founder Ezra Cornell was a Quaker, for increasingly Quakers (e.g., Clark Kerr) will become influential in advocating and administering this view of higher education. For White, the graduates of universities would become the members of the legislature, they would staff the newspapers, they would penetrate the whole of America and eventually the world. For future reference, we should note that this view of the American university was firmly entrenched before 1910.

There is a third faction, which is easily confused with the second. This faction, advocating what has been called *liberal culture, aims not to serve society but to run it.* It is called liberal in the old-fashioned sense that it advocates educating the whole man and not engaging in narrow specialization, But in subscribing to the belief in a well-rounded man, it comes close to advocating liberalism in the sense in which I have been using it. That is, the well-rounded man is the fully developed man, the individual who has reached his full potential not only economically but morally, esthetically, and socially as well. There is nothing sinister per se in the cultural version of this conception of the university, and in fact there is much to be said for it.

But it is capable of becoming more than cultural snobbery. In pressing its opposition to specialization, it comes to place its own private parameters on the search for truth. Thus Hugo Münsterberg can say: "The only scholarship with a right to exist is that which serves the practical need of the masses."[3] But recall that the practical need of the masses eventually is to become like the moral and cultural elite. This is what differentiates it from the purely utilitarian approach. There is also but a short step to the conclusion that the cultural elite, by virtue of being fully developed, should assume the leadership of the whole of society. No one exemplifies this better than Woodrow Wilson, who managed to make the step from the president's office at Princeton University to the White House. In 1902 he could write in *Princeton for the Nation's Service* that in planning for the university he was also "planning for the country."[4]

The fourth and final faction within the university were those who advocated the *research* model, who saw the university as the place for the endowment of scientific and scholarly research and discovery. Invariably, the German universities are cited as the source of this model, and in many important respects they were. Unlike in Great Britain, research in Germany was routinely associated with a university. The American universities imitated it. At the same time, there had always been a research tradition in England, both scientific and scholarly, frequently cultivated by men of independent means, and outside of the university. For these men knowledge was its own end. Something of the flavor of this and the attempt to incorporate it into the British university can be found in Cardinal Newman's *Idea of a University*, published in 1852. I recommend this classic to correct a misimpression about the origins of the research model. It will also serve to dispel the notion that everything has to be explained in economic terms, that specifically the German research model was adopted by American universities in order to serve the march of industrialism. Far from it. There has always been an independent intellectual tradition both inside and outside the university. Although every society has formalized vocational training, not every society has had an independent intellectual tradition.

Not only is there an independent intellectual tradition in the English-speaking world, but whatever one's original motivation for the pursuit of knowledge, the pursuit is perfectly capable of sustaining itself. Many a young man and woman have entered the university to pursue social mobility, but once they have heard the muse they never leave.

The research model of the university is best exemplified in Thorstein Veblen's *Higher Learning in America*, published in 1918 but written before 1910. Veblen identifies the university with its research faculty and characterizes it as the pursuit of idle curiosity. Idle curiosity, or the disinterested pursuit of knowledge, is unintelligible to doctrinaire liberals, for it is the attempt to understand without any prior commitment to draw future policy out of the understanding. It is anti-teleological, for disinterested acts do not fit into any functional system. It is anti-deterministic, because we are free in terms of what we do with it. The past does not determine the future. The ongoing triumph of liberalism is reflected in its ability to convince the public and much of the university community that 'disinterested' is the same as 'uninterested'. Here we may anticipate that the real conflict within the university is not between philistines and serious people, but between the followers of the research model and the advocates of liberal culture.

In terms of the research model we can perhaps best understand the difference between a college and a university. A college is any post-secondary educational institution. A university may, and usually does, encompass a college but it also has graduate schools. The graduate schools include not only those that train future scholars and scientists, but the professional schools such as law and medicine as well. From the point of view of the research model, the professional schools are still vocational. But even within the professional schools a distinction is made between training practitioners and carrying on independent research. The research model, then, identifies the university with researchers, both masters and apprentices.

From this point of view, many of the people who are at the colleges or universities, including faculty as well as students, are not part of the research model. The research model never managed wholly to capture the American university. In fact, the peculiar nature of American universities is that no one of the models dominates. Second, a good deal of what goes on at universities will seem to researchers to be trivial and frivolous, but not necessarily threatening. Third, the vast majority of undergraduates will appear indifferent or even hostile to the values of research, for that is not why most undergraduates go to college. Even the graduate students will frequently appear mediocre. Fourth, given the need to accommodate these other interests, much of university life will revolve around time-consuming busy work. Finally, an administration that must attend to diverse interests will often seem to the researcher to be unsympathetic.

The foregoing is a bare bones summary of Veblen's lament about the obstacles to the research model, but his detailed comments reveal a much richer conception of the university and its problems. To begin with, the university is the only modern institution "on which the quest for knowledge unquestionably devolves."[5] In other words, the organized pursuit of knowledge is unique to universities, and at the same time every other function now performed by universities, from professional training to conferring status, can be performed in other ways and outside the university. Moreover, if the business of the university is to pursue knowledge, then a good teacher must be both a pursuer and someone who can train apprentices or turn students into apprentices. This can be done only in the laboratory and in the seminar, not in the large lecture, which is the preserve of the orators of liberal culture. The bald assertion that research conflicts with teaching is propaganda put forward by advocates of liberal culture.

With regard to the outside world, Veblen acknowledges that while nothing is more important than knowledge, still "the furtherance of civilized life is a larger and more serious interest than the pursuit of knowledge for its own idle sake . . . too serious to be taken care of as a side-issue, by . . . faculty . . . [who are] not men of affairs or adept in worldly wisdom."[6] Here is the antithesis of liberal culture, for here is the acknowledged separation of university and state. Knowledge cannot be in the service of special interest groups because knowledge knows no political or geographic boundaries. In seeking to subordinate itself to the outside world, the university can only compromise itself and become an

instrument for commercial or political exploitation. One of the consequences of making the university the servant of external purposes is the
quantification of university activity, the use of statistics to measure in an
allegedly objective fashion progress toward achieving the specified ends.
We are by now all too familiar with the body count and the numbers
game of worthless publications.

Some of Veblen's most hostile remarks are reserved for his fellow
social scientists. Too often social scientists are occupied with questions of
what ought to be done to improve conditions and protect values that are
already accepted. Consequently, they do not much concern themselves
with finding the "causes" of current conditions, nor do they follow any
argument to its logical conclusion, "in case the conclusion might traverse
the interests of those on whom they are beholden."[7] As a result, social
science all too often becomes a "'science' of complaisant interpretations,
apologies, and projected remedies."[8] Not only is this a fairly accurate
summary for Veblen's time, but, I shall contend, frequently contemporary
social scientists play the same role vis-à-vis the doctrine of liberalism. Far
from attacking the establishment, or critically analyzing current institutions, liberal social scientists engage in "edifying and incisive rehearsals"
of liberal cliches.

FUNDING AND STRUCTURE

The bureaucratic structure of the modern American university was
worked out in the period between 1890 and 1910, and it has not significantly changed since then. It reflected two main facts. First, the serious
researcher in particular and faculty in general did lack the knack for
finding subsidy for their own activity. There may have been one opportunity in the 1880s, during the transitional period from religious denom-
inational control to private secular benefactors, for faculty to gain control
of the university and work out some type of independent subsidy. They
did not take it, partly out of habit, partly for the first reason indicated,
and partly for a second reason. As we have already indicated, the university failed to achieve a unity of purpose. An institution with multiple
purposes, few shared values, and occasional conflicting ones requires a
peculiar kind and degree of academic administration.

The stage was now set for the academic entrepreneur, the college or
university president who engaged in a highly competitive process of expanding the power and prestige of the university, much as a business
executive might do for a private corporation. The very diversity of university purposes proved to be its main source of economic strength; its
diverse activities enabled the university president to seek economic support from diverse private benefactors. Even those who scoff at the way

the university has been a source of social mobility and personal vanity must admit that it has been strengthened by the bequests of large private fortunes, much the same way that the medieval church grew economically powerful through the bequests of those who sought to buy their way into heaven. Even under these admittedly exaggerated conditions, the independence of the university was assured.

This kind of funding was not without its price—it did create a new kind of hypocrisy—but in the end it rested on the awareness on the part of many benefactors that an intellectual elite resided within the university, an elite that inspired both respect and suspicion. To some extent benefactors responded to the notion that the university was the secular embodiment of society's highest values. To a large extent they responded to the recognition that material and industrial progress depended upon the continuous development of creative minds, a creativity that seemed to flourish best in the atmosphere of the academic guild system. Even university presidents stood in awe of the guild system, and this explains in part why the business model was never wholly applied to the university. One simply could not treat professors like employees. They were irreplaceable by virtue of skills that could not be mass produced in any mechanical fashion. For their part, serious scholars and scientists, unlike artists, found that they needed the institution, not only for economic reasons, but for the recognition and stimulation that went with it. Research was taking on and in fact seemed to require a corporate structure. The feudal internal structure reflects the requirements for training academic personnel and at the same time accommodates multiple purposes.

The modern American university owes its power and prestige, then, to two bargains. The first bargain is between the university and its external subsidizers. In return for performing a variety of useful tasks for a variety of benefactors, the university is permitted to retain a high degree of institutional autonomy, even to the point of using funds to subsidize internal activities that are of little interest to the outside world. The second bargain is internal. In return for the freedom to pursue its goal and to compete for resources, each faction (utilitarian-vocational, liberal-culture, research, and many more) agrees to tolerate the existence of the others. What has emerged is not a democratic institution but a medieval one with guild features. The bureaucracy consists of a president who presides over feuding deans and departments, each jealously guarding their prerogatives. Within each unit, the guild prevails, for skill is not hereditary but the product of masters actively recruiting the most talented apprentices. To the outside world this looks like chaos, but it has provided the freedom that makes American universities preeminent throughout the world.

The modern American university, then, is not an institution that rests on a consensus, because there is no common good and no faction will deny the possibility of ultimate conflict. Nor can the president of such an institution maintain order by persuasion alone, for persuasion requires a consensus. Of necessity, the president of a university must, like any politician in power, use coercion, in this case the power to limit funds (hiring, promotion, amenities). But the president is limited by the fact that his power is not absolute either within the institution or without. Universities, like corporations, are still competitive, and few presidents would seek to define the content and methodology of a discipline for fear of becoming the laughing stock of the academic world. There are too many people who will notice when you are not wearing your chemistry department, for example.

Within the institution the president is confronted by factions who, in the absence of a consensus, present every issue in moral terms. He must cultivate a special kind of rhetoric, one whose vagueness will serve both his external dealings and his internal dealings, one that obscures the lack of consensus, one that allows him to plead political necessity, and one that does not too easily betray where he will come down in the crunch. Finally, since there is no given consensus, he cannot always strive to preserve order, but must at times actively seek to provoke controversy.

The most common accusation is that the president has betrayed something or other. This is especially true if he began his career as spokesman for one of the factions. But such an accusation either reveals the lack of comprehension on the part of the accuser about the workings of the institution or is a rhetorical device for castigating a president who fails to support one's unitary vision of the institution.

One can always own up to the inevitable existence of conflict. Yet, there are three ways of trying to avoid the moral conflicts constantly generated by the office of college or university president. First, if the school is not well endowed (especially true of publicly supported institutions), the president may adopt the attitude that the university simply serves the outside funder. He then becomes a technocrat, presiding over quantifiable employees for whose pretensions he eventually develops a sense of contempt.

Second, he may attempt to deceive himself by pretending that there really is a consensus towards which the university is progressing. Here he engages in a higher sophistry by surrendering to the myth that clamor is progress. I call this the teleological trap. Once having fallen into it, he finds neither peace nor progress nor a single faction or individual who will grant him any credibility. His only recourse is to look for a position with some foundation that believes in the progress toward consensus.

Third, he may attempt to run the college or university along liberal democratic lines, engineering a democratic majority through persuasion alone on every issue. Instead of "a" consensus, he presumes to manufacture one on each issue. No institution can run this way. Not even the

United States government runs this way. We democratically elect our officials, but (a) limit their power over individuals and private institutions, and (b) allow the government to make policy and delegate authority without daily referenda. In the attempt to engineer a consensus, at first the institution is disrupted, then it collapses. This is what happened all too often in the late sixties.

The moral fiber of college presidents was revealed during that period of turmoil. The turmoil was provoked by advocates of liberal-culture who made their biggest power play to seize the ivory tower, and it was abetted by a public sold on the belief that a president who cannot maintain order by persuasion alone is incompetent. This is a case of an ignorant public falling into the teleological trap. The moral president either survived through courage and the luck of good allies or he went to the wall of resignation.

At the same time we should recognize that, in the absence of a consensus, what is an end to one person may be a means to another. Scholars for whom the pursuit of truth is an end must recognize that to some university presidents a distinguished faculty of truth seekers is a means to something else, with no guarantee that such a faculty will be always thought of as the best means to that other end—or that the end will itself remain constant.

FEDERAL FUNDING

According to the modern liberal interpretation, federal funding of higher education has a long and progressive history that reflects the increasing awareness within our society that the full development of everyone's potential requires substantial government intervention. The great moments in this history are the Northwest Ordinance of 1785-87, the land grant act of 1862, the Second Morrill Act of 1890, the Hatch Act of 1887, the Smith-Lever Act of 1914, the development of ROTC during World War I, the activities of the Work Projects Administration during the depression, the GI Bill, the Sputnik crisis, and last, but not least, Titles VI and VII, as well as Title IX of the Education Amendments of 1972. In what follows I shall show that no such smooth transition reading is justifiable, and that a quite different account can be given.

From the very early days of U.S. history, education was deemed a matter for private individuals, local communities, and states. No mention was made in the U.S. Constitution of education. In fact, delegates to the Constitutional Convention defeated a motion to establish a national university. Furthermore, a study of the Northwest Ordinance reveals that land grants were intended to encourage migration. The fact that land was set aside for the maintenance of public schools was an added inducement.

No such provision was made in the original colonies, where 98.5 percent of the population lived. Even in 1806, when Jefferson proposed using tariff surpluses for public education, he supposed "an amendment to the Constitution by consent of the states, necessary, because the objects now recommended, are not among those enumerated in the Constitution. . . ."[9]

The Morril Act proposed to establish and maintain colleges for the agricultural and mechanical arts, not for higher education as a whole. It was at first vetoed in 1859 by President Buchanan, who argued that "Congress does not possess the power to appropriate money in the Treasury, raised by taxes on the people of the United States, for the purpose of educating the people of the respective states."[10]The Act was passed in 1862 and signed by Lincoln during the Civil War with a provision for mandatory military training. The Hatch Act of 1887 and the Smith-Lever Act of 1914 were also concerned with agriculture in particular. The Smith-Hughes Act of 1917 was passed amid concern for encouraging vocational skills in areas crucial to the potential war effort. There is nothing in any of this to substantiate the claim of general federal intervention in higher education. The National Defense Education Act of 1958 was a response to Sputnik, to meet "the present emergency" in national defense. Moreover, it contains a clause (Sec.102) prohibiting federal control.

There is, therefore, no national support for and no congressional intent to establish total federal funding and control of either education in general or higher education in particular. Wherein does, then, the pressure come for such federal domination? It comes from two sources, which, as we shall see, are really the same: professional educators and the federal bureaucracy.

Back in the fifties a debate was conducted on whether there should be a national system of education, presumably financed by the federal government. At one level it was conducted as a debate on funding, with protagonists of a national system maintaining that only the federal government could afford the necessary expenditures whereas the states could not. This was a bogus issue, because no matter who disburses the money, the taxpayers, present and future, really foot the bill. Opponents of federal funding did establish one major point, namely, that federal funding usually leads to federal control.

Although the debate concerned only primary and secondary schools, the protagonists for a national system were in fact members of the university community, both those who trained school teachers and those who sought careers in educational bureaucracies at all levels. Here are the first signs of the emergence of the *academic-bureaucratic complex*, comparable in scope and importance to the military-industrial complex, except this time it was an intimate relationship between universities and government bureaucrats, not elected officials. Not only were these the people who adovated the national system, but their rhetoric reveals the full flowering of liberal social ideology:

> The nation as a whole can no longer remain indifferent to regional and local deficiencies in the education and training of youth since the security and welfare depend upon the full utilization of its human resource potentional. —Eli Ginzberg for Columbia University[11]

> The new case for federal intervention in education is no longer the case for convenience or for the values of the intellectual contributions which education makes to national welfare, it is stark necessity. . . . This is not Federal aid to education; it is the Federal creation of education, education of a kind and of a quality which did not exist before; but which the national necessity now demands. . . . Here is no Federal aid to education, here is Federal education for purposes distinctly national. . . . —Harold W. Stoke, president of Queens College, C.U.N.Y.[12]

> Education must be "a primary instrument of national policy."—John A. Hannah, president of Michigan State University[13]

> The university has become a prime instrument of national purpose. This is new. This is the essence of the transformation now engulfing our universities.—Clark Kerr, *The Uses of the University*[14]

Between 1955 and 1960 the number of permanent employees in the Office of Education grew from 426 to 1,022. More than 300 people were hired just to administer NDEA. The movement between an office on campus and an office in Washington was accelerating. Moreover, it was becoming clear that national education was not a response to a consensus but the attempt to create one:

> the greater the proportion of our youth who fail to attend our public schools and who receive their education elsewhere, the greater the threat to our democratic unity.—James Bryant Conant, Harvard University[15]

How does this apply to higher education specifically? In an earlier discussion we indicated that the peculiarity of the emerging modern American university was that it required the academic entrepreneur to provide continuity of funding. The fund-raising president is of course a familiar feature of university campuses. More specifically, there emerged the gambler, the college president who expanded the university in advance of actual resources and then relied upon private donors to bail him out. The best example of this was President Harper of the University of Chicago, an institution endowed by Rockefeller. Competition among universities encouraged not only standardization to some degree but a good deal of reckless expansion in the quest for prestige. Public relations became an art, and college property became, in Veblen's phrase, a way of "housing the quest for truth in an edifice of false pretences."[16] But universities, even the best, did not enjoy continuous success. As Archibald MacLeish pointed out in 1941 with regard to Harvard, "gifts to the University in the foreseeable future will not equal in bulk the gifts of the late twenties."[17]

One solution to this problem was to adopt more modest goals. In the quenchless pursuit of prestige, this was the least attractive alternative. A second solution was to seek other sources of financing, such as the government with its seemingly endless taxing capacity. In fact, the government at all levels actually sought out the university, for the skills and expertise of the scholarly and scientific members of the university community were increasingly viewed as valuable. At the very least, no one questioned the relevance of the physical sciences to national defense. This in itself presents no problem, for the university could contract itself out to the government and be reimbursed for specifiable services rendered. It was, after all, the government that really needed the university. But two things prevented it from happening that way. First, the gambling spirit caused university administrators to expand by taking federal largesse for granted, not as a limited contract. Second, many university administrators did not fear federal control; rather, they welcomed it. They welcomed it because they naturally saw themselves as the future heads of this national educational bureaucracy. Clark Kerr actually proposed a National Foundation for Higher Education and a council of advisers on education. Just recently, education became a separate cabinet position.

Surely, it will be asked, these men must have realized the dangers of federal control. They did not, and the question is why. One easy answer is that when you are already a multi-campus head you lose sight of the importance of individual campus identity. A second easy answer is that when you see yourself as the head of the federal bureaucracy, there is no reason to think that things are going to be different. More seriously, what these administrators shared was the liberal notion that educational institutions, like all other institutions in a liberal society, are means to achieving national ends. Education at all levels becomes the chief instrument of government intervention.

Federal regulation of higher education, then, was not imposed from without by politicians but positively engineered from within the university community. That is why it is so important to spell out the serious differences between private funding and federal government funding. Despite the attempts by a good many social scientists to show that private funding meant domination by "big business," the actual facts are quite different. Not only were universities more free, but these social scientists themselves were the product of such a system. To begin with, not all private funders are the same. There is no cohesive group of private funders any more than there is such a cohesive group as "big business." This creates the space for both different and more independent institutions. Federal funding, on the other hand, is uniform, for its interests are all-pervasive. If you do not like one federally supported institution you cannot run to another and different one. Even the Carnegie Commission looks wistfully back to state support, for they have come to recognize that the "federal government intrudes further than almost any state government has ever gone."[18] Private funders, precisely because of what their detractors call "narrow vision," had no national purpose in mind. Moreover, some of the great philanthropists of the past understood that the university was and should be autonomous in pursuing its ends. Large private endowments often come with strings attached, but they are given once and for all time, that is, they do not have to be renewed annually.

What is the magnitude of the federal contribution? For a good many years the federal contribution to education as a whole has been running about 10 percent of the total annual budget of the entire educational establishment. In 1978 the annual budget of all education was about $130 billion. The higher education annual budget was about $42 billion. State and federal contribution to higher education was about $24 billion. The federal share of higher education was around $13 billion. Almost a third of the budget for higher education comes from the federal government. Some of it is spent for specific contract purposes such as funding research of a particular proposal. But some of it is absorbed by the university for overhead purposes and this part trickles down to other purposes.

Given the size of that contribution, one might ask why the government chose to give grants to innumerable colleges and universities instead of establishing a national university or several national universities? This is perfectly feasible, at least economically, when we note that the permanent endowment of, say, Stanford University is about a half-billion dollars. For approximately one billion dollars the U.S. government could endow a super national university that would not need additional funding every year. There are several reasons. Federal grants began with specific temporary purposes in mind and only gradually mushroomed to such large numbers. Moreover, it is doubtful if current universities would have sat idly by, watching all that money go to a new institution. The empire builders would have fought it. Even now the empire builders are loathe to give up federal money and accompanying controls for one main reason: fear of losing out in the competition to other university empires that would continue to accept the funds.

All this explains why it has not happened so far. Why can it not happen now, that is, why no national university now? Let us use the analogy with an argument once made for TVA (Tennessee Valley Authority). It was said that by running one power system on its own, the government would be in a better position to evaluate the efficiency and costs of private power companies, who need governmental commission approval to raise their rates. The same could be said of a national university. It would enable the government to evaluate the efficiency of grant proposals from private universities. We might add that the "temporary" projects could be better carried out in an institution specifically set up for housing them without a commitment to the permanence of any one project. Even regular faculty of private universities could go to the national university for specified contracted periods of time.

Here the sinister aspects of federal control become more apparent. A hardheaded case could be made that the handwriting is on the wall about the doom of purely private universities. Private wealth on a vast scale is disappearing. As government controls more and more of the economy, this will be increasingly the case. That is, in time a modern liberal government might make sure that no one is in a position to give significant endowments to a university. Needless to add, this activity of government intervention is what is preached in a good many universities. In addition, government regulation of the economy is a major cause of inflation. Inflation is constantly nibbling away at the real value of university private endowments. As former President McGill of Columbia University said a few years back: "We are no longer in all respects a private university."

But there is something even more important behind federal funding. In the liberal vision of society, all institutions must be subordinated to the ultimate teleological purpose of the nation. Any specific institution that is left out is both a threat and a symptom of failure. I have already cited Conant's position opposing private schools. It is clear that the same case is going to be made, although not necessarily by the same people, that private schools of higher education work against national unity. In short, the great vision of a liberal society will require that all colleges and universities at every level reflect national purpose.[19] This is why federal funding and accompanying federal controls must reach out to every institution.

One way of exemplifying this point and the amorphousness of liberal doctrine is to look at the issue of egalitarianism. When Clark Kerr originally wrote *The Uses of the University* (1963) he recognized the pressures of an egalitarian society, but he insisted that in his vision of the university serving national purposes "the great university is of necessity elitist—the elite of merit— . . . equality of opportunity, not equality *per se*."[20] Kerr's vision of the outcome of a fair race obviously differs from the vision of other liberals. When universities were privately endowed, the pressure of egalitarianism was diffuse and offset by "narrow" private endowers who respected the elite of talent. But with the rise of the ethnic vote in America and the women's movement, the pressure has become more focused and concentrated. Clearly, some other liberal vision of the outcome of the race has taken over. Kerr sadly laments in his 1972 postscript that the consensus he envisioned is gone.[21] But make no mistake about it. While liberals may differ in their prophecy of the outcome of the race, it was still the liberal theory that Kerr had in mind when he welcomed government control. Even disenchanted liberals cannot stop the tide they helped to create, largely because they cannot oppose arguments whose structure continues to operate in their minds.

THE ROLE OF THE SOCIAL SCIENCES

Social scientists (many, but not all), including anthropologists, sociologists, political scientists, historians, teachers in schools of education, economists, and even philosophers and psychologists, have played a key role in making the modern American university a handmaiden to the federal government. This is the result of the coalescence of both internal and external pressures. The external pressure, which we shall examine first, arises from envy of the prestige of natural sciences with their generous federal subsidies, and the pressure on social scientists to help solve "social problems" such as crime and poverty. This last influence has resulted in what I shall call a *vulgarization* of social science. The internal pressure arises from a specific intellectual notion of what constitutes social science as an academic or intellectual activity. The internal pressure will be clearly related to the external pressures.

The technological benefits of the theoretical activities of physical and biological scientists for security, health, and prosperity are indisputable. As a consequence the physical sciences enjoy not only prestige but handsome subsidy. Though the natural scientist may have no interest other than satisfying his curiosity, he is never asked to justify his existence. Such is not always the case with the social sciences. Not only is their status as sciences intellectually suspect in some quarters, but there is as yet no list of generally agreed upon contributions to rival physical technology. Although some social scientists may content themselves with simply trying to understand and to offer a coherent account of social life, there are few funders, private or public, who will lavish support on satisfying curiosity. To some this is cause for resentment.

At the same time, there are external interests who are anxious to use social science as a means to their own end. Commercial interests are anxious to know about consumer habits, and political interests are anxious to get whatever help they can to solve such practical problems as what to do with juvenile delinquents. There is a great deal of money for this kind of thing. Not only do some social scientists respond to this commercial and political exploitation, some more whole-heartedly than others, but in so doing they inadvertently accept a certain model of human behavior that is dubious to say the least. They also employ a form of statistical argument that masks ideology in scientific-sounding dress. It is this distortion of science in the interests of some fashionable value that I have called the vulgarization of social science.

We have already noted some examples of this distorting effect in what I have called the trend argument and the hidden variable argument. I'll note one other example here. A statistical correlation is discovered between being a college graduate and earning a higher than average income. Someone then concludes that going to college "causes" the higher income. This conclusion serves a number of interest groups, but it can be challenged. For example, isn't it possible that both going to college and later earning a high income are both themselves effects of another cause, like being ambitious and talented? I do not pretend to know but merely to suggest another explanation to fit the "facts." What about the "facts" themselves? This correlation might be true when only 7 percent of the school-age population goes to college, but will it be true when, say, 60 percent of the population goes to college? It certainly could not be true when 100 percent go to college. These statistical rebuttals would immediately occur to any professional, but not when he begins to serve ideological interests.

The connection between the external pressure and the internal pressure is achieved when we notice that only some conceptions of social science as an intellectual activity can in any way be consistent with the attempt to make social science serve ideological interests. Here a brief synopsis of alternative conceptions of social science will reveal some of the deep-rooted causes of our current perplexity.

The oldest model of social science is borrowed uncritically from physical science. Here we begin with the notion that science is concerned with discovering and explaining natural patterns. Social science is ostensibly concerned with such patterns in the human and social world. Just as in the physical world everything is ultimately reducible to a more fundamental level of explanation (e.g., chemistry is reducible to physics), so social behavior is ultimately reducible to physics as well. Social phenomena are just a higher-level manifestation of the laws of physical science. If the latter are deterministic, then so are the former. This view provides for both prediction and explanation. In fact, prediction and explanation are symmetrical.

Besides being unflattering to social scientists, there are many, many criticisms of this reductionistic model. We do not have to go into all of them here. For our purposes it is enough to note that this conception of social science makes both values and self-conscious change impossible. In the early days of modern science (seventeenth century) many of those who advocated a mechanical model of the universe had the foresight to exempt human beings. Thus we came to conceive of a physical universe that could be manipulated for human convenience. If this model is then transposed uncritically to humans, we end up with social science as the manipulation or control of human behavior. This is not only sinister but leaves unexplained and unexplainable the point of view (the values, the perspective) from which the manipulation will be carried out. There are still those who are encouraged by B. F. Skinner's behaviorism into thinking that all social problems are a matter of conditioning. An element of this is present in the liberal assumption that people are solely the products of their environment.

A second model of social science is the so-called functional one. Here it is asserted that social regularities are *sui generis*, not reducible, that they are empirically discoverable as trends, and that the trends can be explained in terms of some built-in goal or purpose. Every meaningful social regularity has a certain function or goal. The job of the social scientist is to identify, explain, and predict the continued course of trends. This view permits some meaningfulness for values since they are the built-in goals of the trend.

The only question is which unit of reality has the built-in goal or trend. The European continental tradition has tended to emphasize specific institutions as the bearers of the trend: the family or the state or the economic class as in Marx, and so on. Not all institutions unerringly achieve their ends any more than every acorn becomes an oak. This allows us to judge institutions as either well or ill, depending on whether they function properly, that is, consistent with their built-in ends. It makes no sense to speak of individuals altering the institution. Each individual either fits the institution or he does not. In fact, individuals have no reality apart from their institutional standing. From the point of view of our modern social scientist who wants to make himself useful, this approach has a serious disadvantage. It puts the social scientist in a position analogous to an astrologer: he can identify, explain, and predict the trend (or so he would say), but he cannot make individuals act consistently with it. One is at liberty, presumably, to ignore or act contrary to the horoscope. He certainly cannot look for the necessary and sufficient conditions of action, for that reverts to determinism. What he can do is serve as an apologist either for the status quo or the future revolution that is built into the trend. This public relations function of the social scientist is precisely what Veblen criticized.

Functionalists are largely to be found among the sociologists. They take as norm what Max Weber lamented about the future: the inevitability of centralized bureaucracy. In the United States, Robert Merton and Talcott Parsons helped to train several generations in the belief that our social world is a structure of interconnected institutions. This unwittingly leads us to believe that there is a central core or establishment and that meaningful reform is possible only by seizing control of the establishment.

The British tradition, which we share in America, is to identify the individual as the bearer of the trend. Each individual has a built-in goal or goals which he strives to achieve, and this is precisely what the social scientist identifies, explains, and predicts. But just as every acorn does not become an oak, so not every human being achieves his end or functions properly. There are always obstacles to overcome, and it is the function of the practical social scientist to help the individual to overcome those obstacles. Clinical social science has a more familiar name: it is called social engineering.

This approach sounds much more promising for our social scientist who wants to have the same sort of prestige as the physicist and the engineer. But first he must face the problem of all functionalists, namely, how do we get someone to act consistently with his horoscope? "An economist by training thinks of himself as the guardian of rationality, the ascriber of rationality to others and the prescriber of rationality to the social world."[22] First, it must be possible for us to act consistently with the horoscope, that is, there must not be any ultimate conflict among the things predicted in the horoscope. Not only must this be true for each individual but it must also be true of all the individuals who make up a coherent group. In short, there must be ultimate harmony, both individually and socially. Second, like his institutional brethren, he cannot look for necessary and sufficient conditions, for that would revert to determinism. That is, there must be some element of choice. But the choice cannot be free, for if it were that would mean that each individual is at liberty to disregard his horoscope. Disregarding the horoscope consciously is logically impossible, for it would be like choosing not to get what we really want. When this appears to happen it is because we have not correctly identified the real trend. The choice, if it is to be influenced by the social scientist in the right direction, must be "conditioned" (we cannot say caused) by factors that are either consciously known (information) or not known (ignorance) or, if known, are misused (higher-level information) or not used (subtle need) or are beyond the control of the chooser (oppression). This gives the social scientist plenty of leeway to be helpful either as educator or as advocate of social intervention. No doubt it is now clear to the reader that this conception of the nature and uses of social science is none other than the liberal social ideology.

A number of objections can be raised against this notion of social science, but I shall reserve the critique for a later chapter. It is only important at this point that we recognize the crucial connection between:

a. liberal social ideology and a particular conception of social science (teleological),

   b. teleological social science and higher education (liberal-culture and useful social science join hands),

   c. higher education and government intervention bureaucrats.

Needless to add, teleological social science is the science of trends and statistics par excellence. The modern American university, in short, has been subverted by empire builders in the administration who confuse their national ambition with the existence of a national purpose, by enthusiasts of liberal-culture, and by teleological social science. All of these join together in originating and sustaining liberal ideology.

   Nowhere is the ideological character of academic social science more evident than in the area of race relations. Although this book is not the place for an extended analysis of either race relations or theories of race relations, I would like to maintain one thesis and point out another. I want to maintain that little or no insightful work has been done, because researchers have approached the issue of race relations with ideological blinders. A look at the predominant approaches by sociologists since the 1930s reveals a common ideological approach.[23]

   Most sociologists work with a functional model that presupposes that industrialization is the main force determining social structure and consciousness. Within this framework of economic determinism, economic progress is supposed to lead to full assimilation. As late as 1966, Parsons had even worked out a timetable.[24] (Note the proximity of this date to the advent of affirmative action.) But the equilibrium point of full assimilation has never emerged. Of course one could question the theory, but sociologists and other social scientists have preferred to seek those hidden variables that frustrated this utopian homeostasis. The most widely accepted "hidden" variable candidate is supposed to be the attitude of race prejudice (e.g., the work of Gordon Allport) as revealed in socio- and psychometric surveys (forerunners of the statistical trend argument). These surveys lead to the startling conclusion that almost everybody is prejudiced, that is, that the whole society is sick. Such fundamental illness could only be overcome by social engineering from the top.

   So dominant is this view that even those who disagree about policy nevertheless share it. On the one hand, it could be argued—and was by Gary Becker—that government intervention has caused the disequilibrium and frustrated full assimilation. On the other hand, Marxists, who share the same thesis of economic determinism, argue that full assimilation will come with the disappearance of the class conflict problem.[25]

   We shall never have a profound understanding of race relations as long as it is viewed from an unquestioned and fixed intellectual and political perspective. Moreover, the dominant view, like Marxism and Freudianism before it, frustrates self-criticism. Just as critics of Freudianism are dismissed as disturbed people suppressing their problems, and just as critics of Marxism are dismissed as victims or creatures of capitalistic exploitation, so critics of the dominant sociological theory of race relations are dismissed as racists.

The existence of a special interest group among social scientists has led Irving Kristol to dub it the *New Class*. This group is in favor of a centralized government controlling most aspects of social life. Subscribing to the belief that the social world and the individual have objective built-in ends, they as a special class of experts know what these ends are and how to administer them. What most stands in their way is a decentralized social and economic order or one with multiple centers of institutional power—private schools, corporations, and so on. They resent the influence of business and even labor. They naturally interpret these other centers of power as inefficient, sinister, misguided, or selfish.

In 1972 George McGovern received the support of 87 percent of the faculties in social science and the humanities. As Ladd and Lipset have shown in their famous study, the anti-business bias is centered in the social sciences and humanities, but it is just the reverse in the fields of natural science, business, agriculture, and law.[26]

Ignoring this evidence, Robert Lekachman has recently said that college faculties are generally conservative,[27] and that only in some social science departments is a liberal bias present. But it is, contrary to Lekachman, precisely its entrenchment in social science that is most crucial. It is in social science courses that social and political issues are discussed, not in departments of forestry and geology. It is also in the social sciences that journalists and opinion influencers are majors. So serious is this problem that Robert Nisbet claims that "the alleged research presented at meetings of the American Political Science Association always comes out with conclusions that would be acceptable to Arthur Schlesinger, Jr., or John Kenneth Galbraith."[28]

LIBERALISM AND HIGHER EDUCATION

It should be clear by now that the greatest danger to the university is not external but internal. Insofar as dramatic persecutions occur against unorthodox ideas they are carried out by student disrupters acting as the self-appointed thought police of doctrinaire liberalism. But even more insidious is the danger posed by the very success of the university. There is a strong tendency to take oneself seriously, perhaps too seriously, because others expect so much from us. Then, too, if we examine the kinds of people who are drawn to college teaching we find individuals with exaggerated expectations of what can be done. They have been "turned on," and they expect others to share their enthusiasm. After a while they may sour on students, their research may not go well or be ignored, and then of course there is always the drudgery associated with any job. These individuals then become quite susceptible to the charm of the illusion of a great social role for the university. It is much easier to sustain this illusion outside the seminar and the laboratory, much easier to administer it or to preach it.

The first move of liberalism within higher education is to crush internal opposition. This is done by the initially modest appearing assertion that the university must play a socially subservient role. This modesty is frequently coupled with some platitudes about the importance of excellence (here left undefined) in the service of the social good. But here the differences begin. Excellence is being praised as a means, not as an end. The psychological problem is that those who pursue excellence in their research, publication, and teaching must do so as an end in itself, as a passion geared to a specific interest, not the general interest, with a single-minded devotion that frequently breeds conflicts, and in an institutional context that necessarily establishes hierarchies.

The attack commences when a chiding administrator points out that dedicated professionals take too narrow a view and ignore the general interest. Next comes the encouragement of the pursuit of useful knowledge as opposed to frivolous research. This presupposes that somebody actually "knows" in advance what knowledge is going to be most useful. Neither history nor logic provides such a guide, but social ideology does. Next comes the realization that some kinds of variety are ultimately incompatible with teleological liberalism. Variety might be all right as a means and as a temporary device, but it must ultimately give way to a standardized and finalized truth. When those who subscribe to the research model and those who are involved in professional training begin to groan about the decline in standards, the answer they receive is that there will be even greater productivity if the new liberalized university is given a chance. The final attack on excellence consists in redefining it as whatever is consistent with the general interest. In a democratic society, the general interest cannot be served by hierarchies, which are defined as exploitative, and the whole notion of excellence as a personal talent is rejected as a quasi-religious mystery enshrined in the guild system by a priestly class.

Crushing internal opposition means opposing all seemingly feudal hierarchical arrangements and anything that smacks of the guild system. It thus appears to be antiauthoritarian. But this is only appearance. If within an academic department decisions are arrived at by consensus and democratic means, it is still possible for one department or a whole division of the university to remain recalcitrant. Recall, for example, that the natural sciences are not in agreement with the ethos of the social sciences. This would frustrate the overall teleology. Hence it is necessary to democratize the whole university. Among other things this means giving the right to vote on policy decisions to students and perhaps to the groundkeepers. The social scientists implicitly trust these constituencies as allies precisely because the ideology of modern liberalism permeates·our whole culture, and because students are especially indoctrinated in social science courses. This is not democratization but usurpation.

The second move of liberalism within higher education is to establish that there are no legitimate external frames of reference in terms of which it can be judged. Mouthing traditional slogans about university autonomy, the new class would never tolerate outside interests interfering with its operations. In practice this means that if the community at large or relevant funders of the university democratically decide that what the university is doing is wrong, the new class will not allow the outside democratic structure to circumvent its plans. It clearly does not have a fundamental commitment to democracy. Nor does it have a fundamental commitment to university autonomy. These slogans are hypocritically invoked as means to ends.

How does it justify this hypocrisy? It does this by refusing to recognize that there is such a thing as a moral choice or an ethical conflict or even a legitimate political difference. All value judgments or decisions will be based on the purely objective assessment of the most efficient means to achieve the ends built into human nature. Social scientists and fellow travelers in the humanities who teach relevant literature and art will become the experts. The result for the academic world is that social scientists are now not only as important as natural scientists, but in fact are more important than anyone else. Even what constitutes permissible or meaningful research in the physical sciences must be determined by committees of social scientists.

What distinguishes the new high priests from the old priestly class is that the former are scientific. That is, they can explain everything as a technical solution. Older conceptions of morality are acceptable if properly reinterpreted as technical advice involving means and ends, but any alternative to this technique is rejected as superstition.

The new technocrat puts a great premium on people acting rationally. But rationality is what is calculable. Technocrats are rational because they can extract from the statistics policy decisions that are scientifically certifiable from the point of view of liberal social theory. The individuals for whom the policy is made are rational to the extent that we can appeal to their self-interest. Of course, not everybody behaves this way, least of all formerly distinguished but now recalcitrant members of the faculty. They, like the students, must be rationalized to accept what is in their best interest. The technocrat always tries to give people the benefit of the doubt by using persuasion. But when that does not work, it becomes necessary to wipe out all institutions and institutional practices that sustain disagreement, especially vestigial notions of hierarchy and excellence.

The third movement of liberalism within higher education is the reform of external society. One may wonder how an institution that is to serve the social good can at the same time presume to define the social good. The answer has already been given. All legitimate values must have been scientifically certified within the relevant intellectual community. The social experts not only choose the means, they establish the ends. Of course, it will be pointed out that every institution generates a view of the totality of society which is as hospitable as possible to its own demands; in its own image, we might add. The university is no exception. But unlike other institutions, the university, at least until recently, engaged in a critical analysis of interinstitutional visions. It neither ignored, misunderstood, nor distorted demands for rhetorical purposes. The university has always housed its own worst critics. But all that is changing. Liberals confuse their own rallies and teach-ins with critical reappraisal . The only thing they never reappraise is doctrinaire liberalism itself. Under the guise of criticism, the rally turns into a form of mass persuasion and subliminal propaganda for liberalism. Criticism becomes acceptable only if it is a prelude to some course of action, but this presupposes acceptance of the notion that the university serves the social good.

The mass rally is an ideal tool because it is an extension of the large lecture. The large lecture, as you will recall, is the natural home of rhetoricians of liberal-culture. Unlike the small seminar and the laboratory, it conditions students to become passive recipients of someone else's thought. One cannot interrupt and dwell at length on a point anymore than one can stop and reedit what we see in the movies and on TV. In the large lecture, which is the forum of the university's commitment to democracy (educate everybody), the symbol of its cost-conscious efficiency, and the embodiment of the liberal environmentalist notion of teaching as input-output, the university has prepared the technological ground for its own undoing.

There are of course the more subtle forms of reforming society, such as imbuing future teachers and journalists with the liberal ideology and working for the total regulation of every institution in society.

I point out that the university cannot long remain a free institution if all the other institutions within society are regulated. The dependence of one undermines the independence of the others; this is true not only of institutions in general but just as much among the collectivity of universities. This observation may move some, but it falls on deaf ears as well, for to the academic-bureaucratic complex total regulation is cause for celebration.

On Wednesday, February 2, 1983, a TV production was aired entitled "Affirmative Action and Reverse Discrimination" as part of the series "The Constitution: That Delicate Balance." Most of the participants were people who figure prominently in the pages of this book. They discussed a a hypothetical case of granting tenure under affirmative action. In the hypothetical case, there was no prior finding that the university had ever discriminated, and, while all of the candidates were judged equal in publications, the black candidate was judged third in teaching ability.

All of the participants who were in favor of hiring the black candidate uniformly expressed the view that the university is a functional part of society and therefore must serve its political goals as interpreted by them.

Shirley M. Hufstedler (former secretary of education):

> . . . each individual has to have particular essences, in terms of the quality of what that teacher will bring to the whole academic environment. . . . Are they really taking an active role in nonacademic activities that nevertheless affect the student body? What is their relationship with the community? . . . the kinds of relationships which that university must build with the community of which it's a part are really very important in the whole teaching environment of the university.

Juan U. Ortiz, city personnel director, New York City:

> . . . a university does not exist in a vacuum, it does exist as part of society, and I firmly believe, and the committee believes, that the racial composition of this faculty is a very important consideration that must be taken into account. So, therefore, we had three excellent candidates; we feel that given the racial composition that perhaps a member of a protected group should be given an edge.

Ellen Goodman, syndicated columnist, the *Boston Globe*:

> I think that the issue that everybody is dealing with is the real imponderable about this case, which is the utter subjectivity of the word "merit."

Anthony Lewis, columnist, the *New York Times*:

> I think I'm on Ms. Goodman's side in the end, because there is a kind of abstract quality to the discussion of merit as merit. . . . Because there is no such thing as proof of the best-qualified person. The reason for those appointments [U.S. Supreme Court] was that it was felt important to all the people in the country to have not an all-white, all-male court. . . . if we could afford to take that consideration into account in the Supreme Court of the United States, we might be able to afford it for one faculty member. . . .

Eleanor Holmes Norton, former chair, EEOC, professor, Georgetown University Law School:

> The fact that . . . if any element of the society is to be—any profession in the society is to be—subject to affirmative action, all must be.[29]

CHAPTER 4

Federal Regulation of Higher Education

> Surely we have learned that however laudable the goal,
> we cannot trust in the limitless goodwill of government—
> that agencies that are charged with carrying out the law
> have an almost irresistible tendency to go beyond the
> law. . . ."—Congressman John O'Hara (former chair-
> man of the House Subcommittee on Postsecondary
> Education)

Given what we have said in the previous two chapters, we are in a position to understand the events that transpired during the 1970s in the confrontation between higher education and government bureaucracy. First, we shall see how government bureaucracy attempts to apply the concept of affirmative action to higher education. It will move through the three stages we have identified as the platitude stage, the remediation stage, and the realignment stage. Second, at each stage we shall notice that the reaction of the university is mixed, both positive and negative, because it reflects the internal disagreement within the university itself about the role of the university vis-à-vis the external world. Third, given what we have discovered about university funding, presitge, and ambition, we would expect the university to effect some sort of compromise. Finally, given the logic of liberal social ideology, we should expect that each compromise prepares the ground for the subsequent concession and the further eroding of the university's position.

COMMENCEMENT

When the Civil Rights Act of 1964 was passed, universities were initially exempted from Title VI. The interesting question is why? The obvious answer is that the university community as a whole was among the fore-front of institutions fighting to end discrimination. Here we may note that no matter what internal model of the university one supported, there were substantial reasons not only to oppose but to fight discrimination actively. Not only was the university community in general opposed to discrimination, but a high proportion of university professors are leading advocates of liberal or left-of-center political positions urging government intervention to end discrimination. Moreover, this liberal image of the university professor is more true of the prestigious institutions than of the less well known universities and colleges. And as we noted in the first chapter, Southern universities were far more responsive to the 1954 Supreme Court decision in *Brown* v. *Board of Education* than the primary and secondary schools. In the North, the last vestiges of discrimination in higher education admissions had all but disappeared by the early fifties, including quotas in professional graduate schools. In fact, as one admissions officer of a leading university told me in confidence, the universities had been quietly employing a double standard preferential admissions policy with regard to blacks since the late fifties. Any black applicant who in the eyes of the admissions committee seemed likely to complete the program was accepted, even in preference to non-black students with better credentials. Finally, with regard to faculty employment, a poll conducted in 1968-69 showed that 23 percent of male faculty and 20 percent of female faculty were in favor of preferential hiring, that is, "relaxing" the normal academic requirements for minorities.[1] Those percentages were to increase in 1972-73 to 35 percent and 36 percent respectively.[2] As a consequence, the university is the last place in our society where one would contemplate government intervention on behalf of the oppressed.

Be that as it may, in 1970 the Women's Equity Action League brought a class action suit against the entire academic community for discrimination with regard to employment. The League appealed to Executive Order 11246, which until then no one had ever thought was applicable to the academic community. As a consequence of this suit, Revised Order No. 4 of December 4, 1971, added women or sex as a category. And in 1972, the Equal Employment Opportunity Act officially extended Title VII of the Civil Rights Act of 1964 to educational institutions as well as employees of state and local government. For the record, universities with federal contracts over $10,000 are prohibited from discrimination. Title VII specifically refers to nondiscrimination; it does not mention any requirment of affirmative action, nor does Title IX of the Education Amendment of 1972, which does not even mention employment. Affirmative action, you will recall, is a product of executive orders and bureaucratic fantasy.

So it is not to the law that we must turn, but to bureaucratic action. It is in Revised Order No. 4 that we begin our tale of affirmative action in higher education. According to this order, all institutions with contracts over $50,000 or 50 employees need to file affirmative action plans, including goals and timetables. If there is a violation, contracts can be delayed, denied, or cancelled. If charged with noncompliance, the university has 30 days to show cause. If it does not do so to the bureaucracy's satisfaction, it is given a notice of termination and the opportunity for a hearing. In addition to EEOC, the Labor Department delegates its authority to the Department of Health, Education, and Welfare to deal with universities.

Now what might be the university's reaction to Revised Order No. 4? To begin with, if one does not practice discrimination, and if a university possesses members of the faculty who are literate enough to read the law for themselves, it may rightly bring suit against HEW, the Department of Labor, and EEOC for exceeding their authority. It is one thing to deal with paperwork, it is quite another to commit oneself to a course of hiring. Nothing in the law requires this. On the other hand, the law is what the courts say it is, and in 1972 the *DeFunis* and *Bakke* cases had not yet come up. In all fairness, an attitude of caution might be the most prudent course of action. Barring a suit, then, the university might simply refuse to accept government contracts under the conditions so imposed. For reasons we have already discussed, most universities are unlikely to surrender the prospect of federal subsidies if there is any way to keep them.

This leaves as the only course of action an attempt to negotiate with the federal bureaucracy to see exactly what is required in an affirmative action plan, just what the commitment is in goals and timetables. Having settled on a course of action we can begin to try to feel comfortable with it. After all, the university does have allies inside and outside of government, society really needs us, and we have dealt with other bureaucracies before. What we did not see was that what looked like the practice of worldly wisdom in 1972 was really the onset of self-deception.

The first part of an affirmative action plan is paying lip service to platitudes. The university really doesn't mind this sort of thing since the platitudes originate within the university in the first place. We are, of course, all in favor of equal opportunity—to prove it we shall even proclaim it on our stationery. But we want to make perfectly clear that we espouse "equality of opportunity without entering into a policy of equality of group results."[3] Yet into these vacuous phrases begins to creep a more dangerous policy, because not only is the existence of discrimination in the past acknowledged but there is a further acknowledgement of an "accumulated loss of talent [that] is staggering to contemplate."[4] This is quickly followed by advocacy of "a better distribution of women and minorities among institutions and among fields of specialization and ranks," for it "is badly needed."[5]

Even if we grant a possible loss of talent, how does anybody know that the loss is staggering? Is there a way of measuring it? And why is the loss associated with a better distribution of women and minorities? How does one know that the loss concerns just these groups? Despite what is said about equal opportunity for individuals, not predetermined groups, the university has inadvertently accepted the unproved assumption that relevant talents are statistically distributed by group. For all I know this may be the case, but no one knows for sure. At best it is an assumption. Some members of the university community accept the assumption as an article of faith, some accept it as a working hypothesis subject to falsification, and some neither accept nor reject it but subscribe to it because they do not believe that simply saying it commits the university to anything.

The first shock comes when university officials are told by HEW that universities are guilty until they prove themselves innocent. That is, any statistical survey of the university will show that selected minorities and women are not represented in anything like their percentage of the population. Now, the university is not in a position to shoot down this argument by claiming that it is a non sequitur, that there is no necessary connection between percentages of the population and faculty appointments. It has been trapped by its own rhetoric into playing the bureaucracy's game.

Forced to play the game, the universities reply that there has been no underutilization of black and women Ph.D.'s. In fact, a double preferential market has major universities bidding up the price of such black and female Ph.D.'s in a highly competitive fashion. Moreover, the fact that few women have reached the top of their profession reflects facts about family life such as raising children, facts over which the university has no control. Besides, the university is not responsible for the poor educational preparation of minorities at lower levels of the educational ladder.

HEW may now ask, What does the university expect will happen as segregated schooling disappears and as women's liberation encourages more women to seek careers? The honest answer is that we do not know. The political answer is that we should expect a tremendous increase in the available women and minority Ph.D.'s. What does the university expect will be the quality of these new Ph.D.'s? The honest answer is that nobody knows. The required answer is "roughly equal."[6] Then is there any reason to think that there will not be a vast increase in the pool of qualified applicants? No. Will the university give this new pool an equal opportunity? Of course. Would the university be willing to go on record about future expectations? After all, they are only expectations, not real commitments.

The case has now been made for accepting goals and timetables. Let's put the best face on it. "We now stand in a transition period between actual past deficiencies of major proportions and potential future achievement of true equal opportunity."[7] Like all liberal social policies, goals and timetables are *transitional*. And a goal is not a commitment, only a "normal expectation."[8]

No less a figure than Clark Kerr supports the notion of a transitional period. "We hope that the current period of transition will not last longer than the end of the twentieth century—less than one generation."[9]

Here it might be useful to distinguish between a liberaloid and a liberalist. A liberaloid denies that we are instituting quotas; a liberalist admits that there are quotas but maintains that they are only temporary.

So far it looks as if all we have is a paper concession to placate bureaucrats. After all, government bureaucrats have to earn a living and we can at least help them look as if they are doing their job. But what looks to a wily administrator like a paper concession becomes the new gospel in the hands of liberal ideologues. Armed with what looked like a mere platitude, committed liberals engage in preferential hiring of women and minorities. Black and female Ph.D.'s with even minor achievements are to be preferrred over other Ph.D.'s with major achievements. Black and female graduate students are to be preferred over current holders of the Ph.D. degree. There is a mountain of incriminating reports and documents to substantiate many claims of this kind. I was personally faced by four other members of a department personnel committee, all holders of the Ph.D. degree in philosophy and all presumably literate, who told me point-blank that Title VII says we "must" hire women and blacks.

Now that the rug has been pulled out from under the administration by some of its own faculty, what can it do? Having mouthed all of those platitudes about opposing discrimination, the university is not in a position to order its department heads not to hire blacks and women. Nor is it in a position to state publicly that the platitudes were negotiated as paper concessions, not as real policy. Its only recourse is to argue that some of the faculty have misinterpreted affirmative action. But having done this the university has once more passed the initiative back to HEW—which decides what affirmative action is or is not. The university has negotiated away its prerogatives. It has been outmaneuvered by the government bureaucracy and the bureaucracy's allies within the university community itself.

THE CONFLICT

In the midst of detailing the issue of affirmative action in higher education, we are apt to lose sight of the real conflict. At one level it appears to be a conflict between a mindless and inexperienced bureaucracy on the one hand and the university on the other. One author traces our difficulty to the fact that the industrial model is inadvertently being applied—or misapplied—to the university. No doubt the Labor Department just does not understand how the university works:

federal officials . . . press distinguished universities to make commitments
to increase sharply the number of women and blacks . . . in their faculties.
Consciously or unconsciously, efforts are being made, in the name of antidiscrimination, to transform those faculty systems—to make them conform
more closely to industrial patterns of personnel management.[10]

The suggested solution is to appoint to the federal bureaucracy persons
experienced with the university administration:

misconceptions . . . could be avoided if HEW had available for consulta-
tion an advisory panel of persons well versed in the actual operations of
institutions of higher education.[11]

I do not believe for a minute that this is where the conflict lies. On
the contrary, one can make a case for treating the university as an industry. Let us begin with the assumption that all institutions in society must
play their proper roles, and further that the role of education is to prepare
people for the economy. Higher education then becomes nothing more
than an adjunct to industry. The rebuttal proceeds from the claim that
someone has misinterpreted the social role of the university. So what we
have is a dispute between two versions of liberalism, and they are both
liberal in assuming that every institution has to play a role subservient to
the social good.

At another level it might appear to some as a conflict between
federal control and university autonomy. This way of stating the conflict
is rhetorically useful as a way of drawing to the administration the support of classical liberals, who are in principle opposed to any government
regulation. It also represents a dawning in the minds of some modern
liberals that government intervention, which they themselves have advocated all along, is a cure worse than the disease. Thus, this way of stating
the conflict is a backing off, if not a full-scale retreat. But the fact of the
matter is that this too is a misstatement of the conflict. No university has
any intention of rejecting federal control, because that means giving up
federal funds. What is being argued is what kind of control and by
whom. The university strives to play a "vital social role," which means the
university aspires to define the social good, not merely serve it. Here too
the conflict is between different groups of liberals.

It is not an accident that government bureaucrats have singled out
the university, and it is not merely a misunderstanding that leads such
bureaucrats to impose an industrial model on the management of universities. Of course, by its very nature the university provides services that do
not easily lend themselves to autonomous task specifications. Hence, the
profit criterion cannot provide delivery of the services at acceptable levels.
This inherent ambiguity of performance tests makes the university unlike

a typical business. At the same time, modern liberals have traditionally argued that government intervention is justified precisely in tasks that private enterprise cannot or will not perform. For this reason government control of higher education is a natural consequence. Moreover, a review of the major publicized cases allegedly involving discriminatory hiring practices yields an interesting fact: a disproportionate number are public utilities (e.g. AT&T), governmental units, government contractors, unions, and the education establishment. In each instance these entities are largely insulated from free-market competition (they have, in fact, markets with considerable inelasticity of demand) and are therefore best able to engage in nonfunctional discrimination (for example, reverse discrimination) and pass the cost forward to consumers. Finally, I shall argue below that we are not witnessing the misguided imposition of an industrial model but something more sinister.

Government regulators have traditionally assumed an adversary role against business, but affirmative action bureaucrats initially assumed that the university was going to cooperate wholeheartedly. Resistance, however, developed precisely when it became apparent that regulators had not come to correct old abuses but to institute a new social order.

VARIETIES OF CAMPUS LIBERALISM

Who are the major groups of competing liberals? We note that they are all modern liberals in subscribing to the belief that government intervention is necessary to overcome oppression. Yet, there are differences. Group I envisages the outcome of a fair race as still hierarchical (merito-cratic). We are all winners, but some will win more than others. After all, not all oak trees grow to the same size. Only time will tell which are the tallest oaks. Group II envisages a hierarchical finish as well, but the hierarchy will contain no gaps as far as race and sex are concerned (elitist). That is, if blacks are 11 percent of the American population, then in time blacks will be 11 percent of the recipients of Nobel prizes won by Americans. Group III takes the liberal position to the extreme by arguing that everybody will finish at exactly the same place (egalitarian). In short, it advocates total equality.

It is the struggle between competing groups of liberals that accounts for the response to affirmative action in the university. Group I accuses Groups II and III of lowering standards. Group II advocates more imaginative standards, especially during the transitional period. Group III advocates a total reappraisal of standards. Liberalism is perfectly capable of generating this wide variety of competing versions. That is why as long as we use liberal rhetoric, even if we do not believe it, we shall not only be trapped into liberal policies but every policy will give rise to conflicting versions. Short of accepting the egalitarian version, there is no way to make these policies look cumulative.

A perfect example of what I am talking about occurred at Harvard University. President Derek C. Bok issued an "Open Letter on Issues of Race at Harvard" on February 26, 1981. He reaffirmed his commitment to affirmative action. He wants to recruit minority students "because they have unusual opportunities to make important contributions to society after they graduate." Yet he balks at a separate cultural center for minority students because this is inconsistent with greater contact, and he notes the difficulty of hiring more minority Ph.D.'s, especially when out of Harvard's 132 black graduating seniors in 1980, only 2 entered Ph.D. programs. Bok is clearly liberal type I. The letter was in fact a response to pressure from minority students to hire more affirmative action faculty.

About a week after Bok's letter, the *Harvard Law Review* announced that it would be choosing a percentage of its new staff to reflect sexual and racial representation. The *Review* has become liberal type II. When shall we see type III?

REMEDIATION

Modern liberals accept the notion that intervention from the top is necessary to overcome certain kinds of oppression. The top can mean the government and within an institution it can mean the administration. Having adopted modern liberal rhetoric, for any number of reasons, university administrations found themselves committed to "doing something." The original hope might have been that the something would be to provide the expertise for reforming other institutions, including the primary and secondary schools that would then produce students worthy of university life. Presumably one did not have to reform the university. But more doctrinaire liberals, inside as well as outside the university, not only pointed their finger at the university but on their own initiative set about reforming the university. This reform included such things as hiring people who would not otherwise have been hired. The hiring was done in the name of affirmative action. The university administration committed itself to the rhetoric of affirmative action in order not to forfeit federal funds. The controversy then ensued as to what exactly the university had committed itself. On the one hand the university administration was trapped by rhetoric and public image, and on the other HEW defined what constituted affirmative action in higher education. If we keep in mind the social ideology of modern liberalism, then the story is really this simple.

In return for federal largesse, the administration now has to work out what it must render to HEW and what it must continue to render to the search for truth. The second stage of affirmative action was upon us, the remediation stage to make up for the deficiencies of earlier societal oppression.

The answer that underutilization was a problem of supply, not of demand, that is, that underrepresentation resulted not from university discrimination but from oppression outside the university such as inferior earlier schooling, merely postpones to another level the really controversial issues such as assumptions about the distribution of talent and motivation. The first place that universities will be forced to deal with this issue is in student admissions.

Perhaps the most extreme and ambitious attempt to put liberalism into practice was the adoption of open admissions in publicly supported universities. Open admissions was the acceptance of all high school graduates into public colleges, at least all those who could be persuaded and rounded up to attend. Since according to liberal ideology all men are rational animals seeking to maximize their self-interest, it is in every man's interest to obtain as much education as possible. But imagine what happens to students from the black ghetto and their liberal white peers when, say, William Bradford Shockey is invited to speak on campus. These students are totally unprepared for this kind of give and take. The idea that simply exposing people to ideas will somehow make them more rational is a romantic teleological delusion, a subscription to the myth of automatic progress. This concept of open admissions is analogous to liberal foreign policy, the belief that when you introduce liberal democratic ideas parliamentary democracy will automatically result. Here you can just ignore social, economic, and historic factors, in short, the whole institutional context in which liberal ideas themselves may function optimally. Have these people forgotten J. S. Mill's warning:

> It is, perhaps, hardly necessary to say that this doctrine is meant to apply only to human beings in the maturity of their faculties. . . . Liberty, as a principle, has no application to any state of things anterior to the time when mankind have become capable of being improved by free and equal discussion . . . the capacity of being guided to their own improvement by conviction or persuasion. . . .[12]

The other point to keep in mind is that the presence of a large minority undergraduate population can have two other uses. It can become an excuse, under the doctrine of cultural relativism, to hire more minority faculty, and such students are a potential mob to be stirred up by the faculty as the occasion requires.[13] "Open" is a misnomer, for it goes beyond increasing enrollment to actual structural changes in the operation of the colleges.

It should be clear, however, that undergraduate admissions in general is not a controversial area. For quite some time colleges have gone out of their way to recruit undergraduates. If the body is warm, some college will actively pursue you. There is hardly any excuse available in our society for anyone who does not go to college. More important are the questions such as preparedness and retention standards. The refusal to deal seriously with either remediation or grading has led to the steady erosion of the B.A. degree.

Having achieved equality on the undergraduate level, we next proceed to the graduate level. This is important to universities both because it is where serious research begins and because it is where future members of the faculties are trained. So graduate school becomes the focus of the supply argument. If there are not enough black and women Ph.D.'s, then why not train more? Now it should be recalled that the university got into trouble in the first place largely because of its dependence upon federal funding. What is really remarkable is that many leading academicians, as well as the Carnegie Council, propose to solve the problem by demanding more federal aid, this time in the way of subsidies for special graduate programs to train minorities and women.[14] This response to the crisis establishes beyond a doubt two conclusions I have already made. First, the university has no intention of surrendering federal funding even if it means federal control. Second, the assumption that increased federal funding will solve the problem is as clear a commitment to modern liberalism as you can get.

It is by now a foregone conclusion that too many ambitious administrators of the managerial mentality will turn everything into an attempt to get more federal funds into higher education. It presupposes as well that it is the function of the university to solve certain problems such as underpreparedness. Shouldn't we ask ourselves why these problems were not solvable on the lower levels despite years of pouring federal funds into primary and secondary education and a host of other programs of social welfare and reform? Is there any reason to believe that graduate school is the proper level for a solution? Is there any justification for the assumption that talent is statistically distributed by groups such that merely increasing minority and women representation in graduate school will have the ultimate ripple effect? The argument that all this is the university's responsibility—for it too is a guilty party to past discrimination—is a simple-minded acceptance of the thesis that all institutions in society are functionally related and that the guilt of one is shared by the system as a whole. This is not a fact but an article of liberal faith—and a controversial social theory. Furthermore, who is to employ these people after they graduate? Will universities be able to resist the wholly anticipated pressure that if "we" have trained them, then "we" must retain them?[15] If these graduates are not all superior, then are "we" responsible because "we" trained them?

Part of the naiveté of well-meaning people is the assumption that opening the door is all that is required. What these people fail to understand is that opening the door is taken by others to mean that guaranteed outcomes are expected everywhere. This expectation has been voiced in an interview (*New York Times,* December 28, 1982) with Reginald E. Gilliam, Jr., a black, former political scientist at Williams College, top aide to Senator John Glenn of Ohio, and vice chairman of ICC. He speaks of "The increasing numbers of embittered, disillusioned, young, recent black graduates of the Harvards, Yales, Berkeleys, Stanfords . . . initially full of idealism, hope and expectations that their hard-earned degrees would automatically place them on a fast track of professional advancement . . . now finding themselves failing to make partner. . . ." Gilliam explains that failure as their exclusion from the "Washington game, a political process that incorporates the old shibboleths of 'merit' and 'hard work' but is not exclusively that." No doubt Gilliam is making some valid points, but his remarks betray certain expectations of what is supposed to happen.

Unperceived in all of this is that the assimilation of the graduate school to the undergraduate school encourages taking the lowest common denominator as our standard. It is a vain attempt to maintain a level of funding by cheapening the product and by aiming to produce what the external market demands. It is also an attempt to strike a bargain with the devil in the hope that some good will come of it. But if we "democratize" graduate schools will we not soon have to do so with the faculty? And can the first-rate universities survive if the rest of the system is democratized?

The rude awakening for Group I liberals, those who subscribe only to the broadening of opportunities without predetermined results, comes when HEW makes it clear that it has other ideas in mind. To begin with, is it really socially useful to draw off talented individuals into useless subjects like classics and philosophy when those students could be studying medicine and engineering? It is not a question of denying excellence, they say, but of what kind of excellence.

At one Ivy League university, representatives of the Regional HEW demanded an explanation of why there were no women or minority students in the Graduate Department of Religious Studies. They were told that a reading knowledge of Hebrew and Greek was presupposed. Whereupon the representatives of HEW advised orally: "Then end those old fashioned programs that require irrelevant languages. And start up programs on relevant things which minority group students can study without learning languages."[16]

So it will not do simply to broaden opportunities for students. HEW will insist that affirmative action apply to faculty as well, both present and prospective members of the faculty. Here too we begin in seemingly innocuous fashion and gradually progress to something more sinister. HEW guidelines require that each university and college have an affirmative action officer in order to insure that there is no discrimination and that every effort is being made to give women and minorities equal opportunity. Group I liberals agree, for this is just public relations. But wait. It is specified in the guidelines that the officer should be a "person knowledgeable of and sensitive to the problems of women and minority groups." This would seem rather obvious, except that to HEW it means that the affirmative action officer should be a woman or a minority group member herself, preferably both. This does and says a number of things. First, it provides jobs for women and minorities, jobs that would not otherwise have been there. Second, it once more says that universities are guilty until they prove their innocence. Third, and most important, it subscribes to the thesis of *cultural relativism*, the belief that only members of a culture can really understand or be sensitive to that culture.[17]

Not only does HEW impose cultural relativism on universities but it practices it. In response to the criticism that its own staff is not representative of the population, it replies that the staff must be able to relate to the people who bring complaints. Thus, as of June 1973, one-half of the staff of HEW were women, three-fifths were members of minorities, and one-half were black.

The thesis of cultural relativism has had a long history in the social sciences, but on purely logical grounds its critics could always make short shrift of it. In order to make the assertion that members of one culture cannot understand the members of another culture, the person making the assertion must understand both cultures. If the person who asserts it understands both cultures, then the thesis is false because it is self-referentially inconsistent. Not only is cultural relativism logically incoherent, but it is also impossible to accept it and still believe that it is possible to help people. Our practice rejects it. We do not believe that a psychiatrist, or a novelist, has to be neurotic or psychotic to understand and perhaps help people who are.

But in reviving cultural relativism, HEW has reinterpreted it from the point of view of liberalism. To be knowledgeable of and sensitive to women and minorities means to accept the theory that women and minorities are oppressed victims of circumstances beyond their control, and that those of us who are fully developed have a moral and legal responsibility to intervene on their behalf. Anyone who does not accept some version of modern liberalism is unknowledgeable and insensitive, not intellectually and morally developed. Now, at least, we can begin to understand the look on the faces of modern liberals when we say such things as people are responsible for their own lives—it is the look of the elect contemplating the damned.

HEW further insists that women and blacks who are faculty members should have a greater involvement on college and university committees. One immediate problem with this recommendation is that many women and minority members are new junior members of the faculty who must concentrate on research if they expect to gain tenure. The main intention of HEW's recommendation is to put women and blacks into the power structure in order to insure the continued and increased hiring of more women and blacks, as well as other minorities. When HEW accepted Harvard's affirmative action plan it added the stipulation that these representative committees would "have a role in monitoring all appointments."[18] To offset the loss of research time, we may expect HEW to insist that service on committees be a major factor in granting tenure. Then it is no longer necessary to prove oneself; rather, one can escape the traditional criteria by engaging in political activity. Trying to put the best face on this ploy, the Carnegie Commission notes that women and minorities are heavily pressured to serve on committees. But who puts on the pressure? The answer is that most committees now stipulate a specific number of positions for women and minorities. In short, first you instigate the requirement and then you succumb to the pressure. It is rather self-serving, like arranging to be drafted for nomination.

In addition to insuring the presence of women and minorities in the faculty, the Carnegie Council also recommends that special posts be created in the administration to be filled by women and blacks—for example, as assistant deans. This will allow relatively new groups on campus to acquire the experience necessary to move up in the administration, experience that might otherwise take them much longer to acquire.

How does one justify the preferential hiring of faculty and the preferential appointment of administrators? The same sorts of cultural relativism arguments can be used here. First, it is claimed that these new faculty will encourage minority undergraduates to seek careers in the academic world, that is, they will serve as models and mentors. This argument is necessitated by the fact that simply having increased the size of the student body did not lead to the automatic ripple effect. Rather than consider a host of possible hypotheses to explain this, the liberals resort to the hidden variable argument. What proof is there that some people need models and mentors? There is none; it is a speculative attempt to avoid facing potentially embarrassing or deep theoretical difficulties with liberalism. Liberals appeal to the idea that some subtle need is not being met, explaining the failure of the ripple effect from student to faculty. The second argument is even more interesting, for it claims that there is some intellectual justification for preferential appointments:

... differences in sex, race, and cultural experience to provide breadth of understanding and role models, which may be especially important for undergraduate instruction.[19]

Again we raise the objection, where is the evidence that the breadth of understanding can only be provided by people in certain categories?

The academic bureaucratic complex is very much in evidence here. The need to eliminate "covert" discrimination forces the bureaucracy to keep finding new tasks for itself, thereby expanding its numbers and opportunities for promotion. For instance, we shall need a legal definition of who is a "black" in order to prevent whites from "passing" and illegitimately benefitting from affirmative action programs. We shall need a national registration program similar to South Africa's. This in turn will provide great new opportunities for social scientists to collect and study geneologies.[20]

LIBERALISM AND PREJUDICE

The social philosophy of liberalism operates with what we have called a psychologistic view of the relationship between individuals and society. That is, it presupposes that all explanation is ultimately reducible to the motives of individual people. Society is the individual writ large. Since liberalism does not recognize anything as a motive force except individual desires, it is unable to understand that certain events are the unintended consequences of a number of initially unrelated historical factors. Hence, whatever set of circumstances or consequences is not liked by liberals must be ascribed to motives (conscious or unconscious). Thus if there is underrepresentation it must be the result of prejudice or racism. All racism is the product of prejudice. Prejudice and racism are even ascribable to institutions. The university is an institution that is underrepresented, hence the university is prejudiced in general and racist in particular. Therefore, extraordinary steps must be taken to guarantee the presence of women and minorities in the student body, on the faculty, and in the administration.

Are there other possible explanations? Many have been detailed, including some with surprising statistical revelations. One study indicates that women had greater presence in numbers during an earlier period and then the number dropped off at about the time that motherhood was becoming a much more fashionable alternative. As of 1971, single women in their thirties working continuously since high school earned slightly more than men in that category. Another study indicates a great disparity in the average age of members of various ethnic groups. Some groups, such as Jews, have a much higher average age, and hence in those areas

where achievement has some relation to age we should on purely statistical grounds expect much greater representation. Chicanos, for example, have as a group an average age of less than nineteen. We could
hardly expect them to be represented by percentage of the population in
fields and professions requiring a great deal of postgraduate education
and experience. My reason for mentioning these statistics is not that I
think that statistics should be our final guide. On the contrary, I want to
get away from a purely statistical approach and to judge individuals, not
groups. I mention these statistics to indicate what I think has gone wrong.
Those who have used statistical analyses to derive conclusions in support
of government intervention have allowed their analyses to be controlled
by the social ideology of liberalism. They have started off with a conclusion in mind and have looked for supporting evidence. There is nothing
wrong per se in this. But in a scientific approach one also considers
alternative hypotheses and looks to disconfirm one's hypotheses. That is,
one also designs experiments to deliberately try to falsify one's pet
hypothesis. The fact that proponents of government intervention do not
do this once more exemplifies my contention that social science has been
vulgarized in the service of ideology.

The statistics with regard to women are even more interesting.
Between 1972 and 1981 total college enrollment rose by one-third. In
1972 there were 74 women for every 100 men, but by 1981 there were 108
women for every 100 men. The number of men increased on campus by
12 percent but the number of women increased by 63 percent. It could
easily be argued that colleges and universities did not open their doors to
women after being pressured, rather the pressure increased after schools
increased the presence of female students. Second, betwen 1971 and 1980
plaintiffs who sued by appeal to EPA (Equal Pay Act) lost 47 out of 64
cases. Third, when 33 female salaries were raised at the University of
Nebraska, the courts also found that 92 male faculty were underpaid. By
and large the difficulty with EPA suits, as pointed out by both Richard
Lester *(Reasoning About Discrimination: The Analysis of Professional
and Educative Work in Federal Antibias Programs,* 1980) and Pezzullo
and Brittingham *(Salary Equity: Detecting Sex Bias in Salaries among
College and University Professors,* 1979), is that factors other than discrimination may account for the statistics. Regression analysis in mathe-
matics can be applied only when it is assumed that all jobs are comparable. Finally, there is the well-kept secret statistic that black female professionals' median income is 125 percent of white female professionals.
Walter Williams, in *The State Against Blacks* (1982), has suggested that
this possibly reflects the greater urbanization of blacks and the higher pay
to be found in urban areas. The conspiracy hypothesis is just not going to
be an adequate explanation.

Despite these statistics, Barbara Bergmann can write the following in the *New York Times* (January 10, 1982):

> . . . in the absence of affirmative action, women and blacks are routinely passed over in favor of less qualified white men, as attested to by mountains of evidence presented in hundreds of Federal courtrooms.

One of the special problems facing women in our society is the relationship between a career and family responsibility. Given the traditional pattern of family life, including assigning to women the major responsibility for child care and subordinating the careers of women to that of their spouses, it is not surprising that (a) some women choose not to have families, (b) some women surrender their careers, and (c) of those who maintain both, some impoverish their careers or subordinate them. It is therefore not surprising in the academic world that women as a group are not as well represented at the top of their profession.

Clearly it is not the university's responsibility if family life has developed as it has. There are perhaps good arguments for changing family life. But it is the university's responsibility to maintain the best faculty possible, regardless of any other consideration. What women, as well as men, will have to realize is that life requires the making of moral choices: I may have to choose between one potential spouse and another or no spouse at all, depending upon what other things I want. In short, it is not always possible to have one's cake and eat it too. There is no guide in these matters, and a good deal of the conflict is potential and frequently involves factors beyond our control. The necessity for making these kinds of choices is part of the moral dimension of life.

But it is precisely the moral dimension of life that liberalism denies. Given its theory we can understand why. If I am a liberal then I believe that I have innate built-in ends, all of which are consistent, and all of which have to be satisfied if I am to fulfill myself. In short, I have a nature. Moreover, every institution is to be judged in terms of whether it allows me to fulfill my true nature. Hence, if I am a woman, and I want both a career and a family, then in order for me to fulfill myself I *need* both. If university hiring, retention, and promotion practices are not conducive to having everything I want, then there is something wrong with the university. Therefore, any policy that changes the university to suit *my needs* is justified. Not only can I have my cake and eat it too, but the ends clearly justify the means. What liberalism has done is to substitute a seemingly technical solution for a moral problem. It is all perfectly consistent, and that is why the only way to refute it is to challenge the idea that human beings have a nature to be fulfilled.

So prejudice, like every other concept, has been subtly redefined from the point of view of liberalism. Prejudice now simply means any practice that prevents people from fulfilling themselves. Hence those of us who oppose such policies are prejudiced. Not only has liberalism created and mounted this massive assault on every institution, but it wages a relentless campaign against those who choose not to fulfill themselves. Any woman who does not want a career is castigated. Even the notion of comparing what different groups have, the *gap,* is designed to get some group to define itself in terms of what other people have. Any black who chooses not to become "white" is also castigated. Nor should we be misled by rhetoric here. I have also heard it argued that each group has its own special end, and therefore double or multiple standards have to be used. This is just a perversion and typical of the ability of liberalism to split into many versions.

ADMINISTRATIVE COPING

There are 34 congressional committees and 74 subcommittees concerned with the 150 laws affecting higher education. In the last twelve years the number of pages on higher education in the federal law has grown from 90 to 360. From 1965 to 1977 the number of pages in the *Federal Register* on higher education regulations grew from 92 to 1,000. As the state bureaucracy grows, independent institutions are forced to build up their own bureaucracies in order to negotiate with the state bureaucracies. This requires further increasing the power of deans and presidents at traditionally decentralized institutions. Some academics not only advocate this direction but want college presidents to be as powerful as corporation presidents. They even aspire to "capture" the regulators.[21] It is hoped that by controlling salary increases, departmental budgets, research funds, travel allowances, and approval of outside grants, college presidents can insure the progress of affirmative action.[22]

It is impossible to cope with liberalism from the administrative point of view. The reasons are really quite simple. First, human beings do not have natures; rather, each and every one of us has a multiplicity of conflicting desires. Second, there is no generally agreed upon liberal view of what is really basic. Hence, every person and every organized interest group simply plugs into the liberal formula whatever is demanded at the moment. It is therefore not possible to arrive at any consistent policy. The only way out is to impose upon people some belief about what is in their best interest, and this of course is the ultimate totalitarian implication of egalitarian liberalism—it is what we shall get when government intervention becomes total.

One example of inconsistency has to do with the issue of nepotism. Nepotism is the bestowing of benefits on the basis of family relationship instead of merit. In the academic world it usually involves giving a job to a spouse. In order to circumvent this practice, which frequently worked against highly qualified women who lost out to less qualified women who happened to have a spouse in a key position, the university frequently adopted antinepotism rules, which prevented both spouses from being employed in the same department or school. Frequently, there were laws to reinforce the rules. Within the past decade, not only has the number of women going to graduate school increased, but the number of marriages of two professionals has increased. Sometimes one spouse is hired and the other is not because of antinepotism rules. But frequently the unhired spouse is better qualified than any other applicant. The irony now is that the better person has to be rejected because of the regulation. As a consequence, a big drive is underway to undo these antinepotism rules and simply judge people on the basis of merit. All this is perfectly understandable. What disappoints me is the fact that liberals do not recognize that the problem was created by regulation in the first place. Why not generalize and recognize that any regulation is going to have these counterproductive effects? Of course, I know that nepotism is still being practiced, but regulation made it worse. Does this argument not hold elsewhere?

Government pressure to promote equality of result, in the form of threats to cut off federal funding, leads administrators to compromise and ultimately to distortions of fact. If an administrator subscribes to liberalism, he may even be guilty of duplicity. Under the illusion that they are still in control of the situation, typical well-meaning administrators who want to maintain standards will accede to a compromise that they consider a sop to government bureaucrats. For example, they will institute a scholarship or internship program, without realizing that they have entered a game they cannot win because the rules have been defined by liberal logic. Nor do they realize at first that such concessions will be used as evidence against them, as admissions of guilt. Nor do they realize that such concessions will commit them to further steps from which they cannot go back. For as we shall see, such seemingly minor concessions admit people to the university process, which those people by their very presence will eventually cause to be redefined.

Here the example of the business world will be of no help. In the business world new hirees do not determine policy. The university is different. It is collegial—faculty help to define policy. So new hirees cannot even be shunted off into a dual but meaningless and redundant administration. Finally, as we shall see, the job of seeking truth is just not going to get done, at any price. In fact, what happens is that the university changes its product.

Setting up special *ad hoc* programs like ethnic studies is a case in point. It may begin as a platitude, a way of paying lip service to various sorts of social pressure. Giving these programs space on campus is not the same thing as making them part of the university. But soon platitudes give way to compensation, so that these programs gradually acquire responsibility for overcoming the disadvantages of women and, especially, minority students. Finally, the people in the program gain full faculty status, including tenure. To deny them tenure on the grounds that they were never intended to become a full-fledged part of the university is to provoke uprisings and the charge of racism or prejudice. Once the spokesmen of these programs gain full faculty status, they also obtain a role in shaping overall university policy. The tail begins to wag the dog. To try and offset this by multiplying ethnic groups with special programs is to magnify the corruption inherent in such special access programs.

What sorts of ideas might flourish in a black studies program? The following statement is from Dr. Leonard Jeffries, head of the Black Studies Department at CCNY, as published in April, 1982, in *The City College Alumnus:*

> Based upon serious studies and analyses that have been made, we are quite clear that Africa is the origin of mankind . . . and those societies and cultures that moved into high culture and civilization were developed around African peoples. . . .
>
> It is difficult to even raise these questions because of racism. It is difficult to deal with it with you because I would have to say that that which has been inherited from the Judeo-Christian heritage has an African root and origin which we have not effectively dealt with and, in looking back at Black Studies, it becomes quite clear that the values that come out of our Judeo-Christian heritage were institutionalized in processes and institutions in the Nile Valley thousands of years before there was a Jew and before there was a Christian. If we're going to talk about a legacy to mankind in the Nile Valley, around African peoples, it will reverse the whole process that has elevated the Greeks to a pinnacle in society, and we now raise the question, "Where did Greece inherit its traditions and its cultures?" We have to go back to the Nile. . . .

Ethnic studies programs are very often no more than subterfuges for circumventing the normal hiring process, and they serve as well to entrench doctrinaire liberalism. In practice, conservatives are rigidly excluded from appointments to black studies, ethnic studies, Chicano studies, and women studies. Hence these departments serve as additional reservoirs for left-liberal sentiments.

Ironically, the reason why the government went to the university in the first place is that the university was the home of special intellectual skills. The conflict comes when an institution producing people with these skills is pressured to achieve other aims that are inimical to those skills. No doubt in time government will learn to discount the university in a manner similar to businesses, instituting their own tests in the wake of B.A.'s being given to illiterate people. Of course, the liberal assumes that he knows the ultimate end, so, for him, there can be no real conflict here.

But herein lies the rub. Only those with no fixed belief in fixed ends can pursue the notion of an open truth. This insight was at the heart of Veblen's warning that knowledge knows no political boundaries.

A comparable dilemma is faced by the Soviet Union. It wants creative scientists who will help to maintain a competitive level with Western science and technology. But in encouraging such creative thinking in the sciences, it finds it spilling over into other areas. Is it pure coincidence that leading dissidents such as Sakharov are also scientists? Can one encourage questioning of preconceptions in one area and one area only, or is this a habit of mind that knows no bounds? Analogously, encouraging the questioning attitude in physical and biological science is bound to lead people to question the liberal ideology. Given our political system and the prevalence of the liberal ideology on both domestic and foreign affairs, I cannot but be pessimistic about the ultimate outcome of a showdown. Raising objections about the dangers inherent in research in the natural and biological sciences is just the opening wedge of a political onslaught.

The worst form of self-deception in these matters is the argument about variety. In the name of variety and in praise of variety, liberals go about undermining the very props that true variety needs. Variety is a necessary condition but not a sufficient condition of productivity. In any case, a standardized quota conception of variety is itself a way of undermining true variety. It is at the same time a perfect instance of using the language of freedom and liberation to impose a messianic vision on society. Only liberalism can accomplish this in the same breath.

What our administrative Machiavellians and specialists in "realpolitik" have overlooked is that the new egalitarianism in all its forms will not permit the old hypocrisy to work. These new "other" people are against real diversity, and they are demanding the same status and control that goes with the traditional university. They will achieve it precisely because acquiesing in federal regulation in order to obtain federal funds undermines the institution. The most dramatic example of this is the litigation explosion. Federal control and making the university the servant of an ideology encourages every grievant to go outside the institution and to litigate. The breakdown and the impotence of internal due process is the ultimate consequence of the teleological trap, the mythical consensus that makes every institution a means in some societal end.

REALIGNMENT

If anyone had any lingering doubts about where we were headed, they were all dispelled by the next set of events. We left off our discussion of HEW with the education amendments of 1972.

In studying the "Summary Statement . . . Sex Discrimination Proposed HEW Regulation to Effectuate Title IX of the Education Amendments of 1972," officials at Stanford University discovered (in Section 86.34) a proposal to have government bureaucrats monitor the curriculum in higher education to "establish and use internal procedure for reviewing curricula, designed both to ensure that they do not reflect discrimination on the basis of sex and to resolve complaints concerning allegations of such discrimination, pursuant to procedural standards to be prescribed by the Director of the office of Civil Rights." When informed of this, then (1974) Secretary of HEW Casper Weinberger expressed his own shock that such things were being considered and reassured Stanford University that he would never approve of it. This was not the only time that Weinberger came to the aid of the university, but it underscores how much the university was at the mercy of the administration holding office.

It is increasingly clear that behind the facade of pursuing justice and granting equal opportunity, something more radical and dangerous was taking place: an attempt to redefine the university and American culture as well. In the name of a social ideology, what was taught, what was published, and what was thought was being reshaped to fit that ideology. Little by little, stories began circulating of repressed research. In 1978, Professor Gerald Lesser of Harvard was asked by his colleagues—as well as threatened anonymously—not to publish the results of his comparative study of verbal and reasoning skills because it might be "misinterpreted and used to foster racism."[23] At U.C. Berkeley in 1973, it was proposed that no research be undertaken if anyone's reputation might be damaged—read this as no publication of research showing that minority students are having trouble achieving in higher education. These regulations were rescinded after great controversy, but note that if they had become national policy, this book could not have been written. The mentality of the people we are dealing with should now be seen for what it is.

If Title VI and Title VII of the 1964 Civil Rights Act were to apply to higher education, then so would the executive orders and Revised Order No. 4 of the Labor Department dealing with affirmative action. In July of 1972 HEW issued a 100-page draft of guidelines for the application of affirmative action to higher education. This draft was revised and issued in October 1972, and was largely a repetition of Revised Order No. 4. This order was in turn amended under Revised Order No. 14, published on February 14, 1974. Here we begin to confront realignment:

> Neither minority nor female employees should be required to possess higher qualifications than those of the lowest qualified incumbent.

This reduction to the lowest common denominator was just too much to swallow. In response to unexpectedly heated opposition, Peter

Holmes, director of the Office of Contract Review, issued a memorandum taking back what Revised Order No. 14 said:

> Colleges and universities are entitled to select the most qualified candidate, without regard to race, sex, or ethnicity, for any position. The college or university, not the Federal Government, is to say what constitutes qualification for any particular position.

But this memorandum does not really take it back; rather, it opens up a new front, for it goes on to say what is apparently innocuous:

> . . . no standards or criteria which have, by intent or effect, worked to exclude women and minorities as a class can be utilized, unless the institution can demonstrate the necessity of such standard to the performance of the job in question. . . .

What is the new front? The new front is that the university is going to have to prove that its traditional standards are relevant to the performance of the job. This is supposed to be nothing more than the old *Griggs* doctrine. But in September, 1978, new guidelines were issued that spelled out how universities were supposed to validate their standards. The intent is wholly predictable. If under any set of circumstances the desired numerical balances are not achieved, it will be necessary to redefine the job in order to arrive at the predetermined results.

> Whenever a validity study is called for . . . the user should include . . . an investigation of suitable alternative selection procedures and suitable alternative methods of using the selection procedure which have as little adverse impact as possible. . . . Whenever the user is shown an alternative selection procedure with evidence of less adverse impact and substantial evidence of validity for the same job in similar circumstances, the user should investigate it to determine the appropriateness of using or validating it in accord with these guidelines.

In case you missed it, "adverse impact" is the younger sister of "underutilization." In case you are wondering where HEW got the idea for alternative selection procedures, consult the AAUP statement and those indiviuals who advocated models and mentors as a subterfuge for hiring women and minorities.

Moreover, the traditional notion that instructors are hired because they are potential scholars and that is why they need a Ph.D. and that is why they have to publish and that is why they have to meet all the traditional standards, all this is swept away again by redefining the jobs.

If job progression structures are so established that employees will probably, within a reasonable period of time and in a majority of cases, progress
to a higher level, it may be considered that the applicants are being evaluated for a job or jobs at the higher level. However, where job progression is
not so nearly automatic, or the time span is such that higher level jobs or
employees' potential may be expected to change in significant ways, it
should be considered that applicants are being evaluated for a job at or
near the entry level. . . . A "reasonable period of time" will vary for different jobs and employment situations but will seldom be more than 5 years.
Use of selection procedures to evaluate applicants for a higher level job
would not be appropriate:

(1) If the majority of thoes remaining employed do not progress to the
higher level job,

(2) If there is a reason to doubt that the higher level job will continue
to require essentially similar skills during the progression period, or,

(3) If the selection procedures measure knowledges, skills, or abilities
required for advancement which would be expected to develop principally
from the training or experience on the job.

Anyone who thinks that these guidelines were formulated by people who
do not know the academic game had better read the fine print. The fine
print neatly closes off every avenue of escape.

If anyone thinks that these guidelines are going to affect only community or junior colleges, or second- and third-rank institutions, he
should read on. For contained within these guidelines is the first formal
and explicit attack on the guild system and the concept of excellence. How
does one know or extablish that Professor X is a more distinguished
scholar than Professor Y?

When an informal or unscored selection procedure which has an adverse
impact is utilized, the user should eliminate the adverse impact, or modify
the procedure to one which is formal, scored or quanitified measure or
combination of measures and then validate the procedure in accord with
these guidelines, or otherwise justify continued use of the procedure in
accord with Federal law.

Now, ladies and gentlemen, prove to me that Beethoven is better than the
Rolling Stones. No matter what you say, it is always open to someone to
ask why one factor is important as opposed to some other.

This kind of argument has been made many times in many contexts.
Here is one version:

Who is the best pitcher for a professional baseball team? Simple arithmetic
tells a large part of that story. Hence, prejudice is more easily discernerible.
Who is the best candidate for a philosophy instructorship? Not so easy.
Judgments about the quality of a person's scholarship may differ widely
and no mechanical resolution is possible. When purely objective rules of

selection are absent, a sex-biased choice is more easily rationalized. . . . Hiring goals serve as a check on the workings of such prejudice; by voluntarily acceding to that check, we free ourselves from culpability.[24]

One curiosity about this argument has been overlooked. If professional decisions are that difficult to make, then how does one know that any decision has been prejudiced? It would seem that in order to extablish that a decision was prejudiced, one would first have to establish that a candidate with better credentials was rejected in favor of a candidate with lesser credentials. But if there is no sure way of establishing this, how could one ever know or come to believe that prejudice operated in the first place? This argument is self-contradictory. But liberals operate with a different logic. Because they operate with the premise that all abilities are equal (either by group or by individual), sheer statistical evidence establishes the existence of bias. With that assumption, it becomes obvious that realignment was built into the whole discussion from the very beginning. Can anyone use the statistical procedures recommended by HEW to validate the theory of liberalism? Only if one accepts the ideological norms can these results be obtained.

A few years back, administration officials were amazed that officials of HEW did a statistical analysis of every rank and every field and every subfield at major universities. Why pick on the big schools, why be picayune about every little distinction? Now it is clear why. If women and minorities are able to achieve statistical parity in higher education as a whole, that is not enough. Invidious comparison is still possible. It is especially important that they achieve parity in the best schools. And if they achieve parity in the best schools but not in every department, then invidious comparisons can still be made. Finally, if they achieve it in every level of every department but some subfield of knowledge is not proportional, then a gap still exists. Any evidence that groups may vary widely must be eliminated, otherwise the liberal assumption about human nature cannot sustain the policies recommended.

In any other context many of us would welcome the challenge to validate selection procedures for hiring faculty. On purely intellectual grounds it would be enlightening to articulate intellectual values, positions, and presumptions, both our own and those of our colleagues everywhere. It might, for example, be instructive to point out how some people confuse being articulate with being insightful, how some confuse rudeness with originality, and how some confuse iconoclasm with creativity. It would be most instructive to show how often the quality control of the guild system has been replaced by the soulless training of technicians. No doubt we all have our private axes to grind here. But I suspect that this useful exchange will not be the outcome.

We must remember that validation is a statistical procedure, and that it is imposed by liberals who believe in teleology. So while some of us will set about showing that what we are looking for is a certain entity, call it Y, and that we have reason to believe that quality X leads to Y more often than any other quality, we shall run up against a challenge. First, HEW will ask if the correlation of X and Y is strong enough, and if it is not, then HEW will suggest alternative qualities, like S or T, which, strangely enough, will have some correlation with percentage of the population. And if it should turn out that X is very strongly correlated with Y, then HEW will challenge our use of Y as an entity controlling our choice. They will ask if Y is really a useful means of achieving Z, where Z is some extra-university value in terms of which the university is to be judged. It will also turn out, strangely again, that Z can only be achieved, for sure, by hiring people in proportion to the population. Even if they cannot destroy Y, then they will suggest additional entities, such as Z, on the grounds that the university must achieve a variety of ends. We are not being asked to prove our objectivity; rather, we are being challenged to explain why we are not pursuing the liberal version of society.

Even in fields where the evidence is seemingly incontroversible, such as athletics, something must be done. One would have thought that the liberal position would be to allow women, for example, an equal opportunity to make the varsity team and to discontinue double-tracking in the athletic department. But what cannot be denied must be redefined. Liberals advocate equal funding of women's teams. So it should be clear that what is behind the policy is the granting of equal benefits, not bringing about equal opportunity. The purpose of having teams will be investigated and suitably redefined. Where differences are alleged they must be denied; where they exist they must be redefined.

So far, I have been arguing about the threatening nature of federal guidelines and about the various responses. Is it possible to present recent evidence for the convergence of these two points? The answer is that the 1982 AAUP Guidelines on Affirmative Action (as published in *Academe*, January-February 1982) represent just such a convergence.

As is to be expected, the AAUP endorses hiring the "best qualified persons," it endorses the "rights of individuals" as opposed to group entitlement, and it stresses that while sexual and racial qualifications might be pertinent to hiring, they certainly are inappropriate for "reappointment, promotion, or the granting of tenure." The guidelines also prudentially remind us that if academics do not do the job, the federal government will. All of the aforementioned would certainly satisfy the classical liberal.

But a closer look reveals a very different conception of what is going on, something that indicates a modern liberal direction. To begin with, the title of the guidelines is "Recommended Procedures for Increasing the Number of Minority Persons and Women on College and University

Faculties." It is a foregone conclusion now that the real objective is increasing participation, not eliminating bias. Of course, the two things amount to the same thing if a number of assumptions are made, and the guidelines proceed to make those assumptions. "Where the principle of nondiscrimination is truly operative, the expectation is that all groups, where large enough units were considered would achieve adequate representation." We are told that "in the interest of *diversity* a faculty might make the academic judgment that it would be desirable to have more men or more women or more black or more white persons among the faculty or student body." We are told that if candidates are "approximately equivalent," then "in the interests of diversity, affirmative action considerations might control the final selection." To insure the desired results, all appointments should be "monitored," "search committees should be sensitive in reading letters of reference for indications of bias," minority candidates should meet with current minority faculty, and criteria with "adverse impact on affirmative action efforts" should be reevaluated. Once more the criteria are guilty until proven innocent.

One final point is worth driving home. The university is not going to save itself by claiming at this late date that its major function is the production of knowledge. For the production of knowledge is not itself an unassailable goal. After all, we would not, for example, condone Nazi-type experimentation on humans without their consent just to advance medical knowledge, even if it meant saving lives. There are always other values in terms of which any one value can be challenged or checked. Thus we should not be surprised that some would use the university as a means to some other desirable goal, desirable to some at least. But what is different about this case is that a particular series of norms is being imposed not only on the university but upon the very process that criticizes and analyzes norms in the first place. What we can debate now, even from within our bunker, will no longer be possible when we have completely liberalized the university.

CHAPTER 5

Fact and Myth about Affirmative Action in Higher Education

> If we can have affirmative action programs for star quarterbacks we can have affirmative action programs for people that society's discriminated against.—Joseph H. Califano, former secretary of HEW (1983)

My purpose in this chapter is to examine the structure and content of the arguments that have been offered in support of preferential admissions. I shall examine each specific argument individually. The embarrassing ease with which the individual arguments may be refuted will give us pause for thought. There is an Alice in Wonderland quality about these arguments until we realize that they are not really isolated arguments but bits and pieces of a much larger scenario. In the next chapter I shall present a formal analysis of that scenario.

A wide and varied number of arguments have been put forward by a wide variety of individuals and groups. Sometimes these arguments are presented singly and sometimes in clusters. It is clearly not the case that someone who endorses one such argument or cluster necessarily endorses another argument or cluster. In any case, I shall rebut each individual argument and cluster. More importantly, the seeming variety is often a symptom of thoughtlessness on the part of the espouser or it is the succumbing to rhetoric, the use of any emotional plea as long as it works and independently of whether the arguer believes it. Often it is well intended. Often it is sinister. Frequently it is an exercise in self-deception.

We may pause before continuing with the main thread of our argument to consider some reader response. It will be said that I am being very unfair here to some proponents of liberalization. The essence of the complaint is that I have misrepresented or distorted their argument by attributing to them policies to which they do not subscribe. For example, it

101

will be said by one reader that she advocates proportional hiring only from the pool of women Ph.D.'s and nothing more. She certainly does not subscribe, or so it is asserted, to radical equalization. My response to this is that any argument that is used to support her policy or any argument that is used to substantiate her charge of past discrimination can be generalized to support the most radical polices. It is not a question of whether an individual personally draws the implication from an argument but whether the logic of the argument could allow someone else to draw that implication. Not only do other people draw the most radical implications but the way has been paved for them by the well-intentioned people who will soon find themselves victims of the very process that they have helped to initiate. No doubt my analogy will be misunderstood or misrepresented, but these seemingly well-intentioned proponents of social justice will ultimately find themselves in the position of the first and second estates who, for their own reasons having refused to support King Louis XVI, find that they are themselves the first victims of the ensuing reign of terror.

ADMISSIONS POLICIES

Although the opposite impression is sometimes created, it is a fact that women, blacks, and other minorities did gain admission to colleges and universities, including graduate schools, long before affirmative action. Affirmative action, therefore, is not the policy of gaining admittance for blacks. However, the blacks admitted, for example, were small in number, where small is defined by reference to percentage of the population. Affirmative action is a policy of increasing the percentage.

Many of the blacks admitted to universities prior to affirmative action were admitted on the basis of a differential admissions policy. That is, the traditional or conventional standards were suspended in part. This was done for two reasons. First, in known individual cases, conventional standards did not give a true picture of potential. Second, a truly voluntary and experimental policy for increasing black participation in university and graduate school and professional life was already in existence, largely at the instigation of liberals. This program was always modest, carefully monitored, and done discretely. Ironically, forcing universities to justify their admissions policies may actually lead to a decrease of this second category. Nevertheless, it should be stressed that many of the blacks admitted prior to affirmative action did in fact meet conventional standards, some brilliantly. One of the consequences of implementing affirmative action is to funnel all blacks into a separate admissions procedure. This technique allows affirmative action advocates to claim that affirmative action admittees are highly qualified by citing some of the high scores of those blacks who would have been admitted anyway, and raises the average score of affirmative action admittees by lumping all blacks together. Of course, this may taint otherwise highly gifted blacks, but then they are so much fodder for liberal cannons.

Some universities and graduate schools at one time had overt or covert quotas by race, national origin, religion, and so on. Some medical schools had *long quotas*. For example, if Jews are 2 percent of the population they were given 5 percent of the admissions. Jews were supposed to be grateful because, after all, they were getting more places than they "deserved"; and they should not complain even if some Jewish applicants with outstanding credentials were rejected. Affirmative action occasionally prides itself on asking for a *short quota*. For example, if blacks are 11 percent of the population, HEW may only ask that 8 percent of the entering class be black. Critics of affirmative action are supposed to be mollified because that is less than what blacks "deserve." Of course, what affirmative action people fail to realize is that even a short quota for group A is in fact the imposition of a quota limiting groups B, C, and D. Even long quotas are quotas, and that is what some of us thought we were always fighting.

Some universities had and have geographic quotas. In part these quotas reflect public relations: the attempt to create a national image, generate prestige, and help in subsidizing the university through alumni contributions. More often than not, these quotas were applied on an "all things being equal" basis. Geography was an edge to some who already met conventional standards. The same point can be made about many of the other differential criteria used for admissions, such as musical skill. Affirmative action quotas are unlike geographical quotas because affirmative action quotas entirely circumvent or are substitutes for conventional standards.

At the same time, we should recognize that differential criteria were used for other purposes, mainly economic. Children of wealthy alumni, outstanding athletes who could instill pride in the alumni, politicians who could grant favors—all found themselves or their children or friends admitted to something for which they could not otherwise qualify. Without attempting to justify this practice, I merely note two things about it. Failure to gain admittance to one university because an athlete was recruited instead did not exclude the applicant from another school. Here we are beginning to realize the difference between graduate and undergraduate schools. Law schools and medical schools as a whole inevitably exclude, whereas undergraduate colleges do not. Affirmative action advocates persistently ignore the distinction between graduate and undergraduate schools.[1] Moreover, differential standards in this case did not mean total reorganization of the university. Affirmative action is not just an admissions policy, it is a policy that revolutionizes the whole structure and content of higher education.

This last point is one that should be stressed. To the extent that universities have adopted policies aimed at serving the outside world in diverse ways (staffing the Boston Symphony as well as the New England Patriots) and coincidently increasing the prestige of the university in all walks of life, it was always done with a wary eye toward maintaining the high internal standards and the diverse traditional activities of the university. Affirmative action, on the contrary, inevitably subordinates the university to outside interests and to the winds of political fashion.

One of the most remarkable feats of university administration in the first half of the twentieth century was its ability to serve the community at large and at the same time maintain institutional autonomy and pursue its own internal goals. A case could be made that financial independence was a necessary condition for this achievement. A further case could be made that institutional autonomy allowed the American universities to achieve a standard of excellence that influenced the very aims of the community at large. In short, the very value of the university vis-à-vis the community at large was enhanced by institutional autonomy.

Some affirmative action advocates would ignore this achievement and attack conventional standards as irrelevant and hypocritical. After all, it is said:

> We do not live in a society in which there is even the serious pretense of a qualification requirement for many jobs of substantial power and authority. . . . the higher one goes in terms of prestige, power and the like, the less qualifications seem ever to be decisive.[2]

But this obscures another important distinction. The university and the community at large are not isomorphic. Maybe it is not functional for all positions in the community or even all positions within any one institution to be certified by a credentials committee. Maybe there are and ought to be other considerations. But what does this imply about the university? It certainly does not imply that the university ought to mirror the practices of the community at large. Within the university those standards are functional; and it is, I believe, overall more functional for the university to be different both for its own aims and coincidentally for society as a whole. Part of the reason that doctrinaire liberals miss this point is that they insist upon interpreting the social word as a monolithic teleological whole.

Finally, we should stress that high admissions standards are not synonymous with a rigid commitment to numbers. Every university admissions committee is keenly on the alert for the unpolished diamond, the individual who is much better than the scores would indicate. Curiously, advocates of affirmative action like to point out that someone who is admitted with lower scores frequently turns out to be the academic star of the class. This is certainly cause for universal rejoicing. But note the contradiction! To become the star of the class is to meet in the highest degree the conventional retention standards. If this is a good thing, then advocates of affirmative action cannot say, later, although they shall, that conventional retention standards are dispensable.

TWO WRONGS MAKE A RIGHT

An affluent society like America can afford to give people a second and even a third chance. No matter how many times you fail to qualify, there are frequently other opportunities. This is beneficial because a number of late bloomers are always to be found. The decision, however, always has to be made at some level about the allocation of scarce resources, so there is always some point at which qualifying rounds come to an end. This is no longer true of the undergraduate programs. One now has to make special efforts to stay out of college. Increasingly this is becoming true of many graduate subjects. But the situations are not exactly the same, so some comment can be useful here.

Since graduate schools are or used to be unequivocally engaged in training professionals, admissions criteria were much more stringent. In order to justify an increase in minority admissions, one argument that surfaced was the claim that no merit system had ever really existed in higher education. Institutions of higher education have been known to apply double standards of admissions in favor of the rich, the powerful, the friends of the rich and the powerful, and especially athletes. Those who now invoke the "good old days of excellence" argument to exclude minorities are, it is said, simply being hypocritical.

This is a curious argument. There is a parallel that would go something like this. All those with special discount admissions coupons (rich, powerful, athletes, and so on) are rationalized by the admissions committee as helping to keep the university financially solvent. A winning football team is important for boosting alumni support. Now that the government is the biggest single funder, the special wards of the government are to be given discount admissions coupons. This is clearly a version of the two-wrongs-make-a-right argument. But the second wrong is still wrong. So is the first.

Since I have not put myself in the position of justifying the first wrong, I am at liberty to point out how much greater is the second wrong. To begin with, double admissions standards are not always accompanied by double retention standards. Nor is there any commitment on the part of the university beyond graduation. On the contrary, admitting poorly prepared minority students inevitably becomes a commitment to changing the curriculum, grading, and the responsibility of the university beyond graduation. Along with the gentlemen's "C" we must add the black "B." Moreover, it should be noted that "jocks" do not affect the quality, structure, and nature of either teaching or faculty research. Admitting minorities under liberal aegis directly affects the daily life of students, teachers, and scholars. In fact, it is intended to have that influence. Finally, graduate schools do not field athletic teams, so the analogy starts to become increasingly strained.

Critics of Alan Bakke are fond of pointing out that prior to the Supreme Court decision the dean of the Davis Medical School was permitted to admit a few students at his own discretion. The presumption is that such admittees did not meet the conventional standards and were thus accepted because of political influence. This is highly plausible. But as a result of the national attention given to the *Bakke* case, the dean no longer has that discretion. The moral of the story is not that our society is corrupt but that corruption can be overcome, and in the name of excellence.

One is always confronted with the story of some minority student who, when admitted with a discount, ultimately blossoms into a super student. We all have had such experiences, and they are meaningful because the minority student was required to meet the same retentions standards as every other student. But this is the exception, not the rule. Time and time again I have discovered that people are totally unaware of the fact that for the vast majority of minority students this never happens. Most minority students who enter with a discount do not, even with proper remediation, catch up. The sad fact is that many never catch up all the way—even through professional schools, even to certification exams beyond professional schools. Whatever the explanations for this, nobody any longer seriously claims that there is a known remediation procedure at *any* cost that will close the performance gap in the academic world. That is precisely why there is such an effort to redefine performance outside the academic setting. In this way, the gap is closed by once more redefining the game. It is this external political pressure that constitutes the greatest threat to the university.

DEPRIVATION AND THE GAP

Blacks as a group do not score as well on college board exams as do whites as a group. The standard explanation of this gap is that schools with largely black student bodies are inferior to schools with largely white student bodies. The inferiority is measurable in exact economic terms. Even where noneconomic factors are mentioned their absence is traced to economic factors:

These schools are often overcrowded, housed in old and rundown plants, with equipment, programs, and extracurricular activites of a quality far below those of the middle class and suburban schools. . . . Experience in taking standardized tests (and the likelihood of success on them) varies inversely with such conditions endemic to the ghetto or barrio school. Students in noncollege bound classes obviously will not practice on college board exams.[3]

There are two responses to this type of argument. In the most extensive analysis of American public schools ever made, James Coleman found almost no relationship between expenditures and the quality of the educational output.[4] In a follow-up study, Christopher Jencks concluded: "Variations in schools' fiscal and human resources have very little effect on student achievement—probably even less than the Coleman Report implied."[5] The conclusion of the Coleman report had noted that "race is not the operative factor." Even in those cases where *carefully selected* black students are allowed to transfer to a largely white school and perform better, it was found that "the apparent beneficial effect of a student body with a higher proportion of white students comes not from racial composition per se, but from the better educational background and higher educational aspirations that are, on the average, found among white students."[6]

If one listens to the liberal social scientists one is told that the state of the art allows for exact measurement or proof.[7] But when one tries to get at the real records, one is told that such records and present techniques would do a great deal of damage.[8] Who is one to believe?

One direction in which liberals might go is to pursue this problem at another level, such as the family environment. After all, Orientals are easily distinguishable and are among the most disadvantaged and discriminated against in our society. Yet of all groups they are least in need of affirmative action in education. I shall leave to the reader to speculate on the many reasons why this is not taken too seriously. On the contrary, the new tack is to argue that the whole idea behind testing is wrong in the first place. It is precisely because admissions tests do correlate well with academic performance that a new approach is necessary to defend affirmative action.[9]

. . . [That] standardized test scores and higher education performance are highly correlated is unsurprising, for the tests are meant to mirror institutional requirements. They stress the very linguistic and logical skills the university prizes.[10]

Instead of providing better preparation for blacks so they too can play the game in greater numbers, we should change the rules of the game:

As the students change, the curricula will presumably change in some degree, and the correlation of performance with admissions standards should also change. Where curricula and evaluation procedures have been redesigned to reflect the special needs and interests of minority students, rather different correlations seem probable. . . .[11]

This subtle move from ending discrimination (let them play) to changing the game (realignment) will be apparent throughout this survey of arguments. It reinforces a point I made earlier about the differences between the Jackie Robinson case and affirmative action now understood as realignment.

IMPROVING UNDERGRADUATE EDUCATION

Given our heterogeneous society, and given the importance of undeniable oppression in our past history, it is an important part of our educational responsiblity to make all undergraduates aware of the past and teach them how to deal with it. Therefore, it is concluded that the presence of minorities on campus is an important way of improving undergraduate education.

There is a big gap here between the means and the end. Let us take the end for granted. Is this the only means to achieve it? First we may ask for evidence that throwing diverse peoples together really achieves the end. I know of no study that establishes this. In addition I offer the following considerations. Will one learn as much about human suffering or different mores by talking to any randomly selected minority group person as one will by reading a good book about it or seeing a dramatization? To some this may sound silly, but there is a point behind it. Simply having undergone an experience does not entail one's comprehension of it or one's ability to communicate it. In fact we can argue that, depending upon the person, his moral character, and his conceptual ability and background, the experience is very different for different members of the same group. One might learn more from reading Ralph Ellison's *Invisible Man* than from academic slumming; no amount of journalism or statistical reports or personal interviews could convey the corruption of Soviet society as convincingly as Solzhenitsyn's *Gulag Archipelago*.

At the same time we should recall that not everyone who undergoes an experience takes away the same thing from it. Not everyone who survived Auschwitz drew the same conclusion; some left with an abiding sense of amorality. Analogously, some who leave the ghetto and the barrio for the campus bring with them an equivalent sense of amorality. "Street wisdom" is often no more than a euphemism for being able to exploit first. So after we finish romanticizing life among the poor, it will be necessary for the more radical members of the faculty to make sure that the experiences of the ghetto and the barrio are properly interpreted not only for the rest of the population but for the minorities as well. It appears, once more, that we are not adding new subjects to the curriculum but are engaging in social activism.

We should also keep in mind that a college or university is necessarily an artificial environment. What might be the consequences for white students if the overwhelming number of blacks they meet are academically mediocre or worse? What about the effects on blacks of being thought of as guinea pigs or of being patronized? The real results are that black students, at least, prefer not to be patronized and end up forming their own enclaves. The same people who recommend this alleged improvement in undergraduate education then turn around and ask for a large enough number of minority students so that they can create their own community.

One example might help us to understand this conflict. We are all familiar with the violent events on the Cornell campus in 1969. One liberal interprets it as being provoked by the isolation of a small number of minority students in a rural community.[12] His recommendation is to increase the size of the minority student body. An alternative interpretation would reveal that in an endeavor to lead the liberal parade, Cornell recruited a number of black students who had good academic records but who were out of their depth at Cornell. Most of the students involved were on probation, despite redesigned schedules and grading. If they had been allowed to attend another college with a slightly less competitive student population, they would in all probability have done very well. Instead of being at the bottom, they could have been at the top elsewhere. These students were victims of liberal experimentation.

Of course a great deal depends upon what one means by improving education. Integrating the institution and sensitizing whites means getting them not only to "understand" but to sympathize and finally to accept a radical liberal vision of society and the behavior that goes with it. So the first lesson is to reject traditional conceptions of education.

> Education is, after all, not an end in itself. . . . If education is to be more than simply book learning and sterile research, groups present in the total community must also be present in the academic community.[13]

And what exactly will these students do when they come to campus?

> The academic community has the capacity to contribute more heavily toward the solutions of such seemingly ineradicable problems as segregated housing, ghetto schools, employment discrimination, and other forms of racial isolation. . . . Students bring the problems, and the effects, of the ghetto and the barrio into class and into the professor's office with them. Thus a potent, if unintended, catalyst for change may now be at work.[14]

Once more we have witnessed the movement from the rhetoric of platitudes to the rhetoric of messianic salvation. This is not letting more players into the game but changing the game.

There are still some who harbor the notion that campus unrest during the 1960s was a mere reflection of the Vietnam war. On the contrary, I have been arguing that the student body has been deliberately politicized. In an interview in the *New York Times* (January 3, 1982) a few days prior to his inauguration as mayor of Atlanta, Andrew Young spoke about how future student unrest would be directed against the Reagan administration's policies. His comments were not sociological observations but indirect encouragements of protests against policies with which he personally disagreed. Moreover, anyone who thinks that campus intolerance is a thing of the past probably has not followed accounts of how Jeane Kirkpatrick was prevented from speaking at Berkeley, the University of Minnesota, and even Smith College. When given an opportunity to apologize to the U.S. Ambassador to the United Nations, the student senate at Berkeley voted 16 to 12 against the apology. So as late as March of 1983 we are confronted by students who have probably never heard of J. S. Mill's essay *On Liberty*.

DIGNITY AND MOBILITY

The most bizarre argument I have come across is the contention that since upward mobility in our society requires a college degree, giving minority students degrees will aid their mobility, increase their self-respect, and terminate the prejudice associated with lower status. Taken literally, the argument is a self-contradiction. What is being demanded is an equal opportunity to become unequal. A college degree confers status, unfortunately, because it is a measure of difference. If everyone has it, it is no longer status. The only way to save this part of the argument is to recognize the liberal teleological notion behind it wherein a degree is a symbol of full development. The egalitarian direction of this revised argument is too obvious to need comment.

Moreover, I would want to question the notion that self-respect involves having what other people have. This sounds more like keeping up with the Joneses than cultivating self-respect. We should also be reminded of the oft-made point that how we got things does a lot to determine whether we respect what we have. Of course if I accept the liberal contention that self-respect is a direct concomitant of full development, the argument takes on a new light. In place of a moral conception of dignity we have been given the political technique of realignment. Finally, I should like to point out that prejudice is not the simple product of associated lower status. Anti-Semitism has hardly abated in the modern world because Jews are so successful. Quite the contrary. The issue of prejudice is much too complex to let this one get by. The case here is just the reverse. The more that minorities are the perceived beneficiaries of preference, the more prejudice is created.

LAW SCHOOL, THE BAR, AND SOCIETY

The claim is made, specifically on behalf of minority students, that many who gain admission with a discount are well qualified and will succeed. Second, a report by the Newman Commission and a survey by the American Bar Association are frequently cited as evidence that academic retention standards have not been altered for minorities. The difficulty with accepting these reports is that there is little or no statistical evidence to buttress them. Curiously, all those federal agencies that are so busy collecting statistics on race, sex, and ethnicity do not have the time to collect information on this. Most states, moreover, participate in the Multi-state Bar exam, where final results are not given a racial or ethnic breakdown.

On the contrary, the little evidence we do have reveals some very glaring contrasts about "success."[15] If the following information is not representative, it is always open to the challenger to collect the wider information and disseminate it, if he can or will.

New York State had its own bar exam. It was challenged as discriminatory by black law school graduates who failed the exam. Here were their statistics. From 1969 to 1975, 82 percent of black law school graduates failed the bar exam, whereas the total failure rate was only 28 percent. From Columbia University 6 out of 13 blacks failed; from Harvard Law School 9 out of 15 failed. The information collected in California was no better: 78 percent of those taking the bar exam passed, but only 36 percent of the minority students passed. After repeated retaking of the exam, the failure rate at UCLA for minorities was still 61 percent.

The first conclusion to be drawn is that we need more statistics, and that we must challenge those who use statistical arguments and make ethnic, sexual, and racial surveys not to be so selective in what they survey or the information they release. Second, based upon the information available, I would say that most minority students accepted as discount admittees (not to be confused with those who enter by the regular route) are not a "success." Third, I would question the contention that the same evaluative criteria are being used on minority admissions students as on others. Really now, how is it possible for such extraordinarily large numbers to graduate from Columbia or Harvard Law School and not pass the bar exam? One can hardly use the argument that these students do not know how to take tests, for how did they complete their course work? Is it not possible that these special admittees are being graded differently?

This last remark would be difficult to prove for the obvious reason that no one really wants to admit it. That is why a survey is inadequate. To use a covert double standard is immoral, it is patronizing if not racist, and it is illegal. To admit it is to run the risk of lawsuits and possible termination of employment. Then, why would anyone do it? There are many reasons, but one simple one is that, given the climate of liberal and governmental pressure, it is easier to pass someone with a higher grade than it is to have to explain why you did not pass him or why grades for minorities in your class are consistently lower. One gets off the hook by passing the initiative for quality control to the bar exam. Throughout higher education there has been a subtle erosion of standards, characterized by passing almost anyone and the ripple effect this necessitates in other grades, that is, inflation of grades.

Of course we know what the response to these arguments will be. Revamp the curriculum, reform the faculty or hire different faculty, and, finally, either change or eliminate the bar exam. When you think of it the liberal argument is really rather neat. If the minority students get by, then the liberals were right, and if the minority students fail, then the more radical liberals were right. In any case, it all reinforces my contention that we are not dealing with getting people into the mainstream; rather, we are dealing with attempts to divert the mainstream.

In evaluating admissions, there are four suggested ends considered. First, there are institutional ends; second, there are purely educational ends (this is determined interinstitutionally); third, there are professional ends (such as the bar exam); finally, there are societal ends or needs or demands. The case for minority discount admissions is made at all levels. It has been argued, first, that the quality of the educational experience for all students is better if the student body is integrated; second, that minority students as a group can, with proper remediation, really compete at this time; third, that minority students can be successful professionals.

We have challenged all of the first three contentions. Even if they are suitably modified (like accepting students who have a real chance to pass the bar exam), the numbers involved at this time are not going to be anywhere near what liberal protagonists demand. It is now time to examine the fourth level: societal needs.

It all sounds so familiar. Did you know that there is only one black attorney for every 6,000 black citizens, while there is one white attorney for every 630 persons? This statistic is supposed to establish that black citizens as a whole are not getting adequate legal services. This conclusion follows only if nonblack attorneys are either unwilling or unable to serve the black community. No one has established that they are unwilling. It is more plausible to suggest that economic considerations of black clients may adversely affect the legal services they obtain. So the argument has to be that even with the best of intentions, nonblack attorneys are unable to serve the black community. Why? The answer has to be cultural relativism.[16]

Cultural relativism works both ways. Not only do nonminority people not understand, but minority people are justly suspicious and unable to deal with nonminority attorneys. The rebuttal of the first half of the contention of cultural relativism is that, even if it is true, there is no reason to believe that nonminority attorneys cannot learn how to deal with minority clients. We can even imagine a quasi-liberal suggestion of creating a whole new bureaucracy of legal-midwives who mediate but are not themselves attorneys. This suggestion also leads into the rebuttal of the second half of the contention. Not only can the suspicion and distrust be mediated, but, assuming that nonminority attorneys are not a special class of oppressors, we should not allow false perceptions to dictate policy. We can and should respond to these false perceptions in a sympathetic manner, but we cannot allow them to determine policy without perpetuating them. It is our responsibility to correct the perception, and this is a more urgent and apparently a more achievable task than training competent minority lawyers. But here, too, we must be careful. To what extent is the perception of being a victim manufactured by self-serving minority interest groups? To what extent is it the product of buying liberal rhetoric about realignment?

There is also a blatant hypocrisy in this argument. If a restaurant owner, for example, hired only white waiters or waitresses because his clients felt more comfortable with whites instead of blacks, liberals would scream discrimination. Here they are able to see that one does not cater to such tastes.

But there is a far more important reason for objecting to the idea that minorities should be served only by minority attorneys, especially the new breed of discount admittees. Given persistent low scores or outright inability to pass the bar exam, is it possible that we are saddling minorities with second-class legal services? I am well aware that there is no one-to-one correlation of bar exam score and "success" as an attorney and that there are other elements involved in being a good attorney, but the spectre of previous liberal arguments haunts my vision. I recall the argument that all-black schools with all-black faculty were inferior because of the fact that they were uniracial and because of the lower educational achievement of black faculty as a whole. Why would that argument not apply here? What makes anyone think that it will not be applied?

There are two possible scenarios: (1) with the creation of more black judges, black attorneys would be more "successful," that is, it is the beginning of further realignment all along the line; scenario (2) a national legal service in which people are assigned to an attorney by lot and with the proper racial-sexual-ethnic mix in order to overcome the charge that segregated legal services are inherently inferior. This is a form of legal (professional) busing. In addition to a national health service, we shall have socialized law. No doubt this too is a transitional measure, but it is just what we are in transit to that worries me.

MEDICAL SCHOOL AND THE ALLOCATION OF SCARCE RESOURCES

No profession exercises more quality control than the medical profession. And to the extent that no one, including the American Medical Association, is wholly satisfied with those quality controls, my ensuing argument is going to be even stronger. The time, expense, and faculty involvement in training doctors is an enormous tax on our resources. As a consequence, admissions decisions have to be scrutinized with extreme care. This shows up in two important ways. First, the age of the applicant becomes an important factor. "All things being equal," an older student is at a disadvantage, for the younger student is likely (in a statistical sense) to live longer and to be able to render greater use of his acquired skills. Second, given the great commitment of resources, no medical school would want to have a high drop-out rate. More than 95 percent of medical students eventually obtain their M.D. degree.[17] In short, there is not and cannot be an open admissions program to medical school, and, unlike lower levels of education or other fields, you cannot go elsewhere if you are rejected. As a result, entrance to medical school is practically tantamount to guaranteed employment, status, and so on. Admission to medical school is, in practice, not an opportunity but a reward.

For these reasons the case of Alan Bakke's suit is especially significant. When his application for admission to Davis was denied, a career in medicine was effectively closed off for him. Did Alan Bakke "deserve" to be admitted? In the case of medical schools, unlike almost all other fields, the candidates who just barely miss out are not marginal candidates. This is a simple reflection of the fierce competition for the necessarily limited number of seats available. The minority candidates who were given special admissions, therefore, did not displace the bottom of the barrel in medical school but highly qualified candidates. To say that the minority candidates were "qualified" or even "highly qualified" is beside the point. The question is whether they displaced "better" qualified candidates or significantly superior candidates. It may not be the end of the world if you have an incompetent philosophy instructor or a mediocre attorney, but it can be a matter of life or death if you do not have the best physician available. Given the number of malpractice suits being filed, I do not see how anyone can take this issue lightly.

Here we have come to the ultimate crunch. If a minority student has attended an integrated school on the primary and secondary levels, has been given a scholarship to a prestigious prep school, has been admitted to an Ivy League college or university and given special support and remediation, and is still not able to muster the highest credentials, what justification is there for (a) further committing scarce resources, and (b) eliminating someone with the highest credentials?

Time and time again, affirmative action advocates seek to redefine the issues. The issue is not whether a minority candidate is "qualified" but whether he or she is the most highly qualified. The issue is not whether they graduate but whether they graduate with honors. Of the sixteen minority students admitted in the original class to which Bakke applied, only thirteen graduated. This is a staggering failure in view of the close to 95 percent-99 percent success rate of the nation's medical schools as a whole. Do affirmative action people admit error? Of course not. What they will contend now is that the faculty was racist or insensitive, and that an affirmative action faculty is needed.

All of the arguments that were given for law school are also given for medical school.[18] There is no point in repeating either the arguments in favor of special admissions or the rebuttals. There is, however, one suggestion and one new argument I would like to discuss.

The suggestion is that instead of having either the medical profession exercise quality controls or the government regulate medical practice, why not introduce a true free market system? Anybody who wants to practice medicine should be allowed to, and it would be up to the patient to exercise judgment and discretion. This would be a case of the traditional "buyer beware." Just to help it a little, we could require everyone who puts up a shingle to state, among other things, (a) if he has a medical degree, (b) where he obtained it, (c) what year, (d) what courses he took and what grades he received, (e) what internships or residencies he has had, (f) what medical societies he or she belongs to, and so on. To help the middle class we might even have a recommended-surgery index in which we state the percentage of times a recommendation for surgery was supported by a second and third opinion. It is now up to the patient to decide. No doubt this would put a strain on medical training, but then I suppose some schools would earn better reputations than others.

There is obviously nothing racist, sexist, or whatever in this proposal. It even allows for a great deal of innovative practice. Perhaps its greatest asset is that it would de-emphasize all those theory courses and put a premium on clinical practice. For example, one physician or a group of physicians could take on a number of apprentices who then would learn the job on the job and not in a classroom or artificial laboratory.

One objection to this suggestion is that it does discriminate by virtue of the fact that minority members who aspire to a medical career would be at an economic disadvantage in obtaining funds for attending a medical school or some innovative internship program. We also do not want to recreate our problem by having the government decide who does and who does not get the limited supply of medical scholarships. One solution is to continue the practice of the loan that is interest free until graduation, and then have the practitioner repay the loan with interest while he earns his living as a physician.

A second objection is that some physicians will continue to have an unfair advantage because they will have attended some of the traditionally oriented medical schools, which will no doubt continue to be exclusive. I do not see how anyone can make this objection. First of all, why should anyone take those reputations seriously? Only if there are objective criteria for evaluating medical training and performance can a school really deserve its reputation, and if there were objective criteria (which liberals constantly remind us do not exist), then we would not have entered this discussion in the first place. We could just have let the medical profession continue to decide who should become a doctor and forget about double standard admissions. If there are really no objective criteria, the schools will soon lose their unwarranted reputations as liberals publicize the nonexistence of objective criteria and as the innovative practices continue to upstage traditional medical training.

I doubt very much if liberals will take my suggestion seriously, despite their inability to devise a crippling objection, but I shall hold off a bit in explaining why. There is one more argument to be considered. There is, we are told, one white physician for every 750 persons in the general population and only one black doctor for every 3,500 black citizens. There is then the familiar claim that blacks receive inferior medical service and that an increase in black physicians can meet that need. I am not going to repeat what I said when we faced this argument about attorneys. Rather I want to challenge the argument in a different way. Let us assume for the sake of argument that we "need" more black medical schools. Why not simply expand those existing schools (including special travel and living fellowships) or create additional new all-black medical schools? These schools would have the added advantage of dealing with the special problems of black medical students. Since all-black medical schools were already in existence liberals cannot use the argument that expansion of medical schools in the sixties and seventies was confined only to preexisting schools. In fact, several new medical schools were started, including Davis. Nor can they argue that whites would have objected to this, because no one ever seriously objected to those two schools. It is the liberals who challenged exclusive schools in the first place.

I think doctrinaire liberals will object to my earlier free market suggestion, and I think that they will object to my claim that more black physicians could have been trained in all-black medical schools. Why? The reason is that liberals are not primarily concerned with innovative standards and they are not primarily concerned with increasing medical service to the black community. What the liberals want is a liberal society in which every group is represented in every institution at every level. What they want is that Harvard Medical School and Stanford Medical School should produce black physicians to the tune of 11 percent, who would then go on to become a significant and powerful group within the medical profession and society as a whole. What they want is an ideally integrated society where no statistical or invidious comparisons can be made. In short, what they want is realignment—on their terms.

CHAPTER 6

The Illogic of Affirmative Action

> . . . endeavouring that they should all start fair, and not
> in hanging a weight upon the swift to diminish the dis-
> tance between them and the slow . . . but if all were done
> which it would be in the power of a good government to
> do, by instruction and by legislation, to diminish this
> inequality of opportunities, the difference of fortune
> arising from people's own earnings could not justly give
> umbrage.—John Stuart Mill, *Principles of Political
> Economy,* II, chapter 1, paragraph 3.

INTRODUCTION

It is impossible to take affirmative action at face value. Its advocates
either do not understand it and its connection with prior social movements such as civil rights, or they are deliberately camouflaging the novel
policy of affirmative action by ingenious attempts to argue that it is a
continuation of past policies. We have tried so far to expose these
subterfuges. It is now time to cut through the rhetoric and to expose the
underlying structure and purpose of the policy of affirmative action.

Affirmative action has been defined by its official advocates as the
policy of placing minorities in the position that the "minority would have
enjoyed if it had not been the victim of discrimination."[1] We have called
this *realignment,* in the context of the shackled runner. The policy of
affirmative action is by definition linked with the concept of "discrimination." In examining the concept of "discrimination" in this chapter and
how it functions as part of the larger argument, we are going to show that
the concept has been subtly redefined to fit the new purposes of affirmative action. Our analysis will show, both in this chapter and in succeeding
ones, that the new concept of "discrimination": (1) is theoretically impossible to specify, (2) is practically dangerous to administer (requiring a new
social order reminiscent of the corporate fascist state—see next chapter),

and (3) presupposes a teleological view of human nature that is just plain false.

THE ARGUMENT FOR AFFIRMATIVE ACTION

As a result of their long history of being discriminated against in American society, blacks have not been able to realize their full potential.[2] This, in turn, has led to their not being able to acquire the maximum amount of merit that accrues to those who live in a society where merit relates in some fashion to developed potential. If America were a truly just society, it would seek to provide for the full development of everyone's potential, and it would see to it that merit was fully equated with social roles (jobs, etc.). Thus, if blacks were allowed to develop their full potential, they would play an increasingly significant role in our society. Moreover, since the innate potential of blacks as a group is roughly proportionately equivalent to the potential of whites as a group, the merit of the groups is roughly proportional, and hence the roles of the respective groups should be roughly proportional. So, for example, if blacks are 11 percent of the total population, then roughly 11 percent of all doctors could be expected to be black. A just society is thus committed to eliminating discrimination and compensating those who have suffered from its effects. One form of compensation is to give to those individuals who have been denied full development of potential the roles they rightly would have had if they had not been the victims of discrimination. Affirmative action is just such a measure and therefore is a legitimate form of compensation in a just society. There are four key concepts in this argument, which we shall examine:
1. discrimination
2. potential
3. the distribution of talent
4. compensation

DISCRIMINATION

Let us begin by distinguishing discrimination from prejudice. Prejudice is a psychological attitude that characterizes individuals. Discrimination is a social policy of exclusion directed against members of some readily identifiable group. The existence of prejudice is not evidence of discrimination. The existence of prejudice is neither a necessary nor a sufficient condition of discrimination. Those who refuse to endorse the policy of affirmative action are not necessarily denying the existence of prejudice. Moreover, prejudiced individuals do not always practice discrimination.

In fact, such individuals may sometimes grant preferential treatment to the very people against whom they are prejudiced. This they may do from guilt, shame, or self-protection.

Prejudice is a prejudgment presumably based on a *lack of experience,* and perhaps acts in a way that precludes the acquisition of the kinds of experience that would contravene it. On the other hand, it is certainly possible to acquire negative judgments from experience. For example, it is a fact that certain neighborhoods populated largely by lower-class blacks are high crime areas. It is not prudent to walk in such areas at night. However, we have no specific word for these prudential judgments. While discrimination based upon a false prejudgment is unfair, the acquisition of criteria from experience and their application to life is precisely what we think of as sound judgment.

Therefore, we must not only discriminate between prejudice and discrimination, we must discriminate between prejudice and ordinary prudence, prejudice and hasty generalization, prejudice and the fallacies of division and composition. We must also be alert to the fact that prejudice is used as a pejorative term to characterize those who refuse to interpret their experience along lines favored by doctrinaire liberals. The most powerful and persuasive subliminal argument used by advocates of affirmative action is the confusion in the minds of most people between prudence and discrimination.

In the context of U.S. history, discrimination can be factually identified with Jim Crow legislation, identifiable with segregated schools and separate facilities in general. If this is the definition of discrimination, then we can note that in the past not all blacks were subjected to this kind of discrimination. Moreover, this form of discrimination has been outlawed.[3]

The argument, of course, is more complex. Still keeping the definition of discrimination confined to purely factual states of affairs like Jim Crow legislation, it can be argued that such legislation produced specific long-term effects. This considerably broadens the scope of the term. To take an example, if having attended a segregated school or having been denied the opportunity to become an apprentice in a union prior to the 1964 Civil Rights Act impairs the capacity of a black to compete in today's economy, then it is plausible to suggest that discrimination and its effects have created a problem for us now. But if discrimination is broadened in this way, then we must establish that discrimination in this sense is the *sole or major cause of the impairment of capacity to compete.*

This is a much more difficult thing to do than most people seem to realize.[4] First of all, one would need an independent measure of capacity or potential in order to determine when and by how much it had been impaired. Second, how can we rule out other hypotheses? Is it not just as plausible to argue that events prior to Jim Crow legislation—such as the institution of slavery—may have established patterns of behavior that are at the root of impaired capacity? If slavery is the culprit, then we should note that it was a practice in Africa before the colonies were established. How do we know that some ancestor perhaps of the Ayatollah Khomeni may not have been the ultimate source of our problem? How would all of this apply to blacks born after 1964, a considerably large percentage? Is there some way to trace an intergenerational impairment of capacity? Is it possible that government programs such as welfare may be a larger factor? How far back into the past are we to go in order to arrive at some estimation of what is equitable? It would seem that there is no rationale for stopping at one place rather than another. As Justice Powell put it, this concept is ageless.

If we must take into account events prior to the arrival of blacks in the United States as slaves, then we must also take into account the alleged oppression of European and Asian immigrants prior to their arrival in the United States. The concept is quickly getting out of hand. Notice as well the final absurdity of this direction. If the object of affirmative action is to restore blacks to the position they would have had before they were impaired, then it might follow that blacks are to be repatriated to Africa! Most blacks would reject this suggestion, and I think it tells us a lot more than affirmative action advocates want us to hear.

At this point a radical transformation takes place in the argument. *Discrimination ceases to refer to a purely factual state of affairs and becomes a theoretical term.* This transformation is already implicit in the notion of "discrimination and its effects." This transformation might even be more accurately described as a metamorphosis.

This new conception of discrimination can be called the collective-participation model of discrimination. Here discrimination is a property of groups, not individuals, who are prevented from participating fully in social life. Participation is understood much more broadly than simply in economic terms. Since the problem created by this kind of discrimination is collective, then the remedy can be collective and can effectively bypass providing empirical evidence on an individual basis.

Lest anyone think that the second conception of discrimination is purely hypothetical, let me quote one recent policy definition: "Discriminatory acts can be viewed as acts that have a negative impact on minorities and women."[5] What are the consequences of this definition? Perhaps the most important is that if a merit system should as a contingent matter of fact have negative impact, then a merit system would be a discriminatory system. Moreover, this definition precludes the possibility of certain people being discriminated against, specifically white males.

I think that enough has been said to indicate that the argument for affirmative action is not a straightforward argument that begins with facts and some consensual norms and then proceeds to make recommendations. On the contrary, the very meaning of concepts like "discrimination" has been transformed, and we have uncovered a potential conflict of norms that may be at the heart of this controversial issue.

To sum up, we must distinguish two conceptions of discrimination:

discrimination$_1$ — those past public policies that have impaired and continued to impair the functioning of blacks. The difficulties here are:

    a. How much impairment is there? It seems next to impossible to determine this. The most remarkable thing about this possibility is that, although it is the most popular one and the one most often invoked, no serious empirical support is ever provided for any of the contingent elements that compose it.

    b. Other than outlawing such practices, what should be done about this impairment?
        1. compensation, where applicable (see later section in this chapter).
        2. remediation
            a— depends upon availability of resources
            b— must be shared with all victims, not just blacks.
            c— this is a negotiable political-economic matter, not a right.
        3. neither compensation (1) nor remediation (2) is realignment.[6]

discrimination$_2$ — all practices, private or public, past, present, or future, that inhibit full participation.

    a. Affirmative action as realignment is a policy for this alleged form of discrimination.
    b. It requires not just a marginal adjustment of personnel but a change in the goals of our society.
    c. Advocates of affirmative action as realignment frequently slur the distinction between discrimination$_1$ and discrimination$_2$.

POTENTIAL AND FREEDOM

The second key concept in the argument for affirmative action is the concept of potential. This stage of the argument makes it clear that we are dealing with a new understanding of discrimination. Quite literally, the argument is committed to the view that someone is discriminated against *if and only if* he has not been allowed to develop his full potential. Part of what this means is that if you have not developed your full potential then you have been discriminated against. This changes the kind of evidence required to determine the existence of discrimination. Instead of establishing the existence of discrimination and then showing impairment of potential, we now find out if an individual or group has reached full potential.

Two general observations come immediately to mind. First, it is not clear that this definition of "discrimination" will apply only to blacks. If it applies to nonblacks as well, and possibly to every individual and group, then we are committed by the ultimate logic of the full argument to a massive and total restructuring of society.[7] This is another reason that the policy of affirmative action deserves careful attention, for its implications are far more radical than is routinely recognized.

The second general problem is to what extent does it make sense to talk about individuals or groups as having a potential?[8] Put another way, to what extent are we asserting psychological or sociological facts, and to what extent are we appealing to norms?

It is difficult to imagine anyone wanting to maintain that each and every individual has a specific potential, such as the potential to be a shoemaker or to be a third baseman for the Yankees. On a strictly empirical basis, I might imagine an infinite number of potentials for an individual and at the same time eliminate a myriad of others. For example, I might have such dexterity that I can be said to have the potential to become a great pickpocket or a great surgeon. I might also have potentials that are socially and economically irrelevant, such as the ability to spit farther than any other human being. Moreover, these potentials might conflict: the development of one might preclude the development of another.

The argument would seem to make sense best as a teleological theory about human nature. What it presumes is that some one or a selected few of these potentials are more truly me than the others and, further, that the successful development of these "true" potentials as opposed to others will bring me something like happiness or satisfaction or fulfillment.

I think it is safe to identify the norms of the argument for affirmative action as those of liberalism. Liberalism, as we have defined it, consists of a basic psychological theory and derivative theories of social structure and political organization. The basic psychology is teleological. Every human being is alleged to have built-in ends. These ends form some sort of homeostatic system such that there is no ultimate conflict. If we fail to achieve an end, it is because of external environmental constraints. The necessary conditions for full development are known as needs. Society, in turn, is the product of interacting individuals. Just as there is no ultimate conflict among the drives of an individual, so there is no necessary conflict among the members of society. Conflict is symptomatic of ignorance or external constraints. Equilibrium is guaranteed by the assumption that no individual can be fully developed unless all are. Given this implicit harmony, there must be an objective social good embracing all other goods. Given this social good we can theoretically construct or reconstruct a society along optimal lines so that not only has each and every individual his rightful place but the total social good is maximized. To the extent that individuals or institutions fail, the state may intervene to bring about the monolithic and collective good.

If such a teleological theory is at work in the argument for affirmative action, then a number of issues must be faced. First, what is the empirical evidence for the existence of such a fundamental thesis about human nature? Second, what concept of freedom is entailed by a teleological conception of human nature? It is here that we shall have to raise questions about the elements of choice and responsibility. Third, what is the relation of the teleological theory here invoked to the issue of determinism, specifically, the causal factors that influence or determine the pursuit of ends?

We begin by noting that there is no consensus either inside or outside of philosophy on the nature of man, or even whether man has a nature. This is not just an academic point but bears directly upon the argument. In short, there is no consensual basis for establishing the true potential or end or ends of human activity. Failure to produce positive evidence by itself does not disqualify the premise, but I think it does put the premise in limbo. For all we know some teleological theory of human nature might be true, but then for all we know any one of a number of teleological theories might be true. The ambiguity of such a position is exactly what allows for a multiplicity of conflicting teleological views. It is because a vast variety of teleological views are widely held that a variety of conflicting positions on affirmative action have been taken by people, all of whom think that they are appealing to the same argument.

I specifically want to focus attention on what I take to be the inherent difficulty of any form of liberalism. The very reason that there are alternative versions of liberalism, potentially infinite in number, is that all liberals subscribe to a teleological theory for which there are no empirical parameters. In short, any liberal can claim anything to be or not to be an ultimate end without fear of refutation on empirical grounds. What the conflict over affirmative action reveals more than anything else is a conflict among such liberal alternatives.

Not only is the argument jeopardized by conflicting interpretations of human teleology, but, in the absence of a consensus or clear evidential support for any one conception of human ends, there can be no persuasive arguments for what stands in the way of achieving those ends. Since we cannot conclusively establish the ends, we cannot conclusively establish the conditions both necessary and sufficient for achieving the ends, and we cannot therefore propose remedies when the conditions are absent. Even if we had a consensus on the ends, we might still have no consensus on the means.

What possible meaning, then, can be given to freedom and bondage ("discrimination") in this context? The argument seems to presuppose the liberal notion of freedom, traditionally defined as the absence of arbitrary external constraints. Constraints are arbitrary if they interfere with the achievement of legitimate ends. In contemporary political jargon, we are not free if our "needs" are not met, specifically our "basic needs." Far from being redundant, a "basic" need is a necessary condition to a legitimate end.

What happens when this conception of freedom addresses itself to what is claimed to be a case of "discrimination?" For example, suppose a local law forcibly excludes me from schools and libraries. It may very well be that under these circumstances I cannot acquire sufficient literacy to pursue my career aims or even discover what careers are available. A good deal of social legislation of the civil rights variety has aimed at and succeeded in large part in removing barriers or external constraints such as those just described. This approach is necessarily limited to removing external constraints. But how do we know when all of the obstacles have been removed? All of the barriers are removed when the anticipated end is achieved. Since alternative teleological theories anticipate different things, they cannot agree that all of the barriers have been removed. It does not matter what is done, for it is always open to an alternative teleology to claim that there is a next hidden variable to be removed.

When confronted with the problem of choice—namely, to what extent individuals who are discriminated against are responsible for their own predicament or how they handle it—those theorists who subscribe to this conception of freedom seem to fall back onto something like Locke's *tabula rasa*. It seems that our choices or decisions are based upon the information available and how we interpret the information. Yet, how we interpret the information also seems to be something accounted for in crudely empiricist terms. Thus, in a special sense, no individual is really responsible for how he reacts to any situation. Any number of philosophers who support affirmative action can be cited as subscribing to such a view.[9]

Even those who wish to get away from conceiving of the social world as the product of isolable atomic individuals hardly fare any better. *That* social and moral phenomena are in some sense influenced by social structure is obvious enough. *How* this social influence affects the autonomy of individuals remains obscure. Despite attempts to detach themselves from naive atomistic individualism, relational social theorists still keep talking about individuals as if they were passive recipients. Nowhere do they deal seriously with how the social actor can mold the audience as well.[10] At least, they don't when they discuss or advocate affirmative action. Moreover, I cannot imagine a form of social discourse that merely reflects existing conditions without providing at the same time a structure for transforming those conditions.

The final philosophical problem raised by the concept of potential is the relationship between teleology and determinism. By appealing to the notion of human potential, the argument seems committed to some teleological theory of human nature. By its concern with factors that objectively deflect from the development of that potential, the argument seems committed to some form of causal determinism.

We are faced with three possibilities. The argument for affirmative action is either (a) teleological but not deterministic; (b) deterministic but not teleological; or (c) a form of teleology that is held along with determinism.

If we choose the first alternative, an autonomous teleology, then we can neither definitively specify those conditions that inhibit development of potential nor offer any remedy against them. The second alternative is even more unpalatable, for a deterministic theory renders the whole enterprise of affirmative action, and any other policy, unintelligible. It is a commonplace objection, for example, to Skinner's behaviorism that it makes social planning a mystery, precisely because it cannot account for or justify those values in terms of which we seek to condition people. No reason can be given for preferring one result to another. The second alternative excludes all consideration of values.

I believe that affirmative action supporters are saddled with the third possibility, an untenable combination of teleology and determinism. A large part of their argument is a blatant appeal to determinism. Although many may grant that past discrimination is a condition of underachievement, few outside of affirmative action circles will grant that it is a cause. Moreover, the belief in and the search for both the necessary and sufficient conditions of achievement presuppose a deterministic universe wherein individual choice and initiative are illusory.

The combination of teleology and determinism serves an important propaganda function. In explaining why people fail to achieve, there is an appeal to determinism. When dealing with complaints that past remediation programs have failed or with evidence counter to their favorite assumptions, affirmative action supporters state their theory in teleological terms. It is impossible to refute any teleological assertion. If most people do not behave as affirmative action supporters say they do, we must remember that they speak about people under ideal circumstances. Finally, they conveniently ignore determinism when they want to blame their critics.

Affirmative action must somehow make sense of itself as both teleological and deterministic. To my knowledge, no one has ever shown precisely how this applies in human social behavior. Unfortunately, what affirmative action and many other social policies offer is speculation in the absence of positive knowledge. It is in fact a crude appeal to ignorance. Finally, there is no guarantee that if we obtained the relevant knowledge it would entail or be compatible with the preferred values or results.

Let me make these points more technically but briefly. A combination of teleology and determinism is a dualism, a theory that human nature operates on two different but related levels at once. It is not logically impossible. But if it were the case, and no one has shown that it is the case, it would amount to a miraculous coincidence. Moreover, such a coincidence need not be positive. We could be determined at one level to seek self-destruction at another level. Finally, there is no guarantee that the same coincidence holds for everybody, that is, we could each be determined (physiologically, genetically, and so on) to pursue different or conflicting aims. The latter possibility has led some theorists to postulate a wider social net that permits a distinction between "normal" and "abnormal" combinations of determinism and teleology. By the time we arrive at this stage we are already flirting with philosophical theories of organic social structure and totalitarianism. There is no space to develop these views here, but the transition to such organic totalities was the path taken by Hegel, it was the origin of the totalitarian element in liberalism, which we shall mention in later chapters, and it foreshadows the egalitarian emphasis on organic participation with which we end this chapter.

THE DISTRIBUTION OF TALENT

The linchpin of the argument for affirmative action is the assumption that the potential of blacks is roughly equivalent to that of whites. That is, it is assumed that the distribution of talent is proportionately equal to the percentage of the population as a whole.[11]

There are two kinds of questions we must raise about this premise. First, what kind of talent is being discussed? Second, what is the empirical status of the claim?

Let us begin with the kind of talent in question. It is usually assumed in the contexts in which this argument is presented that the talents in question are those traditionally recognized in a modern technological society and culture such as our own. In succeeding paragraphs I shall make the same assumption. But we should note the possibility that the argument really wants to assert that there are other talents relevant to a different kind of social world and that we are being urged to change the fundamental values in our society. This is all well and good. But if that is the case, then affirmative action is a very different kind of policy from what we were led to believe. It would then be, to put it crudely, not a question of letting blacks into the game but a question of changing the nature of the game.

Unless otherwise indicated, I assume talents to be those generally agreed upon and conventionally recognized as such. Now, the question is, what sort of empirical evidence do we have for the distribution of talent? The answer is none!

I do not see how, given present knowledge, there can be any such evidence. Racial intelligence, for example, is a bogus issue introduced long ago to advance political programs. Strictly speaking, intelligence or skill would be a property of individuals, not of groups. There is no way in which one "race" can be superior or inferior to another.

A call for evidence is usually greeted with a circular argument. First it is concluded that uneven racial distribution of achievement is the result of discrimination, and then the evidence for discrimination is supposed to be the uneven distribution of achievement. Moreover, the more we argue that achievement is dependent upon the environment, the more plausible it becomes to argue that everyone's native talent is identical. Is this really less plausible than the assumption that talents are proportionately distributed by group? The fact is, and it is a most frustrating one, we do not know—short of actual achievement—how talents are distributed.

Given the traditional American value scheme, it is to be expected that each person be treated as an individual on his or her personal merit, not by reference to any group. There is no reason even to calculate composite scores of groups, for the mere recording is an invitation to invidious comparison and potential misuse. To judge the individual by the composite property of any group is to commit the fallacy of division. Even if it were the case that the composite group scores were not equivalent, it would still be irrelevant for social policy. Of course, if the disparity in composite scores was an effect of something, then such scores would be important. But the causal relation must be shown and cannot be assumed merely from the score itself.

What advocates of affirmative action need is a causal argument linking certain forms of discrimination with the impairment of function. They fail to do this on two counts. First, they provide no independent measurement of talent prior to discrimination and, second, they have not clarified the theoretical interpretation of discrimination to the point where it can be identified independently of the concept of talent.

Advocates of affirmative action act as if the burden of proof rests on their opponents, whereas the burden is really on the advocates. Precisely because there is no objective way to gauge ability apart from some performance, the onus is on those who suggest a remedy for the problem. Switching the onus is a rhetorical tactic designed to embarrass opponents of affirmative action by smearing them with the charge of racism. There is also a blatant inconsistency here. Advocates of affirmative action repeatedly charge that current criteria of academic admission—and in fact all objective criteria—are incapable of predicting future professional success. At the same time they are serenely confident about all retroactive estimations of what might have been (contrary-to-fact conditionals).

Even if one admits that without discrimination blacks would perform better, this alone implies very little. For the sake of argument, suppose that on a scale of 200 to 800 the composite score of blacks is about 300 and that without discrimination the score would be 600. This will still not allow large numbers of blacks to enter those elite institutions where a score of 700 is the floor. Moreover, if we eliminate discrimination for all groups, who is to say that the competition would not be tougher. In fact, this seems to have happened in a sense. Now that everybody knows about special preparation for LSAT and MSAT exams, the scores have risen dramatically over the last decade. A score that guaranteed admission ten years ago will not accomplish that end now. The women's liberation movement has encouraged a large shift in career goals, so that blacks must compete now with women in a way that white males did not have to consider ten or twenty years ago.

Would it be possible to design and perform a crucial experiment on this issue? That is, suppose a randomly selected group of black children are put through a special program in order to determine "what might have been." If all interested parties to this dispute could agree, we might have a crucial experiment. Another crucial experiment that has been proposed is that we practice affirmative action for one or two generations.

No doubt some parties would abide by the results of the crucial experiment, but I doubt all would. Just in case the results are not statistical parity, we can prepare in advance the reasons that will be given for disregarding the experiment:

a.   we chose the wrong sample of children,
b.   too much pressure was put on this group, because they knew they were part of a crucial experiment,
c.   we gave them the wrong remediation (hidden variable argument).

In the absence of clearly defined and empirically correlated concepts, we are given a bizarre statistical argument. Bare statistics about I.Q. differences are rejected out of hand or explained away, but bare statistics about comparative group income are given a magisterial status. We should realize that every simple correlation between a set of social circumstances and the lack of achievement can be met with a known counterexample. In the past it made sense to say that particular individuals succeeded despite persecution and discrimination. Such individuals are our cultural heroes. The present line of argument contravenes a large part of our past thinking on this issue.

The statistical argument also overlooks those statistics that contravene the case. In some activities, like athletics, blacks are not only overrepresented statistically but dominate the activity. Again, is it meaningful to compare group incomes and positions without qualification? For example, the average age of the Jew in the U.S. is mid-forties. The average age of the black is late twenties. Given the fact that in some fields income and prestige have some correlation with age and experience, the disparity would have to be modified downward. Ironically, this would also imply that blacks, and especially Hispanics, are entitled to an even greater percentage of slots at the entry levels.

It is sometimes argued that access to some roles is by reference to test scores and other criteria that bear no relation to those talents actually relevant to later job success. We may be choosing the wrong people by looking at the wrong criteria. This is a very plausible argument and deserves to be developed independently of this context. Yet, the argument makes sense only if we can determine success on the job. If there is an objective measure of success, then why not look into the selection records of various members of selection committees and personnel officers, and if some are more likely to pick future successes than others, then we should rely more on their judgment and intuition. Of course, there is no reason to believe that such intuition will produce the balanced outcome that is at issue or that it will not reflect even more unfavorably on some statistical groups.

The other thing worth noting about the barrage of arguments on standards is that some conflict with others when brought together. Consider this argument complex:

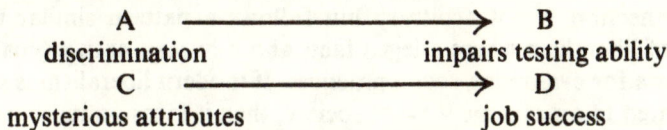

$$A \longrightarrow B$$
discrimination   impairs testing ability
$$C \longrightarrow D$$
mysterious attributes   job success

If C is a mystery, and if C is not identical with B, how do we know that discrimination impaired precisely those real qualities that account for job success? The answer is that we do not. This reduces the evidence of discrimination to mere appeals to pity.

The latest study of standardized tests, a four-year study under the auspices of the National Academy of Sciences, concluded that such tests were not biased and that they did predict later performance. The panel warned against exclusive use of the test but nevertheless insisted that the tests reliably measured what they were supposed to measure.

It is now admitted that it is in fact impractical to take individual cases of "discrimination" and to seek redress for the individuals involved. That is why we supposedly need a policy directed toward minority groups as a whole.[12] If it is difficult to build a case around individuals, how did we arrive at the generalization without specific instances? Why is it practically impossible? It would not seem to be a matter of expense here any more than that consideration would apply to criminal offenses. The difficulty is in proving discrimination as intent and in proving how this alleged 'discrimination' has thwarted the development of innate potential. I suspect that the reason the case is not made is that it cannot be made, and that the inability to document the case is the explanation behind the suggested administrative arrangement, namely, affirmative action. 'Discrimination' is not a fact but a theory used to justify a policy.

As we have already discovered, the difficulty is in providing any clear connection between potential and discrimination. Part of the difficulty is in determining the meaning and extension of potential. Part of the difficulty, as we have also seen, is the ambiguity in the concept of 'discrimination'. There is, however, another interpretation of 'discrimination' that we have mentioned but have not so far discussed in any detail, and it is the version we have called discrimination$_2$ (collectivist-participation). I would now like to turn to this distinguishable version of the argument for affirmative action.

Let us begin by considering the claim that 'discrimination' is not a mere matter of consciously held policies but of cumulative and indirect social forces. It is argued that 'discrimination' is a whole web of social circumstances rather than something that we can isolate. This interpretation of 'discrimination' is an analysis of social life in terms of organic or functional wholes as opposed to atomistic individualism.[13] It is both a methodological thesis about how to understand the social world and a normative thesis about how the social world ought to function. Again, the connection is not arbitrary but follows a pattern similar to other forms of liberalism where alleged facts about human nature (goals) serve as criteria for evaluating social practices. If modern liberalism is seriously committed to an organic view of society, then it faces on its own account special difficulties. The general difficulty is that a practical decision has to be made about how to implement a change in an organic system. Since the system does not operate in such a way that it can be explained by reference to its constituents but must take into account how the constituents interact with each other, two issues must be faced. First, which interactions are in fact primarily responsible for the malfunction of the system? Second, can we focus on selected causal influences and ignore others in implementing change?

What reason is there to believe that focussing on employment and graduate admissions will set the system aright? Let us, for the sake of argument, entertain the counter hypothesis that the major cause of lessened participation is family life amongst blacks. If so, then increased or full participation would seem to require a social or political policy aimed at that relationship. I am not alleging that this is the correct hypothesis. I am suggesting that I have seen no evidence—in fact, not even an argument—to the effect that we know which causes are major. The doctrinaire liberal must present some argument. He doesn't.

The second special difficulty for doctrinaire liberalism under these circumstances is that, having committed itself to the assumption that we operate within an organic system, it must also show that any policy it advocates will not produce a serious disruption of the *entire* system. This issue must be squarely faced. We cannot assume that our remedy is without side effects and that it will operate only on the individual constituents we select.

COMPENSATION

The fourth and final key concept in the argument for affirmative action is the concept of compensation. For the argument to work, it must somehow be shown that compensation is a form of remediation, and remediation is the same as realignment. The reason for this is the important insight that if there are long-term effects of some forms of discrimination, some of them may not be eliminated or eliminable when the original practice is eliminated.

Let us take as an example something not directly connected with discrimination. Someone who is maimed or paralyzed cannot be restored to his original condition. Analogously, a young man unjustly incarcerated at the age of eighteen for a period of thirty years cannot have time restored to him, nor can he pursue many of the careers when he is released that he might have pursued when he was eighteen. Certainly no medical school will admit him. In the same way, those who have suffered certain specific long-term forms of discrimination cannot simply pick up where they might have been. For some, it is literally too late; for others, there are formidable handicaps to overcome.

Is compensation applicable to cases of discrimination, and, if so, in what form? To determine this, let us take some noncontroversial instances of compensation. Let us say that a doctor is paralyzed in an automobile accident in which another identifiable party was at fault. The doctor is likely to receive monetary compensation awarded by the court on the basis of projected earnings. Projected or potential earnings are calculated on the basis of what the doctor was already earning. Next, let us imagine that the doctor is killed in the accident. The doctor cannot be restored to life; the members of his family cannot be compensated for the loss of love and companionship. Again, the only meaningful compensation is monetary, based upon actual earnings. It is inconceivable that the courts would guarantee the children of the doctor a seat in medical school as a form of compensation.

In order for compensation to be paid to the victims of 'discrimination' we would have to (a) identify the party at fault and (b) show that the discrimination caused impairment of function. As far as (a) is concerned, even our doctor could not collect if there were no party at fault or if the guilty party were not apprehended and in a position to pay (e.g., insurance).

Where discrimination is treated as a factual state of affairs victims have been compensated. For example, applicants for jobs as truck drivers were given the first available jobs after a company was convicted of employment discrimination. When 'discrimination' is treated as a theory, the perpetrators are either unavailable, unidentifiable, or nonexistent. Recall that the advocates of affirmative action who treat 'discrimination' as a theoretical term stressed the concatenation of unintentional social forces that produced discrimination. The price they must now pay for that move is to disqualify themselves from using the concept of compensation.

It is this technical requirement of the concept of compensation that critics of affirmative action have in mind when they point out that young white males will be victimized by such a policy. A rough analogy would be to have the doctors who acquired the deceased doctor's patients pay compensation even though they had nothing to do with the accident. This, of course, is not compensation, and it can hardly be mandatory. A more accurate analogy with affirmative action is a situation in which there is no way to trace where the patients went but several doctors are arbitrarily singled out to pay—even though there is no way to establish that they have benefitted personally.

The issue of harming the innocent has come up again and again. Giving preference necessarily denies positions to more qualified non-minority applicants who are not themselves the perpetrators of any of the alleged historical forms of oppression.

All of the responses made to this criticism indicate an appeal to the notion that the social world is an organic whole operating with an inherent teleology. One response is that the harm is only apparent and temporary, but that the system as a whole will benefit.[14] Another response is that although the white male applicant may be better qualified it is because he is the beneficiary of advantages from a previously unfair arrangement. That is, without the system's malfunctioning those white applicants would not be better qualified. Moreover, affirmative action restores the system to its natural state.[15] Finally, it is alleged that the handicapping of white males is not directed toward specific young white males but to the class as a whole. Just as blacks are a subset, so whites are a subset of the total system. Properties of the whole or the subset are not properties of the individual members.[16] In short, the charge of harming the innocent is met with the response that it is not a meaningful charge in a teleological system. If the end is known, and if the means lead to that end, then the means cannot be bad, cannot be counterproductive, cannot disturb the equilibrium, and cannot produce undesirable side effects.

More than anything, this kind of response shows the extent to which the argument for affirmative action appeals to a hidden functionalist analysis of social structure. What appears to its critics as a logical gap between the problem of 'discrimination' and the solution of affirmative action is not a gap once the solution is seen as addressing itself to a different conception of the problem. Belief in this structure also explains why the proposed remedy is political, rather than legal, moral, or economic. The argument presupposes that no meaningful change is possible without basic social restructuring. Hence, the argument for affirmative action is not simply a response to a perceived evil but a commitment to complete social restructuring.

Long ago, when Southern racists in particular used to argue that blacks were inferior and therefore had to be segregated, they would be met by the argument that there were obviously superior blacks. Their answer was that the few exceptions don't count. The only practical way to maintain segregation was to exclude everybody. I suspect that the current response to reverse discrimination by supporters of affirmative action is as disingenuous as the response of the old racists.

With regard to the second requirement in the concept of compensation, calculating the degree of damage, we must repeat that, short of actual achievement in individual cases, there is no empirically meaningful way to identify what someone might have achieved. Herein lies a second crucial difference. In our previous compensation cases there was some way of calculating because there had been some performance. In the case of 'discrimination' there is the absence of performance and hence no way of calculating. One might even question whether compensation would come up for consideration. For example, suppose an outstanding college athlete is drafted by a professional team, but before he signs a contract he is permanently paralyzed in an automobile accident. Establishing potential earnings would be difficult. College stars have sometimes been failures in the professional ranks, and the length of an athletic career is conjectural, given the prevalence of injuries. A high school star athlete would be in an even more difficult position. A person who had never been allowed to try out for the team would just be in a tragic situation.

Even the advocates of affirmative action realize the inappropriateness of the concept of compensation to convey what they have in mind. Hence they assert that to compensate someone is to treat him as if he had his merit intact. What is intended is the restoration of the individual or the group to its rightful position before the damage was done.

The final metamorphosis of the concept of compensation comes when it is further specified that compensation entails giving the victim the role he would have had. This is equating remediation with realignment. How far this is from the ordinary and legal meaning of compensation can be seen with a moment's reflection. The athlete who is paralyzed before he can play in the professional league is not put into the starting lineup. Even if he could play, he would not be permitted to take the place of another and better player. Nor would we routinely change the rules of the game to allow disabled players to participate. What advocates of affirmative action want is a kind of social reform for which there is no clear analogue or precedent. Thus, they utilize the concept of compensation and then jettison it for what appears to be an ad hoc recommendation. This does not of itself invalidate the recommendation, but it does show that an entirely different argument would be needed.

Advocates of affirmative action are not primarily interested in correcting past wrongs but in *creating a new kind of society*. This can be brought out by reexamining the assumption about the distribution of talent. We have already challenged that assumption, but let us for the sake of argument assume it. Let us grant that a cross section of the population has a certain property. How do we know which members of the class in particular have that property? Let us grant to blacks 11 percent of the entering class at medical schools. How do I know which from among the group should be selected? Surely, it cannot be argued that the ones who apply to medical school should be selected, since some of those who did not apply might be the relevantly more talented ones but fail to apply because of the continuing effects of earlier 'discrimination'. Surely, it cannot be argued that the ones with the highest scores in that group should be selected, since some blacks with lower scores even amongst the class of blacks may actually be more talented but are handicapped by past 'discrimination'. In effect, we face the same problem within any group that we face with society as a whole, and therefore all of the arguments propounded by advocates of affirmative action about why traditional standards should not apply also work against applying some version of those standards within any subgroup.

It has not been shown that the right individuals in the preferred group are going to get the compensation. At best, the individual who receives preference can know only that some member of his subgroup deserves the position, though not necessarily himself or herself.

There is, however, one way of salvaging the argument. The foregoing rebuttal rests upon the assumption that merit has some tie with excellence and excellence is identified by the possession and use of a developed talent. That is why, for example, the permanently disabled athlete is not compensated with a place on the team at the expense of a current better player. This assumption, in turn, presupposes some clear conception of the game of life that can be identified with classical liberalism, or even some nonliberal conceptions of social norms. But who says that the rules have to remain the same? Why not redefine the game so that disabled players are subpar only with respect to the old rules or standards; by the new standards they are not subpar. In short, if we redefine all social roles we can minimize the differences among the players and therefore minimize their differing merits. This redefinition proceeds in two steps. First, challenge the notion that most roles require skills that belong only to a few people.[17] Second, redefine merit explicitly to accommodate the *monistic social values that maximize participation.*[18]

Under these circumstances it will not matter very much which black gets the position: fundamentally all people are the same. This is the concept of generic man implicit in the naturalistic teleology behind affirmative action. How do we know what is fundamental and relevant? The answer is whatever produces the correct participatory mix.

What are the consequences of accepting the foregoing new norms? First, it makes 'collective discrimination' a meaningful term and defines a problem whose existence is otherwise difficult to establish. Second, we can now advocate collective remedies such as affirmative action. Finally, it will ease the burden of accepting such treatment, because if an individual benefits, either he deserves it on behalf of his group or in the long run it does not matter which individual gets it.

If I consider myself to be a member of the group-of-blacks, then even though I have not been discriminated against in the sense that my personal potential has not been stunted, and even though I may have benefitted personally from the guilt feelings of some whites, I can call up in my soul a wholly artificial rage about how the group has been shortchanged.[19] In fact, it is quite possible that some day no living black will have been discriminated against in the old objective sense and still the group as a whole can feel discriminated against. Even whites who accept collectivist self-images can feel that blacks have been shortchanged. Of course, we may ask why do blacks-as-a-group deserve 11 percent of anything, and the answer will be that in a truly just society that has recaptured generic man there should be no statistical differences of any kind.

CONCLUSION

The question has never been whether discrimination took place. The question has always been whether the kind of discrimination that has taken place is the special kind required by the policy of affirmative action. Taken at face value, we have concluded, the case has not been made. It has never been shown that discrimination is the sole cause of statistical disparity; it has never been shown that statistical disparity is an acceptable criterion for defining the problem. It is an utter distortion to suggest realignment as a meaningful version of compensation. The view of society as an organic whole is a controversial thesis in social science—not an established fact.

At the same time, we have labored to present a logically coherent version of the argument. We have been able to do so by suggesting a view of society as an organic whole in which the teleological element is participatory. If this version is embraced, then we are talking about a total social restructuring.

CHAPTER 7

The Politics
of Affirmative Action

> *Question.* If you took a public opinion poll and found overwhelming opposition to affirmative action, would you still say that it's the right thing to do, that Government and the courts should do it?
> *Answer.* Yes. I would. There's no question about that in my mind at all. When we are dealing with a question of rights that run back to the Constitution, you don't decide to implement them or not implement them on the basis of how popular they are at a particular time.
> —Arthur S. Flemming, December 7, 1981, after his dismissal by President Reagan as chairman of the United States Commission on Civil Rights.

THE RISE OF ACTIVISM

In its original historical sense, a (classical) liberal was one who believed in liberty, and liberty was construed as freedom from external constraint. This conception of freedom alleges that the individual should be free to pursue his self-interest. Hence we have the original connection between liberalism and the minimal state, freeing individuals from the constraint of the state, and the link to laissez-faire, freeing self-interested individuals from government control of the economy. Henceforth, all versions of liberalism will emphasize (a) freedom from external constraint, and (b) economic oppression. In the nineteenth century, it appeared to some liberals that laborers were constrained by the economic system. This was a form of economic constraint from which individuals should be freed, but there seemed no institution capable of doing the job except the state. Ironically, this was the introduction of state activism to bring about liberty.

Once the state is viewed as the agent for achieving freedom it becomes crucial to gain its ear, if not its heart and soul. Here we begin to witness the movement to make the state the creature of all those who feel constraints on their liberty. The problem is to avoid making the state the creature of any particular individual or interest, or to rescue it from that condition.

Modern activist state liberals claim that they can achieve the new liberation within the framework of parliamentary democracy. But parliamentary democracy was originally worked out in Great Britain and further developed in the United States to frustrate any attempt to use the state in response to every pressure group with either real or imaginary claims of oppression. The system of checks and balances is an elaborate machinery designed to inhibit the activist state. The purpose of majority rule is to block the use of the state to advance the interests of misguided individuals or minorities. Radicals and Marxists have always claimed that it is impossible for them to work within the system because parliamentary democracy is not compatible with the activist state. *Little by little, activist state liberals will begin to undermine parliamentary democracy in their alleged endeavor to liberate the oppressed.*

Modern liberals conceive of democracy as a political system in which everyone has the ear of the government, or in which government represents the interests of all. Thus is born the notion of liberal democracy, the creed of advancing the liberty of all by an activist state that is the voice of all. But democracy is not the will of all, and it certainly is not what Rousseau called the "general will." Political democracy is nothing more than the will of the majority. And, as we have known since the time of de Tocqueville and J. S. Mill, the majority, or what passes for the majority, can exercise its own form of tyranny.

How is it possible for a majority on occasion to be tyrannical? It can be tyrannical if (a) there are fundamental conflicts of interest, (b) there is a failure to respect the interests of minorities, or (c) there is a misperception of interest.

If one is a doctrinaire liberal then he or she believes that there is a generic concept of mankind such that all humans have identical basic needs and that there can be no fundamental conflict among human beings in the satisfaction of true basic needs. Hence, for a doctrinaire liberal, cases (a) and (b) collapse into (c).

Here we shall have to introduce a further distinction between malignant and benign majorities. *Malignant majorities* act to advance the apparent self-interest of the majority. *Benign majorities* act to advance the true interests of all. The benign majority thinks in terms of what interests all members of society have in common. Put another way, the benign majority aims at the heart of teleology, the lowest common denominator. The lowest common denominator is what we all share in common, what we have equally. In short, benign majorities are the forces of egalitarianism.

For a long time it was thought that the misperception of interest was a matter of fact and that the facts could be agreed upon if we had proper education as well as full and open debate. But somehow the universal agreement never materialized. Worst of all, even when the high priests of these alleged facts seemed to agree, that is, even when most social scientists, most of the media, and many church leaders all agreed and pushed these alleged facts in the schools, in the media, and in the churches, even then the majority of the public resisted.

In response to this resistance, a new and final form of liberalism has emerged. It begins with a harsh sense of realism. The benign majority cannot be brought about through education, it cannot be voted into existence, and it cannot be negotiated. Benign majoritarianism must be imposed from the top, by people of vision and will. It must cut through hypocrisy and rhetoric and yet provide inspiration. It must combine the best features of hierarchy and equality. This final scenario is fascism. Fascism is not a reactionary or rightist movement but the fruit of liberalism itself.

EXECUTIVE HEGEMONY

We have indicated that there is a definite trend toward increasing state activism. Precisely because parliamentary democracy is inhospitable to activism, state activism leads to executive hegemony, meaning that political initiative more and more emanates from the top.

Affirmative action is a form of state activism. It is, in fact, a creation of state activism, an effect, not a cause. Let us see to what extent this is true.

Affirmative action derives from the executive orders of Lyndon B. Johnson. When Johnson was a senator from Texas and became leader of the Senate, he argued that Southern senators opposed state activism not out of prejudice but because they feared that state activism of the civil rights variety would inflame prejudice. On the road to national office, Johnson experienced a sudden conversion and not only aided a legislatively inept President Kennedy but went on to preside over the most far-reaching civil rights legislation ever enacted, the Civil Rights Bill of 1964.

Hubert H. Humphrey was Johnson's vice-president from 1964 through 1968. Humphrey ran unsuccessfully for president during the 1968 election, losing to Richard Nixon. In chapter two we noted in some detail Humphrey's explicit denial that the Civil Rights Act of 1964 was intended as anything other than the promotion of equal opportunity. He rejected the charge that it entailed government coercion to bring about equal results. But what happened when Humphrey was a candidate for national office?

During the 1968 election, Humphrey published *Beyond Civil Rights: A New Day of Equality*. In that book, Humphrey made clear that he now favored realignment: equal results, not equal opportunity. Humphrey began with the usual traditional statement about equal opportunity and individualism:

> . . . our standard of judgment in the last analysis is not some group's power (black, white, red, or blue blood) but an *equal* opportunity for *persons*. . . . Do you want a society that is nothing but an endless power struggle among organized groups? . . . I don't. . . . Equal justice under law and equal opportunity for all persons to develop themselves—that is what we seek. [1]

But we soon find that Humphrey was advocating realignment and group entitlement along with the claim that the latter leads to what we traditionally wanted:

> . . . "without regard to race, creed, or color." That is still what we seek in the long run. But in the short run, now, in this new situation, we have learned that we have to pay attention to race and color. . . . *affirmative action . . . must take account of race.* [Italics added.] [2]

> Someday—hopefully soon—we really will be able to drop all the nonsense about race, and deal with each other just as equals and as persons. But first we have some bad history to overcome. [3]

Was Humphrey's change of heart a mini-conversion, a response to newly recognized dimensions of oppression? This hardly seems likely. To begin with, the Civil Rights Act of 1964 had only been in existence a short time, and it was much too early to tell what impact it was going to have. Second, the major tests of Titles VI and VII, specifically the Philadelphia Plan and *Griggs* did not come up until later, in 1969 and 1971. Third, the alleged first case of affirmative action in higher education was the class action suit brought by the Women's Equity Action League in 1970. All of these events occurred several years after the election and therefore even longer after the book was written. By no stretch of the imagination was Humphrey responding to events; rather, he was creating them. That fateful phrase "taking race into account"[4] was not constructed in the late seventies as an effect of events; it originated with Humphrey as a cause of events.

What then is the alternative explanation for Humphrey's turnabout? Humphrey refers to a speech made by Lyndon Johnson as early as 1965 calling for "equal results." Realignment, then, was always in the works. Second, the Civil Rights Act of 1964 finally guaranteed suffrage for blacks in the South and would clearly affect it in the North. This would have tremendous consequences for voting. Blacks would by sheer force of numbers become the dominant voting group in the South, and if they voted as a block could tip the scales in the North. Since 1948, Dixiecrats had already become unmanageable and unreliable Democrats. Politicians are certainly capable of reading the handwriting on the wall.

Humphrey lost to Nixon, but Nixon's victory did not lead to the dismantling of the activist state. The bureaucracy was established by Johnson between 1964 and 1968, and it was largely protected by its civil service status. Most of these civil servants were and are themselves members of minority groups, women, and white male attorneys committed on ideological grounds to activism. When Leon Panetta was appointed in 1969 to head the Office of Civil Rights, he found that among 278 employees, 129 were black and 15 were Spanish-surnamed. This tally does not take account of the number of women.

Few bureaucrats want to assume the leadership of an office for the sake of dismantling it. It is in the nature of the bureaucratic game that you (a) demand a bigger budget for your department, (b) prove you are doing your job by "doing" something, or at least appear to be doing something, and (c) avoid getting a reputation as someone who cannot get along with his staff. Panetta resigned in 1970 as a "protest" against Nixon's lack of enthusiasm for school desegregation.

Nowhere is the power of the bureaucracy better documented than by Caspar W. Weinberger, HEW secretary under both Nixon and Gerald Ford. Even when he became secretary in 1973, Weinberger was opposed to affirmative action, precisely because he saw that it was not part of the original legislation. He complained that his subordinates sought to undermine him by leaking information to their friends. He tried unsuccessfully to change the Department of Labor's regulations that applied to HEW's administration of federal aid to education. Finally, in a conversation with Secretary of Labor John Dunlop both men agreed that the regulations should be changed, but Dunlop could not follow through because his own bureaucracy would be outraged. So, according to Weinberger, we were left with regulations that prescribed strict numerical goals, timetables, and quotas even though he knew they were illegal.[5]

Jimmy Carter's election as president in 1976 meant a return of the Democrats to the White House and a more vigorous pursuit of affirmative action. Carter affirmed his support of affirmative action, and at a press conference he even defended the Davis admissions program, although he fully recognized the potential conflict with "the concept of merit selection."[6]

We have already documented the fight within the Carter administration over *Bakke* and the revision of the original McCree and Days brief in the face of pressure from Califano, Young, and Norton. Some of the changes are worth noting. In place of an original condemnation of the Davis program and support for Bakke, the government brief advised remanding to the California courts to seek more information on whether the Davis admissions program really was a quota. The rejection of "quotas" was first revised to the rejection of "rigid quotas" and then finally revised to a mention of, not a rejection of, "rigid exclusionary quotas."[7]

Two things have emerged clearly. Affirmative action as realignment was from the first a creation of the executive branch of government and has never at any time had even the tacit support of the majority of the members of Congress. Therefore, it has never been a response to a clearly and generally perceived national problem. Affirmative action as realignment is a strategy developed by politicians largely within the executive branch of government. Second, once established in the ever growing federal bureaucracy, it takes on a life of its own, with vested interests both inside and outside of the bureaucracy capable of not only sustaining this policy but of requiring succeeding executive heads to support it.

FABRICATING OPPRESSION

Are there oppressed individuals and groups who cannot negotiate on their own behalf? The prime example to which modern liberals point is blacks. Was this really the case prior to affirmative action? Recall that affirmative action is not to be confused with the voiding of Jim Crow laws or protecting the right to vote or the outlawing of traditional discrimination.

When we get beyond rhetoric, we find that the facts will not substantiate claims about alleged opression. For example, we have already mentioned the Kerner Report, the National Advisory Commission on Civil Disorders, in 1968, which reviewed the rioting from 1964 to 1968 and found an increasingly divided nation. Moynihan has repeatedly pointed out that the commission's own statistics contradict the conclusion. In addition, the University of Michigan's Survey Research Center, which performed the only professional study of the 1967 riots, came to the conclusion that "blacks and whites are in closer contact and more friendly contact than they had been for years earlier." It is clear that government studies too often rationalize a policy that exists in opposition to the facts. It is unfortunate that not as much time has been spent in analyzing the Kerner Report to death as has been spent in challenging the Warren Commission report on Kennedy's assassination.

An exception to the general lack of courage in standing up to bureaucratic misrepresentation is Daniel P. Moynihan. In 1965, Moynihan published a report entitled *The Negro Family in America* in which he argued that the problems of blacks originated in the family, with illegitimacy, female domination, and increased welfare dependency. The reader is left to draw the conclusion that government intervention exacerbated the problem. In 1968, Edward Banfield's *The Unheavenly City* argued against the thesis of an urban crisis. He found that the residual problem consisted of a few million low-skill people, mostly black, who were not "future-oriented" and disregarded ordinary middle-class notions like planning. Instead they *chose* to live from day to day. Both of these studies locate the problem within the individuals involved, not external coercion. In addition, Banfield challenged the hysterical dimension attributed to this problem. Finally, both works imply that a choice on the part of the individuals involved was a factor.

In 1973, Ben Wattenberg and Richard Scammon documented the availability of a better life for those who chose it. In an article entitled "Black Progress and Liberal Rhetoric," in the April issue of *Commentary,* they argued that a slender majority of blacks had already entered the middle class. They documented gain after gain in income and education. In one decade black income had doubled, compared to a 69 percent increase for whites. Without denying the "gap," we note that the frame of reference for statistics makes an important difference in how they are interpreted. Starting from reality, that is, from where blacks were in the past to where they are now, the gains are significant indeed. These are facts. Starting from where some people want or expect blacks to be, that is, from a hypothetical future, there is a serious gap. The "gap" imports a norm into the statistics. Instead of focusing on the gap, we should be discussing that norm. Moreover, Wattenberg and Scammon found some "reverse gaps" of their own. For example, young, married black couples outside the South earned as much or more than comparable white couples.

Moynihan, Banfield, Wattenberg, and Scammon have all located the really serious economic problems for blacks among the female-headed families, who comprise two-thirds of blacks living in poverty. That number is increasing, while black male-headed households in poverty are decreasing. It is difficult to believe that preferential admissions to medical schools is going to help the former. Moreover, a study of the labor market in New York during the early seventies revealed that a large number of high-paying unskilled jobs were going begging at the very time that minorities were dropping out of the work force. As the unfilled jobs increased, so did the unemployment figure for minorities. The report concluded that "any attempt to deal with the supply of labor should take into consideration the possibility that at least a portion of the decline in labor-force participation is due to the existence of attractive alternatives to working" (i.e., welfare).[8]

146 Nicholas Capaldi

The gains made by blacks were substantial, and they were made prior to the advent of affirmative action. At the same time, there is little or no evidence to support the contention that a lack of jobs or discrimination in available jobs is the serious problem. There is, in addition, reason to believe that government welfare is an encouragement to unemployment.

To recapitulate, there does not seem to be a really oppressed group who cannot either individually or collectively negotiate on their own behalf.

The doctrinaire liberal, in an activist atmosphere, shares the general lack of confidence in the possibility of negotiation outside the governmental framework. Hence the doctrinaire liberal comes to believe that a consensus can be manufactured only within the purely political framework. The last heroic role available to political aspirants in this atmosphere is that of champion of potentially overlooked interest groups. Especially in the Democratic party, which is the party unequivocally committed to activism, a candidate must constantly "find" groups who need help in negotiating their interests. Democratic candidates must now engage in a frenetic search for "oppressed" groups.

The conclusion to which we are being driven is that the concept of *group entitlement,* of which affirmative action is a part, is not the cause of political strategy but its effect. Activist politicians are not initially responding to pressure, but rather are creating the pressure. They are manufacturing interest groups, not just listening to them.[9] Social scientists not only discovered the ethnic vote, they have put it into the maladroit hands of political activists.

Blacks remain the favorite pawns of Democratic activists. Their very history by and large is a history of a group discouraged from developing a sense of personal independence. They have institutionalized a client mentality, as opposed to group cohesiveness. There is a difference. Blacks were already, via Roosevelt, the clients of the Democratic party when the full franchise came in 1964. Johnson and Humphrey quickly moved to continue and extend the pattern, the pattern of black clientage within the Democratic party. The worst thing that could happen to Democratic activists would be to have blacks make it on their own.

We should not then be surprised to find blacks among those groups included on the official list as needing affirmative action. The list includes American Indians, the Spanish-surnamed, Oriental-Americans, and women. Recently, immigrants from India have by petition been included. Is there a pattern here to the choices? Is this list, after all, a list of the oppressed?

I think not. With the exception of women, all of these groups have voted strongly Democratic in the past. Moreover, we must pay attention to the fact that the list includes too much and excludes too much for it to be simply a list of the oppressed. Orientals, for example, are now among the most successful of groups.[10] Cubans are Spanish-surnamed but have been among the most successful of very recent immigrant groups (pre-Carter Cubans). They were largely middle-class refugees from Castro's Cuba. On the other hand, it is not clear why other immigrant groups who have suffered are not included. Why not the Greeks, the Italians, the Poles? Why are the Portuguese of New England excluded?

There is a statistic that can help answer our question. Despite the tendency of activists simply to mention the percentage of the population that a group comprises and then establish the "gap" by noting their percentage of high status positions, further analysis available to anyone reveals a very different picture. For example, the average age of Jews in the U.S. is 45. Is it any wonder that they occupy many positions that come only with age and experience? The average age of Spanish-surnamed Americans is under 20! Most of them are children and inexperienced young adults. How could we possibly expect this group to be represented by total percentage of the population in positions that require at least a college education? In fact, every officially designated "oppressed" or "underrepresented" group has a lower than average age and is dispro-portionately made up of young adults. There is one other generalization that we can make. They are the newly emerging voters.

If I am right, then affirmative action's list of "oppressed" people is a list of potential clients for the Democratic party. Further, if my hypothesis is correct, then we should also look for policies designed for permanently molding these people into clients. If these people were to make it on their own and become doctors, lawyers, bakers, and so on, they would acquire the kinds of vested interests that place them across the whole political spectrum, and consequently it would be impossible to treat and exploit them as a block vote. How do we keep them quarantined?

One way is to reinforce some kind of cultural identity that makes it difficult or discouraging to be identified as anything other than a client. Negatively this is done by finding a common enemy, in this case the "white male." Positively it includes such things as ethnic studies at the university level. (Again the bureaucratic-academic complex is instru-mental.) It also involves such things as encouraging black nationalism and linguistic "pluralism." Preventing people from learning English in school is a way of creating permanent clients. The language concession in the case of Spanish is not a concession to anyone except political activists who can now deliver the Spanish-speaking vote. This is not evidence of their special sensitivity to the needs of Spanish-speaking people but an attempt to immunize Hispanics from those social forces that would other-wise propel them out of client status.

At the current rate, Mexican-Americans may outnumber blacks by the end of the next decade. Carter was able to carry Texas in the 1976 election because of Mexican-American ballots. He responded by appointing more Hispanics to federal positions than any of his predecessors. Just in case there are some misunderstandings, let me reiterate. I am not opposing the political participation of nonwhite males. Nor is it unusual for politicians to seek voter support from ethnic groups, or any kind of group. What is new is the attempt to create voter-clientage in the interests of justifying government intervention from the activist point of view. Government intervention in general and affirmative action in particular are not responses to some kind of social crisis but a new form of electioneering in activist democracy.

ACTIVISM UNDERMINES THE DEMOCRATIC PROCESS

Several times in the course of this book we have made mention of the tripartite divison of U.S. government, the division among the legislative branch, the executive branch, and the judicial branch. We have also stressed that this divison was largely instituted and is still defended on the grounds of checks and balances. Checks and balances (along with two houses, cloture, the Bill of Rights, and a three-fourths majority for amending) protect not only the majority but the minority as well. A tremendous frustration index is built into the process against government interference. All of this adds up to a big argument against a big and powerful government and against the domination of any particular branch of government. Then why do we have a big government and executive hegemony?

Part of the answer is in the incremental growth of legislation. Recalling our Anglo-Saxon heritage, we recognize that English-speaking peoples have never adhered to a collectivist theory. English is the only language in which the first person singular pronoun, "I," is capitalized. Social life is made up of a wide variety of individuals, interest groups, and institutions, sometimes going separate ways, sometimes cooperating, sometimes competing, and sometimes in conflict. In such a world there can be no absolute common interest. At best, what we can achieve from time to time is a consensus, an issue by issue consensus.

The great evil in this kind of world is not faction but factionalism, the struggle among interest groups to dominate rather than negotiate. The two-party system is not itself a governmental institution but a political institution largely concerned with negotiating a consensus and minimizing conflict. With just two major parties, each has to compete for the majority of votes over a large segment of overlapping interest groups. The parties can never really be too far apart. This sytem also encourages intraparty negotiating.

Here we note that the expression "minorities" is a misnomer. 'Minority' is a technical term, a legal concept that stands opposed to majority.

The use of the expression 'minorities' is an attempt to give legitimacy to private interest groups, and it signifies as well the lack of a consensus.

The existence of individuals, interest groups, and institutions who negotiate with each other, and the existence of political parties designed to encourage negotiation before we even get to the lawmaking process, would all seem to indicate that government should be minimal. But it is not. To some extent government has grown incrementally and unintentionally with an accompanying bureaucracy to administer it. The bureaucracy remains as the major vested interest group for the maintainance, application, and expansion of all existing laws.

Along with this incremental process has been the somewhat recent and steady decline of the political party as a major institution. A number of factors have contributed to this. First, very few people are taught about parties. One gets the impression from watching TV that the function of the party is to provide a live audience at national conventions. Schools tend to emphasize government, not party, and they tend to stress the lawmaking activist role. Every civics student is drilled in how a law is passed, as if this were the end-all and be-all of political activity. The irony is that in an attempt to avoid politicizing the classroom, liberal ideological notions of state activism have been introduced. Second, political activists, journalists, and academics have all conspired to make the word "party" a dirty word, conjuring up visions of "deals" made in smoke-filled back rooms.

Big government, then, is the result of the legislative branch of government losing control of its own legislation to the executive bureaucracy and the inability of other institutional structures, including the political party, to serve as pregovernmental negotiating agencies. As we have seen, our legislative sytem of government is designed to frustrate the making of laws to serve every narrow special interest group. Activists have therefore turned their attention to capturing the executive branch of government. This, coupled with the weakening of the party system, has led to executive hegemony. In Germany, this process by left-wingers is known as "the long march through the institutions." This process goes with liberal control of the courts. The courts order big government to become bigger; bigger government in turn takes strength from the courts.

Since F. D. Roosevelt's initiation of the activist state, we now await the state of the union speech to find out what legislation the president proposes. The president proposes and Congress disposes. The "better" newspapers keep us informed of what legislation is pending. Careers are built in legislatures by having one's name attached to numerous pieces of legislation. None of this is the result of a long line of unusually gifted and brilliant executive leaders; rather, it is the consequence of our general subscription to activism.

This sort of process feeds on itself. As government intervention grows stronger, the power of the other independent institutions in America grows progressively weaker. As they weaken, they become more incapable of negotiating their own interests with each other. This further reinforces public lack of confidence in these institutions and refuels activist sentiment. As the bureaucracy grows, independent institutions are forced to build up their own bureaucracies to negotiate with the state. We have already noticed this trend in the universities.

It is difficult to unearth the rationale behind all of this legislation. For reasons we have already mentioned, liberalism is prone to infinite proliferation. Moreover, modern liberals sometimes deceive themselves by acting as if each piece of legislation were a technical problem unrelated to other pieces. When asked to provide a general rationale, modern liberals claim that government does what private interests will not or cannot do. If we focus on the "will not," then a conflict is being generated between government and some interest. Coercion is the likely outcome, not persuasion or negotiation. If the focus is on the "cannot" then we inevitably end up dealing with alleged cases of oppression. But there comes a time when all of these bits and pieces have to be put together. It is then that we see some collectivist notion haunting the modern liberal by which he comes to believe that he is part of a special group who possess a clearer vision of the collective interest. We have then stripped state activism to the point where we can see it as a combination of incentive, coercion, and "education" in the true national self-interest.[11]

It is to the judicial branch of government that we must turn in order to unearth the rationale.[12] Two schools of thought presently prevail with regard to the interpretation of law. One is legal positivism (Austin, Hart), the other is so-called American realism (Holmes, Pound, Cardoza).[13] Despite their differences, both have the same point of departure. Both deny that there are moral or philosophical grounds that serve as the origin of law. Both affirm a more technical conception of law, an attempt to think of the law more scientifically and from an allegedly value-free perspective.

Legal positivists stress will and sanction. Law is what the lawmaker declares it to be; it is willed, not discovered. In the absence of decree and enforcement, rules are not laws. For the legal realists, law is not what the legislature intended but what the judge says it is. This shift, especially in the common law tradition in which judicial decision establishes future precedent, is revolutionary. What HEW and EEOC did with affirmative action should now come as no surprise.

On the basis of what principle does the judge decide? The judge contemplates the consequences of his decision as specified by the social scientists.[14] Law becomes an instrument of social engineering for achieving communal ends insofar as they are elicited by the social scientists. Herein lies the self-deception. Under the guise of engaging in a social scientific activity, judges import into their reasoning process the hidden teleology of liberalism. Activist courts are highly vulnerable to ideological pressure emanating from the university and the media. This poses a far greater danger than the competition of special interest groups in the legislative process.

THE RULES OF THE GAME

Affirmative action is inconsistent with parliamentary democracy, and it leads to political practices more consistent with fascism. This may be summarily established by (a) briefly noting what the practice of politics is like in parliamentary democracy, (b) seeing why modern liberals dislike it, and (c) obsrving how the tactics of affirmative action deviate from that model.

In parliamentary democracy the status quo is the starting point. The status quo consists of interest groups organized to protect and advance the common interests of individuals. These interest groups collectively recognize each other. There is no strict proportionality among interest groups; rather, the relative power of each varies over time. In order to be recognized and accepted, a group must have the capacity to either seriously damage or advance the interests of the other groups. The most clearly recognizable major groups at present are business and labor.

Modern liberals are appalled at such a process. First, it is a conservative process, not an idealistic one operating under absolute goals. Second, such a process does not lend itself directly to the pursuit of noneconomic ends (e.g., self-respect), which is probably why many issues are considered nonpolitical. The system seems to work best with general expansion of the economy. However, modern liberal intervention frequently undermines the potential for economic growth and actively seeks to break down those barriers that were erected to protect private life from the vicissitudes of economic ups and downs.

Until 1964, blacks operated as an interest group under the aegis of organized labor. It achieved great progress. Bayard Rustin is still the outstanding proponent of this model for organizing blacks. Now the question is, Can blacks be an interest group outside an alliance with labor? Blacks, per se, and women for that matter, are not clearly definable as economic interest groups. Nor is the rhetoric or practice of rioting a serious threat to established interests. Rioting is in any case a nonmarginal strategy except with an administration that requires the rioters as clients. Compare the response at Watts with the response at Attica. A strike is another matter, but unemployed people cannot strike. The most implausible arguments for affirmative action, for example, are the ones that vainly try to show how affirmative action is going to help nonblacks.

If we negotiate starting with the status quo, we proceed by showing how each party to the negotiation improves his respective position. Labor leaders, for example, frequently recognize that the best argument is what labor can do "for" the company along with a realistic appraisal of what the company can do for the members of the union. Analogously, bringing talented blacks into professional athletics may have displaced less talented whites, but it certainly pleased the fans and ultimately improved the position of the owners and the other players. Analogously, bringing more talented blacks into any area will have the same effect; ergo, the same argument. Certainly, the Jackie Robinson case is a perfect example of how blacks could substantially advance the interests of all by participating. What is not clear is how bringing in less qualified minority members will do much good. We have already shown how inadequately the proponents of affirmative action try to manufacture a case of added value.

A second kind of negotiation involves changing how the parties perceive a situation. Here we have no threat, no promise. The moral argument used to alter our perception is the argument about past injustice and reparations. But this moral argument, we have seen, ultimately rests upon unprovable assumptions and consistently would have to be applied to society as a whole. When expanded to the whole of society, those unprovable assumptions are even more untenuous.

The unmanageability of making amends for the past is recognized even by its proponents.[15] That is partly why they must suggest remedies for groups instead of individuals, for there is no way to establish this highly abstract notion of justice for an individual. Recall the Justice Department's admission that even discrimination could not be established on a case by case basis. But these objections I have made so far are of a practical nature and thus do not penetrate to the theoretical heart of the suggested change in moral perception. The fundamental objection to this suggested change is that it is totally repugnant to our traditional value scheme with its emphasis upon the individual, not the group. A vast number of writers have pointed out how otiose is the prospect of legitimating the perception of people by group such as race. Here they rightly remind us of the morally repugnant aspect of Nazi anti-Semitism. It is no use arguing that Nazi classifications were malignant whereas ours will be benign, because the classifications inevitably restrict some persons, as the DeFunis and Bakke cases made clear. Nor can we accept the argument that the classifications are temporary or transitional, because that implies a return to negotiation of the first type and an abandonment of the moral argument. Finally, confusing the moral negotiation with the negotiation designed to suggest that affirmative action will advance our collective interests does little to instill confidence in the way we perceive the integrity of those advancing the claims of affirmative action.

The politics of affirmative action is an attempt to renegotiate entirely the economic situation as opposed to using politics to mediate a continuing evolution of economic positions. Put bluntly, it attempts to use politics to make blacks an economically viable interest group. This goes counter to the whole system, and it can only proceed by appeal to some abstract ideal. This has consistently brought blacks into an unnecessary and counterproductive conflict with established economic interest groups. Reverse discrimination and quotas are the battlefields. Moreover, the appeal to abstract ideals inevitably generates conflicts with the ideals of other interest groups. Affirmative action is at a loss to deal with other ideals like academic freedom and the pursuit of truth. We end up with fuzzy, unresolvable conflicts or management-defined resolutions like quotas.

Negotiating in the politics of parliamentary democracy is a special skill. It bears some analogy to economics, because dealmaking is a transferable skill, a highly self-conscious action. Blacks have rarely been allowed to develop the skills of deal making. This is the result of paternalism, being the perennial clients of white liberals, and the type-casting of most black politicians as spokesmen of black constituencies—rarely as deal makers in a consensus. This is the unspoken tragedy. Affirmative action perpetuates and entrenches it.

Because of their history and the extent to which doctrinaire liberals have patronized them, blacks are more likely to exemplify the phenomenon Ortega described as *mass man*. That is, blacks have been persistently encouraged to think of themselves as having rights but not obligations, as entitled to what they desire but without the consequences of what they desire. Blacks have suffered most from the doctrinaire liberal attempt to instruct them in the techniques of power politics without educating them in the spirit behind that politics. How could it be otherwise when liberals themselves have forgotten or repressed that spirit? The irony is that the emphasis on rights will undermine the foundations on which rights exist in the first place. The result will be barbarism.

The case for affirmative action as old-fashioned equal opportunity is not only weak, it is downright dishonest. It is a policy formulated in defiance of the evidence. The case for affirmative action as a change in moral perception is not only impractical but also contradicts the fundamental value of the individual. There is only one other case, this time a change in political perception. To say that it is a change in political perception is to say that we must recognize the political (nonmoral, noneconomic) necessity for changing the way we make judgments and the criteria we use. As we shall see in the concluding section, the arguments for political necessity are tantamount to abandoning parliamentary democracy and embracing fascism.

THE CENTRIFUGAL FORCES OF FASCISM

Without having to contest the facts, the case that I have been building against affirmative action, the activism of doctrinaire liberals and bureaucracy can be dismissed by giving it a less threatening interpretation. After all, what is really so new about political chicanery, general corruption, and bureaucratic mismanagement? None of these phenomena were invented by doctrinaire liberals, and none is restricted to our own society or time in history. It is still possible to profit from these criticisms. But this sort of response is a refusal to link all of the phenomena.

On the contrary, I want to insist that the phenomena can be linked in a coherent fashion, that we are not dealing with isolated events. The thesis I shall present in this final section of the chapter is that the politics of affirmative action bears a distinct analogy to the politics of fascism.[16] In order to substantiate this thesis, two things must be done. First, in the logical sense, we must make clear what is meant here by fascism. Second, we must work to dispel the common received notion sustained by both liberal and radical theory, that fascism is a movement of the reactionary right.

The Theory of Fascism: According to fascists, the central fact of all social life is *power*—getting it and keeping it. Any analysis of history, man, the economy, or political institutions that does not recognize the central importance of power is either a falsehood or a form of self-deception or a way of masking one's own attempt to get power. Therefore, all political philosophy is rationalization. Not only do classical liberals delude themselves and others but radical Marxists do so as well. The Marxists were clever enough to see through classical liberalism as the ideology of the ruling class of capitalists, but the Marxists thought they could rise above this by advocating that socialism would bring a classless society and the end of coercive government. Marxists in power behave no differently from the people they displace. Moreover, they are a lot less efficient at running the economy. So doing away with capitalism is not the answer. At the same time, the classical liberal defense of the rights of the individual is a pretentious moral facade for exploitation.

This brings us to the second key concept of fascism: in place of the abstract individual, the fascist affirms the ultimate reality of the *community* (whether it be the nation, the race, the state, etc.). The behavior of an individual cannot be understood in terms of his rational calculation but only in terms of his nonrational, emotional identification with some community. Left to his own devices, a man will behave as if he were in Hobbes's state of nature. Only the imposition of an arational myth can cause an individual to act for and receive the satisfaction of participation in the community.

The Conditions that Give Rise to Fascism: At the heart of modern liberal society is a despair about its own ability to make sense of the world. There arises a kind of moral crisis over its traditional understanding of itself. Such a society advocates that the individual should subordinate himself to the social process because it is advantageous to the individual. And what is advantageous to the individual is the alleged desire to control the physical environment. But what is unexplained is this desire. It is a kind of choice without a criterion of choice.

The result is that high expectations are generated but never fulfilled. There is progress but never enough. What would "enough" mean in a liberal society? Since some individuals clearly have more than others, and since the relation between rewards and effort does not follow any predictable, calculable, or rational pattern, the failure to be satisfied is attributed to vested interest groups. Any serious economic contraction consisting of inflation and high unemployment will accentuate this perception of a "gap" between haves and have-nots. The "haves" will fear chaos and revolution; the "have-nots" are not only disillusioned but their very perception of themselves as "have-nots" induces in them an inferiority complex. When they perceive others in this same situation they come to think of "themselves" as surrounded by a hostile world.

Tactics for Gaining Power: According to fascists, classical liberal methods of generating reform through parliamentary democracy are not effective. Legislatures are all talk and no action. Exacerbating class conflict is an invitation either to repression from the right or to revolutionary overthrow. What is needed is a new sense of social cohesiveness, not divisiveness. What fascists aim to do is bring people together; they are the only party that can preserve capitalism (private ownership) and adopt a paternalistic attitude toward labor and any other group that feels left out. Now, it may seem a tall order to try to hold so many groups together, but fascist contempt for all theory ("all theory is ideological"), along with the glorification of action, is quite an advantage. In place of theory and reason we have vision, creativity, and "will." Instead of arguing people into accepting fascism, that is, instead of persuasion, a new perception of a new set of values is imposed on all peoples by the elite. The elite in this case are the fascists who have vision, creativity, and will. These new values or new perceptions are myths: they are neither provable nor disprovable. Their function is to promote cohesiveness and inspire action. In the end, public morality is not the product of rational persuasion but of endless, reiterated statement.

Exercise of Power: The hallmark of fascist government is the *fusion of legislative and executive power.* Instead of representation by parties we have representation by class. Each class, however identified, has its place and function. This is what is meant by the *corporative state:* each group has a share of corporative power. Noah's ark has replaced the social contract. The state is in a sense one giant corporation. Private ownership is recognized but so is unlimited government control.

The only obstacle faced by the fascist government is the risk of having the incorporated groups behave like parties or factions. This can be avoided by having the executive head appoint the spokesmen and spokeswomen. This comes about "spontaneously."

Enough has already been said to make clear that the closest thing we have to fascism is activist state liberalism for the benefit of groups. The case, as we shall see, is even stronger. What makes it so difficult to get a hearing is that Americans are not accustomed to thinking of fascism as left-wing liberalism. On the contrary, fascism is usually thought of as a reaction of the right. Let us see how this misintepretation has been generated.

Fascism became a major movement between the two World Wars. The most significant event in the U.S. between the wars was the depression and Roosevelt's New Deal. Interestingly, many of the proponents of the New Deal had a great deal of admiration for Mussolini's economic and social development schemes in fascist Italy. Roosevelt's growing disenchantment with Mussolini came over foreign policy, not domestic policy. This, coupled with our wartime alliance with the Soviets, made it expedient to play down the domestic similarities between the New Deal and fascism and to exaggerate the differences between fascism and Stalinism by "seeing" the former as a movement of the right.

But the case is quite the opposite. Mussolini himself pointed out the close similarities of the policies being followed in Russia, Germany, Italy, and the U.S.[17] But the best case was made in 1941 by James Burnham, who argued persuasively that the New Deal was moving in the direction of fascism by using the techniques of mass-mobilization, spurring industry and technology in the service of the state, and creating an elitist belief system.[18] The elite thus springs from the managerial class, what we have come to identify as the bureaucracy. This is not to say that the New Deal was avowedly or secretly fascist. It is to say that the seeds of fascism were already present in the serious formative stages of activist liberalism in America.[19] The full flowering of those seeds comes only with the development of the notion of group entitlement in the final stage of liberalism. But enough has been said to indicate why it was convenient to think of fascism as a movement of the right.

What were the precise elements in Mussolini's fascism that captured the imagination of modern liberals in the late twenties? To begin with, precisely those things that modern liberals do not like about parliamentary democracy are the things that Mussolini superseded. Instead of a conservative process of political evolution, Mussolini was hailed as the great pragmatist, the man who could imaginatively recreate society. In place of pluralistic and competing interest groups, he offered a communal national vision. In place of bargaining about limited economic objectives, he offered moral regeneration of the whole man. Mussolini was also hailed as scientific, his methods experimental, and his excesses temporary. In fascism the state creates a nation.

The parallels with affirmative action are obvious. Affirmative action is temporary. It is a bold and innovative program, an experiment that transcends traditional logic. Its goal is the organic recreation of America, and it is pragmatic certainly in the pejorative sense of bending principles to fit some objective. Like the followers of Mussolini, liberals are fascinated by the rhetoric and theory, and complacently ignore the practice, the real embodiment of affirmative action in the form of a visit from EEOC or a student riot.[20]

Orthodox Marxists, of course, have traditionally denied the leftist orientation of fascism and have chosen to see it as the puppet of reactionary capitalism. This analysis cannot, as we shall see, be sustained by a look at the facts, and recently even Marxists and radicals have begun to play down the old analysis.[21] Now they want to see fascism as some kind of bourgeoisie aberration. At the same time, it has long been fashionable for Marxists and many liberals to use the term "fascist" as a pejorative epithet for rightist regimes they do not like. This has also conditioned the public to think of fascism as rightist.[22]

What the Marxists would like to suppress or ignore are those facts about Mussolini in particular that show the leftist origins of fascism. Mussolini read all of the available works of Marx and Engels, he quotes them and makes reference to them in his writings, he was elected to the Central Committee of Italy's Socialist party by the Marxists, and he became the editor of their journal. Mussolini had his falling out with the radical left and that explains in part the Marxist opposition. But in no way can this falling out be explained as abandoning a leftist orientation. Finally, we now know that Italian capitalists and members of the bourgeoisie did not engineer Mussolini's rise to power. On the contrary, they feared it, tried to find other alternatives, and only in the end acquiesced when they lacked the power to do anything else. In the end, Mussolini's fascism undermined the old establishment and substituted a totalitarian bureaucracy.[23]

We may now turn to Mussolini, the indisputable example of what fascism is. We have already remarked that Mussolini began his political career as a Marxist and socialist. The central concept for him at that time was class. He always rejected the concept of individualism and the rights attached to the individual in classical liberalism. The "class" was for him the important unit for understanding history and social life, and, more important, it was the potential source of moral regeneration. The series of events leading to Italy's entrance into the First World War led to Mussolini's break with Marxism. He came to see the nation, the "people," as the meaningful social unit.

Was this a sell-out to the "right"? It was not. Mussolini never subscribed to bourgeoisie individualism. In fact, Giovanni Gentile, Mussolini's theoretician, specifically criticized it. Nor did Mussolini become just a nationalist; he simply transferred his political philosophy to a new "community." Rather than reject his revolutionary (not reactionary) notion of moral regeneration, he moved it to a different plane. He was impressed by the way the war brought diverse, sometimes conflicting interest groups together in the national interest. He no longer found it possible to explain this in terms of economic class.[24]

Countless authors have documented the similarity of the totalitarian regimes of both communists and fascists. Despite important differences, what these two movements share in common is the subordination of the individual to the group. The group can have different names and histories and explanations, but it all boils down to a rejection not just of classical liberalism but of individualism. Here we begin to understand the importance of the transition from activist liberalism for the benefit of individuals to activist liberalism espousing group entitlement.

Largely with the help of Gentile, Mussolini was able to work out a full rationale not of but for fascism. Basic to this view is the idea that one must "fulfill oneself as a man."[25] This can only be done if man is free. But freedom cannot be achieved just by removing external constraints as in classical liberalism; rather, freedom comes from fulfilling oneself in a group. "Fascism does not face liberalism as the system of authority faces the system of liberty," wrote Gentile, "but rather as the system of true concrete liberty faces the system of abstract and false liberty." No one, wrote Gentile, could be really free if he were being exploited. And how are we to know what fulfillment within the group means? The minority of the elite expresses the group will, for it is "incarnated and revealed in a few or a single individual" in the "will of a political elite."[26] The final antidemocratic affirmation of this view is to be found in the writings of Pietro Ubaldi, who, speaking for the fully developed, said:

> . . . the response of the majority stabilizes itself not at the level of the collective mean, but at that of the most inferior. The problem is psychological, not mathematical: majority opinion cannot constitute the criterion of truth; such opinion is its debasement. Social life requires the tutelage of the less developed by the more highly developed, in order to indicate to them the path to follow. The majority cannot understand, select, and decide the best course; it can only follow. . . . To govern, certain special qualities and gifts are necessary: an inclusive vision, a profound intuition, a supreme will, rectitude, and sacrifice, qualities possessed only by the exceptional, never by the mass. The exceptional must be lifted above the mass in order to elevate them. The people . . . have need of education. . . . These are the laws of nature. The collective mind is akin to that of a minor, unconscious of the ultimate goals, which only a leader can envision. He that is possessed of that vision has the responsibility of imposing that vision upon those who are unseeing. It is obvious that, for a child, certain ends must be imposed upon him, even with force if necessary, should his ignorance make this necessary.[27]

Enough has been said for us to draw some very firm analogues between fascism and liberal activism for group entitlement, especially as it reveals itself in affirmative action. Recall Dubois's glorification of the talented tenth. The first thing to note about affirmative action is that it is not reactionary but revolutionary, a radical attempt to alter society, to "close the economic gap between blacks and whites."[28] Moreover, it is radical in its alleged service of the humanitarian ideals of helping the downtrodden and exploited. Here we begin to trot out the familiar litany of statistics about the gap and suffering:

> The maternal mortality rate for blacks is three times as high as for whites; infant mortality is almost twice as high. Life expectancy for blacks is nearly seven years less than for whites. In 1977, black unemployment rose to 13.9 per cent while white unemployment declined to 6.2 per cent. White teenage unemployment declined to 15.4 per cent in 1977, while black teen-age unemployment reached a walloping 41.1 per cent.[29]

Not only is there suffering, but the suffering is the result of deliberate exploitation by the establishment.

> All preferential Affirmative Action is trying to do is to break the logjam of white male dominance. White males have long enjoyed an overwhelming monopoly in all the centers of power and lucre: government, educational institutions, business, the press, the police, banking, and the major religions. . . . All of them would leave the caste system intact and would keep women and deserving minorities on the outside looking in.[30]

And what is to become of us if we do not do something about all this? Clearly there will be violence, chaos, and perhaps a communist-inspired revolution:

> Hell hath no fury like justice denied. . . . The crimes that breed of despair will harass us. And who knows? Our time may be running out. . . . Terror is the new language of despair.[31]

There is only one solution. It is not to embrace the old classical liberal emphasis on individual rights. It is not to embrace revolutionary socialism or Marxism. It is to allow a new bureaucracy to mediate the conflict, that is, to retain capitalism but without exploitation. The old effete exploitative bourgeoisie will acquiesce because they are afraid of social disruption. And we know this system works because many major corporations and universities who want government contracts will agree to preferential hiring and promotion. Even if we cannot prove anything in court they will agree to it. Their greed and their fear are enough to make the policy a success. In short, affirmative action, like fascism, makes an accommodation with the old "exploiters" for the benefit of the "downtrodden."

But this policy is more than just an expedient accommodation. It is the first step in the creation of a new order, a new social and political reality, a new kind of human being. All along we have been working with the wrong social model.

> Exaggerated American individualism is fixated on individual justice and neglects social and distributive justice. . . . Social justice refers to what we as individuals owe to the common good, the social whole. And distributive justice refers to what a society owes to its people through its governmental officials. . . . To be a person is to be inextricably interwoven, with other persons, in a fabric that spawns obligations—debts we owe to one another by reason of our common humanity.[32]

So the construction of the New Man, and the New Woman, inevitably means the glorification of the group. At first people will rush to identify themselves as black or Chicano or female or what not. And then, in time, we shall all identify with the social whole. The individual truly fulfills himself as part of the group. But we need "creativity" and "sensitivity" to see this:

> Truth and justice lie in maintaining creative loyalty to all three kinds of justice by not letting the individual get swallowed up in the collective reality of the group and by not letting the individual obscure the legitimate demands of the many. . . . We may think we can make it on rugged individualism; we can't.[33]

No doubt only some people can "see" this kind of truth. They will not be burdened by traditional methods of reasoning and the intellectual logic that are in their minds but masks for ideology. Remember the fascist claim that all political philosophy is rationalization, not truth, and you can also recognize that:

> . . . discrimination is too easily hidden under the nebulous claims of merit.[34]

After all, all judgment is subjective. Argumentation is a waste of time with people who are unavoidably culturally biased. The only solution is to "will" the remedy into effect.

> A lot of spurious arguments. . . All miss the basic truth that patterned injustice requires patterned redress. Institutionalized, incultured bias will only respond to policy changes that have clout. A caste system will never be dismantled on a one-to-one basis.

Voluntary methods have never worked. The spirit of individualism says that all that is necessary is to litigate individual instances of discrimination and all will be well. (That, of course, leaves the current system intact.) This is impossible. . . . What is needed is firm federal action with enforcement power.[35]

Affirmative action, like fascism, operates with those social myths that are neither provable nor disprovable yet serve as a call and inspiration to action. One of those myths is that all evil is environmental. Another is that all the buried talent can be raised from the dead only by the miracles of affirmative action.

All along we have been taking arguments at face value and in the spirit of reason trying to track down the evidence for them. All along we have been wasting our time. Affirmative action cannot establish itself as a reasoned, fact-supported arugment. It establishes itself through constant reiteration. "There is a gap . . ." and other key code words serve in place of serious arguments. I have personally confronted HEW people with rebuttals. After politely refusing to listen to me, they told me: "You are right, technically. We are not really dealing with established or establishable instances of discrimination. But don't you see that what we are trying to do is to overcome sexism and racism, and this is the only way it can be done."

This newly discovered "honesty" helps to explain a lot more. One recurring theme I have expressed is that the environmental determinism argument for lack of achievement is, when carried to its *logical* conclusion, an argument for total egalitarianism. There is absolutely no reason to believe that we are not all completely equal in ability. If that is so, then everybody is just as good as everybody else and no one really deserves to be given an important position instead of someone else. We could decide these matters by a lottery. But that is not what affirmative action practices or institutes as policy. Affirmative action is still a hierarchical solution, for it says that some people are more talented than others. It is just that the talent is distributed by "group." Another myth? Perhaps. But I think it is the *elitism* of affirmative action.

Members of a cultural group share basic values and ideals . . . and they interact intellectually by exchanging ideas about these values and ideals, by clarifying, criticizing, and extending them . . . this bustling process of self-clarification. Some call it the cause of all progress. . . . the intellectually most active and advanced of a cultural group play a crucial role in the above mentioned process of self-clarification. . . . W. E. B. DuBois makes this point about the talented tenth of every group. . . . preferential hiring of qualified blacks . . . will give them the opportunity to play their crucial role in the group.[36]

In short, models and mentors are needed, not to show women and minorities that it is possible to make it, but to lead women and minorities. The models and mentors are the fully developed members of the group with the duty to raise up or to speak for the rest of the group. Models are affirmative action's counterpart to fascist tutelage.

The equality movement is a subterfuge for elitism. It seeks to eliminate competition and substitute a system that is monopolistic, prestige competitive, and emphasizes high security. The employment game will now be played in terms of paper qualifications (recall the validation of standards). The emphasis on minimal qualifications will not help the masses but primarily helps the elitist stratum who can get the paper qualifications.

Remember when we were told that preferential admissions was only a temporary expedient? Don't believe it. Affirmative action will recreate the fascist corporative state, but instead of representation by groups such as labor and capital, we shall have representation by race, sex, and ethnic background.[37] The government will be run by a bureaucratic committee consisting of two of these and one of those and two of them. . . .[38]

It can't happen here, you will say, because we have a democracy. Fascism is antidemocratic. The response to this is twofold. First, I remind the reader of what has been said in the earlier part of this chapter about the decline of the legislative branch of government and the rise of executive hegemony. Recall as well what was said in an earlier chapter about how the bureaucracy can undermine the very will of the Congress.

The illusion that past democratic practices in themselves will prevent the rise of fascism is the result of a serious misunderstanding about both the practice of parliamentary democracy and its relation to public opinion. Liberalism was long kept on a leash by moral, religious, and a host of other traditional institutional values. But modern social science has set about, in the name of science, to undermine those values, and when it succeeds liberalism will turn into fascism. The undermining proceeds in a number of ways. Narrow positivism in the academic world constantly attacks the possibility of a philosophical foundation for values. Once imbued with this attitude, the only mode of analysis left is pure description along the lines of realpolitik. But "pure" description of the exercise of power can only breed cynicism. There is a whole style of teaching that leaves students with nothing but a numbing contempt for public life. Moreover, positivism insists upon a technological conception of knowledge and this inevitably prepares the way for the view that knowledge is for the sake of manipulation. Even Marxism, when it no longer can be taken seriously as a theory, remains as a language and a set of ubiquitous categories whose only function is to castigate all present institutions. Little by little these attitudes emanate from the classroom to the media.

The vacuum of values is filled by pseudo-social science masking a mindless teleology.

The hypothesis that I advance, namely, that affirmative action is a form of fascism, brings together a number of intellectual tendencies that we have already documented. Fascism is a form of social engineering imposed from the top. As a form of engineering it seeks to solve social problems by technical means. To do so presupposes that there are valid laws and structures that can be apprehended by an elite group, structures that can be and must be dealt with without the consent of the individuals who compose the community. Moreover, such social structures must implicitly contain norms, and this is possible only if the norms are teleological. Without the presumption in teleology, all predictions, all exercises in futurology, would be senseless. The assumption of such a teleology permeates the entire rhetoric of affirmative action, all the way from the belief in a "mainstream" to the attempt to give people a "job with a future."

The best evidence of the rise of fascism is the direct attack on democracy that proponents of affirmative action have just begun to launch. This attack is epitomized in an article by Derrick A. Bell, Jr., entitled "The Referendum: Democracy's Barrier to Racial Equality."[39] The background to Bell's piece should be clear enough. Many individuals and groups are dissatisfied and frustrated for many different reasons with our governmental process. Polls continue to indicate that popular sentiment is against the laws that are passed and the policies that are administered. The referendum is one form of opposition. The referendum is the clearest expression we have of the will of the majority. It is the final democratic obstacle to zealots for social change. So we might anticipate that what Bell is going to tell us is that we have to fear malignant majorities.

What makes a majority malignant? According to Bell, majorities are malignant not because they vote their interest in opposition to the interest of the minority but because they actually vote against the social interest, which includes themselves. Why do they do that? Because majorities are victimized by the social-class origins of racism. In short, majorities behave like ignorant, shortsighted children who do not know and cannot by themselves come to recognize their true interests.[40]

Racism is not simply a disease that afflicts some whites and leaves the rest untouched. It is a pervasive influence, though it manifests itself most virulently among those lower-class whites who have been and remain convinced that their own insecure social status may best be protected by opposing equal rights for blacks. This view is contagious and perhaps incurable. It results in white support for policies limiting the rights of blacks even while simultaneously, if more subtly, those policies also limit opportunities for less advantaged whites.[41]

Affirmative action is a case in point.

At the college and professional school levels, upwardly mobile whites like Marco DeFunis and Allan Bakke and their hosts of lower- and middle-class supporters focus their legal and political attacks on the miniscule ten percent minority admissions programs carved out after much effort and sacrifice by blacks, ignoring the obvious fact that traditional admissions criteria favoring family and class contacts effectively provide upper-class, mainly white, applicants with preferential access to ninety percent of the available positions.[42]

Bell prefers to trust to the legislative system despite all of its short-comings. The inevitable result of a referendum is exclusion of the right participatory mix in the determination of the social interest.

. . . the initiative and referendum processes in general prevent meaningful participation by minority groups. As more legislation is passed through direct ballot, minorities are increasingly excluded from participating in decisions affecting the entire society.[43]

In light of what we have said about the decline of the legislature and the rise of executive hegemony, about how affirmative action originates in the bureaucracy, not in the legislature, in the light of all this one must conclude that Bell believes the elite are better entitled to decide the social interest than the majority.

One of the common criticisms of fascism has to be with its emphasis on elites. This is not to say that we must subscribe to the view that all decision making must be reducible to the town meeting model. That model is often impractical. Every institution, even political ones, must operate with some sort of elite. The major difference, however, in the political realm at least, is that elites should be subject to recall. Everywhere we should be able to remove them either by law or by election. The referendum is the ultimate lever to protect ourselves against elites. Even the U.S. Constitution allows for its own amendment. But the kind of elite with which we are dealing in the case of affirmative action is much more tyranncal. Partly it is an elite embedded in a bureaucracy over which even our elected officials have little power. They are twice removed from us and our control. In addition, the notion of group entitlement is designed to create enclaves that cannot be subject to recall. Finally, the peculiar power of the "enclave" in activist politics is that it seeks a "veto" power without any check or potential "veto" over itself.

In this chapter I have discussed the "how" of our march toward liberal fascism. It is now time to make a few concluding remarks on the "who," that is, on who is responsible. There are four main groups who, in varying degrees, are responsible. First, the largest group consists of those many misguided, compassionate people in our society who can always be counted upon to respond uncritically to the rhetoric of activism. Here the moral strength of our society is also its weakness. Second, we have had many occasions to note the ubiquitous role of the liberal theoreticians of activism, the social scientists and members of the academic-bureaucratic complex who not only provide all the arguments but also mislead people into thinking that our problems are technical and therefore can be solved by some mechanical social manipulation of society. They are the technical elite. Third, we have the activist politicians who, in an increasingly centralized and bureaucratized social structure, think that they are exploiting the sexual, racial, and ethnic vote in their personal struggle to gain some position of advantage. They are the bureaucratic elite. Finally, we have those members of activist organizations for women and minorities and whatever else who are the fully-developed mentors of their respective clients. They are the emerging power elite.

Make no mistake about it. Affirmative action is not a temporary realignment. Although we are often told that "preferential admissions" can "be regarded as a temporary expedient," the bureaucracy will keep moving the fruition point a little farther away as we seem to approach it. How will we know when we have arrived?

"It may not be easy to tell when that time comes, however. . . ."[44] Affirmative action, whatever its origins, is now in the hands of liberal fascists.

Conventional wisdom has it that since the Civil Rights Act of 1964 both the government and sensitive institutions, private and public, have sought by various means to overcome the legacy of discrimination. Bluntly put, the formula is: discrimination is the problem and affirmative action is the solution. On the contrary, it should now be clear that affirmative action in all of its guises is the predetermined policy for which people have busily invented the problems.

What is this predetermined policy? Its goal is group entitlement. This means at least the following (here we shall use blacks to stand for all groups): (1) blacks-as-a-group should be represented at every important institution in our society in at least the proportion they constitute of the population as a whole; (2) the interests of blacks-as-a-group will be permanently protected by a perpetual organization of black leaders with semi-official status intra-institutionally, inter-institutionally, and extra-institutionally; (3) this organization will monitor every activity of every institution in order to see that the interests of blacks-as-a-group are protected; (4) the ultimate aim is to achieve veto-power over all social policies which the leadership deems threatening to that interest. Goals and timetables will disappear, but their place will be taken by a new structure, the corporative state.

Several criteria come to mind for determining when equal opportunity has been achieved. There must be substantial equality between minority groups and whites in wages, unemployment rates, housing conditions and oppor-tunities, admissions to colleges and professional schools, and membership in trade organizations and unions. Moreover, minority groups must be substantially represented in corporate board rooms, banks, the guiding bod-ies of the major political parties, Congress, and the state legislatures—in short, in positions where basic economic and political decisions are made.

When practical realities reflect our egalitarian aspirations, then we will have a true tradition of equality. Until that day comes, however, we must take affirmative action to remedy past wrongs, to realize the human potential of black Americans and to transform egalitarian wishfulness into pragmatic experience.[45]

CHAPTER 8

The Impossible Dream

> Be assured that freedom of trade, freedom of thought, freedom of speech, and freedom of action, are but modifications of one great fundamental truth, and that all must be maintained or all risked; they stand or fall together.—*Edinburgh Review* (1843).

AFFIRMATIVE ACTION, THE UNIVERSITY, AND LIBERALISM

American universities suffered a number of traumatic shocks in the late sixties and the early seventies. The upheavals, the criticism, and the soul-searching were interpreted in a number of ways. The rapid expansion of institutions of higher learning undoubtedly created many problems, especially by increasing the number of students and faculty who had no clear conception of university life. It was also a period when many people outside the university were making increasing demands upon the institution. Then, of course, there was the Vietnam War. At the same time there are always those with legitimate complaints about the operation of any institution who hoped that some of the seamier as well as the less human aspects of university life could be eliminated. Nor should we fail to mention the longstanding enemies of American society who are ever alert to exploiting a crisis. There are a number of specific critical issues which can be viewed singly or in various combinations, and, depending upon how one packages the problems, one or more combination of explanations for the problems will be stressed.

My interest was initially engaged by one specific problem, namely, preferential admissions of students and preferential hiring of faculty. In the early seventies when such policies were first being proposed I examined the arguments for them and soon found that they could not be

separated from the conflicting viewpoints about the proper role or roles
of the university. At least two issues seemed to be intimately related, the
issue of preference and the issue of what constituted university life.

The connection between the two issues helped to clarify at least one
aspect of the arguments for preference. From the very beginning I had
been struck by the absurd and almost *Alice in Wonderland* aspect of
some of the arguments for preference. Taken by themselves they could be
struck down, almost dismissed rather than refuted. On the other hand,
when those arguments were seen not as assertions of fact or logical points
but as reflections of a particular view of university life, they had to be
taken more seriously. We all became increasingly aware of our divergent
views about institutions of higher learning. Differences of opinion that
were at one time cohabitable now led, under the pressure of events, to
open conflict. So while the external pressures on the university were there
and real, it now became apparent that the crisis of the American university was internally generated. I am convinced that without the internal
conflict the external pressure could easily have been resisted. I am more
than ever convinced of this because I have come to realize that even the
external pressure is fueled from within the university community itself.

The connection between the two issues clarifies another aspect of
the arguments for preference. As our survey indicates, there have traditionally been a number of competing views of what American universities should be. The arguments for preference clearly reveal that the
internal pressure within the university comes from a particular source,
what we have identified as the liberal-culture faction. This faction, in turn
and as its name indicates, expresses the social ideology of doctrinaire
liberalism. Thus it is doctrinaire liberalism that is the origin of both the
arguments for preference and for a particular view of university life.
And the arguments for preference reveal this connection better than any
other issue. Not only does the social ideology of liberalism explain the
advocacy of preference but it accounts for a host of other controversies
within the university, especially politicization.

In order then even to understand the arguments for preference it is
important to understand the liberal theories of man, society, the state, the
economy, and every other institution. Moreover, if the rejection of preference is to be sustained it will be necessary not only explicitly to reject
liberalism but to offer some kind of rebuttal of it. Debates about preference and the role or roles of the university are thus part of a much
wider controversy. Government regulation of higher education is but one
example of a policy of modern liberalism.

One might be tempted, in view of the foregoing, to go straight to the
heart of the matter, to engage in a critique of the political philosophy of
liberalism and to treat in a subsidiary fashion the implications of liberalism for preference and higher education. But the matter is not quite
so simple. To begin with, education is a crucial institution in the theory

of doctrinaire liberalism; so it is not feasible even to explain doctrinaire liberalism without great stress on education. Not only does doctrinaire liberalism provide a special and very important role for the university as it conceives of it, but doctrinaire liberalism is in turn sustained by those members of the university community who embrace that ideology. Not only do some members of the university community have a vested interest in the continuing influence of doctrinaire liberalism, but they in turn are largely responsible for its pervasive influence upon public opinion and public policy. Therefore, the way in which modern liberalism is held as a position and the way in which it is presented and discussed, as well as not discussed, cannot be understood apart from factors peculiar to modern university practice. In short, arguments for preferential admissions and hiring cannot be understood apart from controversies about the roles of the university, and the latter in turn cannot be understood apart from its symbiotic relationship with doctrinaire liberalism.

In the course of this book we have been led to a brief examination of the theory of liberalism.[1] Our treatment has aimed not to be comprehensive but selective, emphasizing those factors that bear directly on preferential treatment within the university. Liberalism itself has undergone a profound transformation usually noted by the distinction between classical and modern liberalism. The transformation explains both the presence of multiple versions of liberalism and the capacity of liberalism to generate a prolific number of variations. The internal dialectic within the university community about preference is understandable once we note the existence of a variety of liberalisms. Even the inability of classical liberals to oppose decisively preferential policies is made clear once we see that classical liberalism cannot challenge certain basic premises of modern liberalism precisely because it shares them. Moreover, once the basic premises are isolated, they can be not only forthrightly challenged but also indicted as incoherent. The incoherence of liberalism lies precisely in its being an empty set of formulas from which one can infer contradictory policies and any number of alternative versions. This peculiar blindness that liberals have about their own theory both requires some sociological analysis and reinforces the need for some historical explanation of its development.

THE EVOLUTION OF LIBERALISM

Although the word *liberal* is very old, its use as a political term of designation dates from the early nineteenth century in Britain. The Tories, or conservatives, used it at first as a derogatory expression to characterize their Whig opponents. As a result of the Reform Bill of 1832, the Whigs formed the Liberal party by joining with the newly enfranchised industrialists and business classes. The Liberal party's acme of power was from

1846 to 1874. Thereafter, it was challenged by both the conservatives and the more radical Labour party.

From 1825 to about 1870, liberalism, as expressed in and influenced by the thought of Jeremy Bentham, advocated laissez-faire as opposed to the feudal privileges of the landed aristocracy and mercantilism, and it pursued the broadening of political liberties, especially the franchise. From 1865 on, liberalism underwent a metamorphosis. It increasingly supported government activism, especially labor legislation (the so-called factory acts), Irish Home Rule, and the notion that the state exists to advance the welfare of all individuals. After 1870, the main theorists of this modern liberalism were T. H. Green and L. T. Hobhouse. As a result of the depression that began in 1873 and the Irish Home Rule controversy, the Liberal party split in 1886, with many businessmen deserting under the leadership of Joseph Chamberlain to the conservatives. The remaining liberals increasingly depended upon the coalition of special interest groups which it represented: the Irish, labor, nonconformist groups, and so on.

In the U.S., liberal ideas were clearly at work in the thought and policies of Woodrow Wilson, but those ideas crystallized with Roosevelt's New Deal.

Classical liberals had argued for the existence of an ultimate harmony in the social world. Modern liberals have argued that the necessary conditions for this harmony could only be guaranteed by state activism. Both have tended to see the harmony in largely economic terms. By the third quarter of the nineteenth century in England the nature of the social harmony, not its existence, began to be questioned. The leading figure in this movement was T. H. Green.

It was Green who imported Hegel into liberalism. The German philosopher G. W. F. Hegel was the first in the nineteenth centuy to have addressed himself to the issue of the nature of the social harmony. The classical Greeks, as Hegel reminded us, had distinguished the polis from the marketplace. Modern political philosophers from Hobbes onward had made the state the creature of preserving economic institutions, but in so doing had denied the moral function that the Greeks attributed to the polis. Hegel attempted to overcome this dichotomy. He once more attributed to the state the moral goal of fostering human excellence and the good life. But as a modern, Hegel had to argue that civil society (i.e., the economy) was a moment in the progress toward a higher form of unification in the state. Hegel was hostile to popular suffrage; he believed in "functional representation" so that the state is an organization each of whose members is itself a group; he believed that the individual consciousness, unless mediated, remained both empty and destructive. All forms of contemporary collectivism owe their intellectual origin to this aspect of Hegel's thought.

Green incorporated Hegel's notion of an organic society into liberalism. We have already seen the importance of this organic conception of the community in our discussion of the argument for affirmative action. It was Green who argued that poverty breeds moral degradation. It was Green who argued that the ultimate goal of social life is full moral participation. The purpose of state activism is to promote moral development. It is the duty of the state not only to overcome poverty but to make sure that individual citizens are qualified to fulfill some social function and contribute something to the common good. Human personality is to be realized by finding a significant part to play in the life of society, not a smaller institution. Merely providing individuals with opportunity is not enough since opportunity implies the possibility of failure. To provide *positive* freedom is to provide the "capacity of doing or enjoying something worth doing or enjoying."

The ultimate collectivism inherent in modern liberalism is thus fully apparent in Green. Not only do we have state activism but it is state activism designed to guarantee full participation. It is not enough to provide basic needs and opportunity. Terms like "oppression" are extended far beyond their economic and legal confines to describe anything less than "full" participation. Green's critics did not hesitate to point out the collectivist implications of his views. But like all liberals, Green could only interpret collectivism to mean the subordination of the individual to the state. Neither he nor his followers could see that the idea of an innate human teleology, which it is our duty to develop in ourselves and in others, is the liberal counterpart to collectivism.[2] It was Green and his disciple Hobhouse who finally spelled out the implications inherent in a notion of human teleology culminating in social participation.

> The greatest happiness will not be realized by the greatest or any great number unless in a form in which all can share, in which indeed the sharing is for each an essential ingredient. . . . distinct and separate personalities may develop in harmony and contribute to a collective achievement.[3]

The collectivism is embedded in the notions that (a) I am only truly myself when I am true to my basic human nature, and (b) my basic human nature is definable in terms of what I share with others in a collective achievement.

Hobhouse went on to formulate a doctrine of "orthogenic evolution" (as opposed to Spencer and the social Darwinists). He turned that evolution into a teleology of progress in which all living organisms become not only more organized but also more cooperative. The ultimate common good requires the compulsory participation of everyone. Still claiming faith in democracy, Hobhouse went on to spell out the details of a welfare state: ceilings on wealth, new financial policies for dealing with monopoly, welfare, and public services. To the very end, Hobhouse believed that his policies were direct implications from the laws of social development that sociologists like himself would discover.

WHAT'S WRONG WITH LIBERALISM

Liberalism used to mean the advocacy of individual liberty. Now it means the advocacy of state paternalism—a paternalism on behalf of some communal ideal. A number of complex factors have contributed to this switch. I have stressed one, namely, the malleability inherent within the theory of liberalism itself. I have also argued that such malleability is the result of a historicist teleology, and that it can lead to sinister forms of collectivism such as fascism.

The teleological view of individual human nature implies that there are certain necessary conditions that have to be met in order for each individual to achieve or attain or realize his built-in ends. These things that the individual *must* have were called rights by the classical liberal. The modern liberal calls them needs. By calling them *needs,* the modern liberal accomplishes several things. First, he appears to be making a scientific or empirical claim rather than a value judgment. Second, "need" implies something fundamental rather than something frivolous. The list of needs usually starts with "life." Third, the concept of needs gives the modern liberal a powerful rhetorical weapon, for if anyone denies that a need exists he can be charged with insensitivity or worse. Fourth, since a need is a necessary but not a sufficient condition, the modern liberal can never be criticized if the granting of a need does not lead to the result anticipated. Since needs are only necessary they can be established statistically rather than causally. Since they are statistical they are calculable, e.g., teacher-pupil ratios or income. Fifth, needs are not necessarily known to those who have them. Hence an opening is created for the educational awareness of needs. The majority may have to be educated about its true needs. Thus is provided the justification for an activist state with an increasing bureaucracy that feeds on itself.

The bureaucracy in its turn and in response to criticism manufactures the concept of the "subtle" need. No matter what form of state activism is employed to solve so-called social problems, it does not work. Hence there must be a subtle need we are missing, and the responsibility of the bureaucracy is to develop new approaches to it. Moreover, if anyone has his identifiable needs met and does not develop himself or "realize" himself, that does not prove that the need was not a necessary condition. It merely proves that there are additional subtle needs. The statistical approach is preserved. The concept of subtle need also effectively subverts the concept of a minimum need, the mainstay of old-fashioned socialism. Minimum needs were always inflated, but now we know why. Minimum need was always understood to mean all of one's minimum needs, which must mean, if it means anything, all of one's needs. "Minimum" is thus redundant. It is also a concept subject to fashion and changing social circumstances.

The second great need after life is liberty or "freedom." The modern liberal takes over the classical liberal notion that freedom is the absence of external constraint. But whereas the classical liberal used this to infer the conclusion that there should be a minimum of government constraint, the modern liberal infers from it the full panoply of state paternalism. How is this possible? Freedom has been turned into a means, a necessary condition. Or, rather, we should say the modern liberal spells out that freedom as the absence of external constraint can only be a means in a teleological system. Once freedom is conceived of as a means, the modern liberal searches for the accompanying conditions of freedom, and this usually turns out to be economic and political. We are told that in order to make men free we must do something else, usually support the programs of an activist state.

Any theory claiming that freedom is an end in itself cannot be teleological. In a teleological theory we must be free to do something else which is our true end. Anything, absolutely anything, done in the name of achieving the officially designated end can, consistent with this view, be said to be increasing one's freedom. Freedom has in fact simply been redefined to mean satisfying needs. All this is clearly traceable to Hobbes. Although he argued that freedom is the absence of external constraint, he also noted that the absence of all restraint is not total freedom but the state of nature. Hence he advocated an absolute sovereign. Of course there must be restraints, so it is only arbitrary restraints that should be removed. Unfortunately, "arbitrary" is defined as what is inconsistent with the teleological system.

The sense of freedom, let us call it freedom$_1$, introduced by Hobbes is the absence of external constraints. A different sense of freedom, let us call it freedom$_2$, developed in the continental tradition and culminated in Hegel. It says that freedom is fulfillment as part of the social whole. Freedom$_2$ is collectivist. The switch from classical liberal to modern liberal can be seen when freedom$_1$ is equated with freedom$_2$; that is, when it is assumed that in the absence of external constraint we are led to fulfill ourselves. Taking the equation seriously and not metaphorically also leads to a problem we have noted earlier, namely, the conflict between determinism (external constraint) and teleology (fulfillment). The trouble is that liberals simply do not agree on what fulfillment is.

On the one hand, the equation leads to the collectivist nightmare of fascism. On the other, it encourages a host of false expectations that inevitably lead to political frustration. Blacks and women, for example, have been led to create some romanticized versions of participation in which they would be constantly euphoric, always personally loved, and considered personally indispensible in every decision. Since they cannot find it, they assume they have been left out, and what is more that other people have this participation and are keeping them from it. Apparently the notion of fulfillment implies that there can be a society in which conflict and agonizing moral choices do not have to be faced. All this nonsense is encouraged by liberal teleology. The result is not a society free of alienation but a totalitarian society. By handing over the moral initiative to big government, we do not liberate blacks and others but perpetuate a cultural tradition of political dependence. Finally, cultural pluralism is ultimately incompatible with a monistic liberal vision of "the mainstream."

What modern liberals argue for, and must argue, is a specific conception of the good life. The good life must have a specifiable content without which life is incomplete. If it is possible to give that content, then it is our duty to do so. If, having given it, people do not use it well, it is because they are still victims of past oppression. Even more subtle psychological needs must be met.

The difficulty with the concept of the good life is that there is little agreement on what constitutes it. This is the problem of such abstract teleologies as we have already discussed. Everyone plugs in his own version. Very often one gets the impression that for modern liberals we can never reach the ultimate moment of fulfillment—but somehow it is there! Sometimes there is general agreement on what impedes the good life, and then we have a crusade to remove some selected external constraint or other. Sometimes modern liberals become so obsessed with identifying and removing external constraints that they lose sight of any end. Here egalitarianism creeps in, now understood as the equal right of all to the same quantity of resources. We are all entitled to seek self-fulfillment by removing the restraints created by a lack of equal access to resources such as wealth and power. This in turn leads to the romanticized version where we envisage a world without conflicts and frustrations—a world where we transcend the human moral condition. This is why no matter how much the situation is improved economically, there is always going to be the "perception" of a discrepancy between the real and the ideal.

More often, the good life is defined comparatively. There are two things to be noticed about such comparisons. First, they have an air of scientific detachment about them. We are offered statistics comparing one thing with another, such as infant mortality, income, etc. Such statistical comparisons establish a gap, which is to be closed by state activism. Thus public policy seems to be a mere technical solution to a technical problem. But comparisons must be between one *group* and another. This brings us to the second point. Who is to establish the relevant reference group?

Only a fully developed human being could possibly serve as the ultimate referent. Moreover, one would have to be fully developed in order to know what full development is. Doctrinaire liberals appear in their own eyes to be the most fully developed individuals in our society. They alone can make the disinterested decisions; they alone can educate the rest of us. Is it any wonder then that the university is the oracle of doctrinaire liberalism?

Doctrinaire liberals also have their lunatic fringe for whom one item on the agenda of activism becomes a messianic obsession. Such is the case at present with affirmative action. It is a way of trying to guarantee system-wide optimality. Consider the following possibilities:

Game I: group x excels over group y in game A

Game II: group x excels in game A *and*
group y excels in game B *and*
the social value of A is equal to the social
value of B

Game III: group x excels in game A *and*
groups x and y are equal in game B

Game IV: groups x and y are equal in game B

Games II and IV are preferred by doctrinaire liberals over games I and III. Game IV is also ultimately to be preferred to Game II.

There will be time enough to consider fine shadings if and when proportionality comes within view. Proportionality also has the virtue of objectivity, and keeps the process of goal determination from being politicized . . . also avoids the virtually impossible task of determining the extent to which representation has in fact been distorted by structural disabilities.[4]

The extremes of doctrinaire liberalism are infinite. It simply depends upon what inhibiting factor one chooses or fastens onto and what end one envisages. Liberal teleology is not based upon actual past instances of fulfillment but lies somewhere in the vague future. It is something to be achieved, a call to action. This also explains why history has to be periodically rewritten. Here we can also begin to fathom the fascination with schemes of human homogeneity. This is when liberalism becomes shrill, doctrinaire, and totalitarian.

Doctrinaire liberalism is the most pervasive social ideology in our society. Everything tends to reinforce its pervasive influence. We have raised the question of why this is so and how it came about. The root of these views can be traced philosophically to the post-Renaissance assumption of the primacy of method and the attempt to forge universal techniques for solving all problems, whether intellectual or practical. This attempt triumphs in the domination of nature but aborts in reshaping man and bringing him too under the control of technicians. Men become unable to know themselves or to evaluate the world they have created.

The social sciences have, since the eighteenth century, mimicked what they understand to be going on in the natural sciences. Thus, the social sciences have advocated a value-free notion of the study and understanding of human nature and social institutions. Questions of value are data to be explained or explained away in nonevaluative terms. Values cannot themselves be ultimate premises of explanation, so social scientists must seek the prior causes and conditions of values. At the very same time, social scientists have attempted to be useful, like engineers who are the useful extensions of physicists. But in order to be useful one must have some end in mind. Even trying to solve a problem presupposes that someone recognizes a situation as problematic. That is, someone must have certain values in view in order for the social scientists to be useful. The question now becomes, How are we to understand the values by which the social scientist becomes useful to society?

Since value-free social science prohibits values from being themselves ultimate, the social scientists must explain those values as the effects of certain antecedent conditions. Moreover, if the antecedent conditions were different for different individuals or groups of individuals, the resulting values would be different and there would be no objective basis for deciding which values to foster. The social scientist must then postulate the existence of certain universal conditions by which objective values are determined. He needs the notion of a basic human nature. There is, however, little evidence for or agreement on the existence of such a universal human nature. This difficulty is obviated by maintaining that there is a basic human nature potentially but that its actuality is inhibited by external conditions. This kind of theoretical explanation is what we have called teleological, and the resulting view of man we have identified as psychologism. Liberal social science is thus committed to environmentalism, and this commitment is not scientific but ideological. Environmentalism has been made an unassailable article of faith.[5]

The implications of environmentalism and its subcategory of cultural determinism are by now obvious. First, moral choice and, along with it, moral responsibility and freedom are eliminated. Freedom is redefined so that it is no longer an end but a means to something else. Questions of value are now reinterpreted as technical questions to be answered by experts. The unlimited potential for meddling has been opened. Finally, despite liberalism's formal adherence to the ideal of democracy, the perception of oppression and inhibiting conditions, along with the belief in expertise, inevitably pushes doctrinaire liberalism in the direction of benevolent despotism, the contemporary form of which is fascism.

What this benevolent despotism really amounts to is the belief that some members of the intellectual community comprise a technical moral elite whose mission it is to raise up the rest of us. This moral elitism is the expression of a monstrous pride and arrogance. Liberals themselves tend to express their position as a kind of compassion for the downtrodden and the oppressed. The critics of liberalism by and large try to make sense of absurd liberal policies by attributing another motive to liberals: namely, guilt. The critics assert that in a system of seemingly irrational reward schedules those who have benefitted accidentally will want to do something about those who have suffered accidentally. Redistributing the wealth is also a way of redistributing the guilt. But I do not think that either the compassion hypothesis or the guilt hypothesis is a full explanation.

To begin with, we must distinguish between compassion, pity, and sympathy. To sympathize is to be able to understand or even to share the sorrow of another. I might sympathize even with someone's wrong-headedness, having been there myself. To feel compassion is to go beyond sympathy and to want to help. Help takes all forms, including having the courage to tell people just how wrong-headed they are. Compassion itself implies no sense of superiority. Pity, on the other hand, is sorrow for another's misfortune or suffering along with a slight contempt precisely because the victim is regarded as inferior.

Liberals do not feel sympathy or compassion or even guilt. What they feel is pity. The effects of pity on human beings as opposed to compassion can be disastrous. If the helping hand of liberalism is a necessary condition for achievement or development, then this means that the victim could never have made it on his or her own, could never have made it without the liberal.

The liberal intellectual is in his own view the prime example of a totally liberated and fully developed individual. He is superior to reactionaries who may be defined as beneficiaries of the system who do not feel pity. He is superior to the uncouth and grasping masses who need his help. That is why he can recognize the shortcomings of the downtrodden. In fact, the worse they behave the more they need his help. The liberal intellectual is the ideal person to lead us to what is truly and eventually in the best interest of all.

The element of moral elitism helps us to understand several things. First, liberals see themselves as somehow outside the normal process. Their role is to guide and control the system from their superior vantage point. Nor was there ever any question about the elitist status of members of the community of university liberals. These liberals were just as shocked as everyone else to discover that some of the uncouth were responsible for administering affirmative action. However, their response was not to question or reconsider liberalism but to try to work out a deal wherein their control was maintained. These are the liberals who want to make affirmative action work by taking control of its administration.

We may crystallize this last point by invoking the well-known thesis that technological elitism leads to political tyranny. By first capturing and then imposing their ideology on social science, liberals threaten to become the new tyranny. The reduction of moral issues to technical issues is a necessary prerequisite to establish that policy is determined by consulting experts instead of by making moral judgments. This also reinforces our contention of the close connection between liberalism and the university. Without the aura of "wisdom" (expertise) surrounding the university, liberalism would never have maintained and extended its hold on public policy making.

Finally, the elitist element will help us to understand what otherwise seems altogether self-contradictory. That is, elitism explains why liberals advocate quotas, which are at one and the same time an advocacy of equality and an advocacy of hierarchy. A quota is the conceptual apparatus for maintaining elitist control with the appearance of being democratic.

ALTERNATIVES

A large part of this book has been devoted to a sustained critique of liberalism in its modern form. We have also been concerned with explaining why such a weak theory has managed to obtain such a strong hold on policy makers and the public alike, to say nothing of the academic world and the media. The influence of doctrinaire modern liberalism has a great deal to do with the problems of the alternative approaches. Doctrinaire liberalism is sustained, in part, by the weakness of its major antagonists. It is also sustained, in an even larger part, by the fact that the enemies of liberalism often share its basic philosophical orientation, and this is why they cannot overcome it.

We must begin to reconstruct our social faith. This is difficult, but I think that we have learned enough about what is wrong to begin reconstructing what is right. Social ideals cannot be manufactured out of thin air. Nor are they discovered by a scientific elite. Rather, they are implicit in our past practices. The inherent logic of our practice must be examined, ideals extracted and refurbished for present use. Our tradition is in our practice, not in liberal ideology. We must not confuse what some intellectuals say with either our traditional values or how ordinary people understand those values.

Our tradition is epitomized in Anglo-Saxon jurisprudence, a tradition of multiple precedents—not a deductive set of first principles. It is a tradition that evolves out of the past, not one that progresses to a mythical future. It is a tradition of individualism, not collectivism. We must not confuse this individualism with the classical liberal-utilitarian interpretation of it. Individualism means that human beings are autonomous moral agents, responsible for their choices and living according to self-imposed rules. This individualism is the result of older and stronger currents of thought. It existed as an ideal in the Renaissance as well as in the Reformation. It even has medieval roots in the dispute about whether the active intellect was found in an individual soul or a group. But most relevant for our purposes, it has deep roots in the Anglo-Saxon tradition of common law. The great danger to this tradition is some utopian metaphysical vision that fosters paternalism by making the state the judge of what the individual is.

What doctrinaire liberalism has lost sight of is a conception of the common good that need not be a total unity. We in America have always operated with, and still operate with, a sense of community, which is the result of an *inherited* and *negotiated* harmony of *complementary* interests, a working consensus. Our community exists because of what has happened to it. It has been shaped by its heritage. Consequently, any debate about the future must start with the question, What is good for a community with our heritage? Doctrinaire liberalism fails to ask this question because it does not recognize that a community exists in time as well as in space. That is why it is so important to get the history right and not to succumb to ideologically distorted visions.

Notes

CHAPTER 1

1. "Racially segregated schools for minority children are perceived as inferior schools.This is the social reality. The following factors are inevitably associated with this reality: low morale of teachers, inadequate facilities and supervision, poor teaching and low motivation on the part of both pupils and parents. These are the factors which determine the overriding fact that *racially segregated schools are educationally inferior schools.* More compensatory programs and increased funding will not change this fact as long as American racism is the dominant reality in American society. . . ." [Italics added.] Testimony of Charles Morgan, Jr., for the American Civil Liberties Union before Subcommittee No. 5 of the House Judiciary Committee.

2. One of the issues we shall have to discuss is the validity of studies by social scientists and the extent to which they can be used to formulate policy. At this point, one thing seems clear. There is a definite ideological bent in what is accepted or rejected as evidence.

Consider the following statement by Charles Morgan, Jr., ibid.:

Is pupil integration any more likely than increased expenditures to achieve our goals? A basic finding of the 1966 Office of Education study, 'Equality of Educational Opportunity,' (the Coleman Report) was that a child's own family background was by far the most important influence on his school achievement and later life experience. Some have concluded from this finding that the schools are virtually powerless as a positive influence on our children, and that the effort, instead, must be in the area of jobs and income. . . .

The conclusion that the schools are powerless to increase and improve their impact on the young is wrong. As the Office of Education study found, as the Commisison on Civil Rights' own study, 'Racial Isolation in the Public Schools,' later confirmed, and as the Harvard University report recently reaffirmed, the social and economic backgrounds of a child's classmates bear very significantly on his or her achievement in school. It therefore does matter greatly that disadvantaged children not be educated in isolation." [U.S. Civil Rights Commission.]

Now consider the contention of Gloria J. Powell in *Black Monday's Children* (New York: Appleton, 1973), in which she argues that black children in segregated Southern schools have significantly higher self-concepts than black children in desegregated schools and even higher self-concepts than white children.

Without settling the issue here, I do wish to note one inconsistency. Liberals frequently stress psychic damage where objective compensatory programs fail to make a significant difference. Nevertheless, they define oppression by objective criteria such as income. One thing that has not been seriously investigated by liberals is the existence of psychic rewards experienced by members of any subculture. Partly this reflects ideology, but it reflects as well the assumption that society is a monolithic whole. To begin considering the possibility that society is a plurality with a plurality of standards of success, etc., would seriously undermine liberal ideology.

3. *Freedom At Issue* (New York: Freedom House, September-October 1978).

4. Ibid., p. 6.

5. Mr. Jones was subsequently appointed by President Jimmy Carter to the U.S. Federal Court as a judge.

6. *Freedom At Issue,* pp. 7, 12.

7. This section of the chapter, slightly amended, originally appeared in the *Washington Star,* Section F, May 6, 1979.

8. "When groups which have suffered discrimination are heavily under-represented in the privileged roles resulting from selectivity in higher education, there are grounds for making special efforts to find, prepare, and admit qualified individuals from those groups. In any race, if each runner begins at a different starting line, how can choosing the winner by judging who finishes first be a fair measure of accomplishment?" Clark Kerr, "Solving the Selective Admissions Dilemma," in *Phi Kappa Phi Journal,* Vol. 58, no. 1 (Winter 1978), p. 5. Clark Kerr was chancellor of the University of California at Berkeley from 1952 to 1958, and president from 1958 to 1967. From 1967 to 1973 he chaired the Carnegie Commission on Higher Education, and since 1974 has served as chairman of the Carnegie Council on Policy Studies in Higher Education.

9. The following statement appeared in the *New York Times* Op-Ed page during the DeFunis controversy. It is by James E. Coleman, a law-school graduate about to become a clerk for a federal district judge in Detroit: "Imagine that what is involved is not competition for jobs but instead a relay race between two teams, one black, one white, with the finish line being a particular goal sought by both—a job, admission to law school or promotion. . . . Shortly, however, a hurdle appears for the black runner . . . and continue to construct more subtle barriers in the black runner's path. . . . Each time the baton is passed, the runners on both teams are fresh, but to win, the black one would have to make up ground lost because of the obstacles. . . . The decision that has to be made then is whether to ignore this and pretend that the race is fair, or whether to eliminate the artificial advantage the white runner has.

It is precisely this problem that racial quotas addresss. To ignore the advantages created for whites by past discrimination against blacks is to ignore reality."

10. The conception of social life as a race originally appeared in the writings of Thomas Hobbes. Hobbes originated the social ideology of liberalism. For a brilliant analysis of the concept of equal opportunity see Antony Flew, *The Politics of Procrustes* (Buffalo, N.Y.: Prometheus, 1981), Chapter 2.

11. The whole issue of heredity vs. environment is a special problem that exists only within liberalism. Since meritocrats believe in individual differences in ability, it is irrelevant to them how these differenes are reflected in group statistics. On the other hand, elitists defend the assumption that talent is distributed proportionately. For this reason, it is the elitists who have provoked the Jensen literature and the subsequent controversy. No meritocrat would ever have taken

the problem seriously for the purposes of public policy. Since elitists insist that they know the distribution of talent independent of actual performance, they ironically invite consideration of group properties and therefore group differences. Egalitarians solve the problem either by opting for total environmentalism or by redefining what is to be considered a talent.

CHAPTER 2

1. Title VI and Title VII (*Congressional Quarterly*, HR 7152- PL 88-352).
2. Humphrey (110 *Congressional Record* 12723).
3. Williams (Ibid., 1433).
4. Clark and Case, (Ibid., 7213, 7218).
5. Celler (Ibid., 1518).
6. The very first use of the phrase "affirmative action" goes back to the Labor Relations Act of 1935. It requires employers who had engaged in anti-union acts of intimidation to notify employees that those acts were illegal and discontinued.
7. Order No. 4 (Title 41, *C.F.R.*, 60-1.40).
8. Underutilization (41, *C.F.R.*, 60-2.11).
9. U.S. Commission on Civil Rights, *Statement on Affirmative Action*, October 1977, Clearinghouse Publication S4. Members of the commission: Arthur S. Flemming, chairman; Stephen Horn; Frankie M. Freeman; Manuel Ruiz, Jr.; Murray Saltzman.
10. Ibid., pp. 1-2.
11. Ibid., p. 12.
12. Ibid., p. 2.
13. Ibid., pp. 7-8. This is a quote from *Rios* v. *Steamfitters Local 608*, 501 F. 2d at 631-32.
14. Ibid., p. 2.
15. In the first chapter of *Affirmative Discrimination*, Nathan Glazer discusses the problem of liberal disagreement over the "direction" of legislative history.
16. U.S. Commission, op.cit., p. 1.
17. Ronald Dworkin gives his liberal ideology away when he says the following:

> But legal practice should not encourage legislation by a contest of floor speeches. . . . Is it not wiser to insist that floor speeches cannot settle a politically controversial issue unless they are recorded in actual amendments. . . . It seems better that inherently ambiguous provisions be clarified by principled arguments of judges trying to respond to contemporary problems and opinions, rather than by the accident of which small group of congressmen spoke more often than its opponents fifteen years ago.
> Of course, if there is good reason to suppose that that small group expressed the will of Congress, then judges might well be required to defer to that will. But if, on the contrary, there is reason to think that Congress had no will and took no decision on the issue at all, judges would do better to respond to a more contemporary assessment of principle, even though they might disagree among themselves about how to assess it. That opinion may be debatable, but it hardly supposes, as Senator Hatch says it does, that "the Supreme Court has a sort of divine right to do as it pleases" when Congress has already done something else. [*New York Review of Books*, May 15, 1980]

To begin with, Dworkin misrepresents the facts. In the case at issue, those who spoke were the sponsors and floor leaders of the bill. Moreover, provisions were added to the bill to prevent misrepresentation. There is an inherent absurdity in Dworkin's position. If Congress took no stand on the issue, say, of realignment, then realignment is not part of the law. If realignment is not part of the law, then it is illegal for any government bureaucracy to enforce it. At best, the Supreme Court should advise Congress to take a stand. To adjust the law is not to invent the law. It is certainly not to impose a social ideology and a dubious sociology. This would amount in practice to doing what Senator Hatch warns us against. To take Dworkin seriously would give the Court control over all aspects of life not already legislated. It is in fact to replace representative democracy with judicial hegemony.

18. *Time,* July 10, 1978, p. 25.
19. U.S. Commission, op.cit., p. 6.
20. Ibid., p. 11.
21. 29 *C.F.R.* Part 1608.
22. U.S. Commission, op.cit., p. 5.
23. Ibid., p. 10.
24. Ibid., p. 8.
25. Since the British do not have a written constitution, no British court has the power of judicial review. We note as well that the chief executive in Britain, the Prime Minister, is elected by his or her party and not by the public at large. It is not likely under the circumstances to have executive orders in direct opposition to the wishes of the majority party.
26. In an attempt to discredit Bakke, it has been pointed out that there were some whites with even higher cumulative ratings than his, and that these other applicants neither were admitted nor did they sue. First, we are not told if they were admitted somewhere else. Second, we are not told that if cumulative scores alone were used, Bakke would not have been admitted. Others would have been admitted first, but the special admittees would not have been admitted—so additional places would have been there for Bakke. Third, the crucial point is that the Court only intervenes when an interested party sues. Failure of other interested parties to sue does not validate the Davis admissions program. Analogously, the suffering of blacks in the South under Jim Crow is not excusable because no black sued before the *Brown* case of 1954.
27. Ibid., p. 6.
28. Burger, *Swann* 402 U.S. 1 (1971), p. 16.
29. *Griggs,* 401 U.S. 424 (1971).
30. U.S. Commission, op.cit., p. 8.
31. Ibid., p. 10.
32. *International Brotherhood of Teamsters* v. *United States,* 97 S.Ct. 1843, 1856-57 (1977).
33. U.S. Commission, op.cit., compare p. 2 and p. 8.
34. Powell, *New York Law Journal,* June 29, 1978, pp. 21-26.
35. *Time,* op.cit., p. 23.
36. Ibid.
37. Ibid., p. 24.
38. *Los Angeles Times,* July 6, 1978.
39. Education Amendments of 1976, Public Law 94-482, 90 Stat. 2233, adding section 440 (c) to the General Education Provisions Act, 20 *U.S.C.* (1976 ed.) 1231i(c).
40. 123 *Congressional Record,* 6106.
41. Ervin (110 *Congressional Record,* 5612): "The word *discrimination* as used in this reference has no contextual explanation whatever, other than the provision that the discrimination "is to be against" individuals participating in or benefiting from federally assisted programs and activities on the ground specified.

With this context, the discrimination condemned by this reference occurs only when an individual is treated unequally or unfairly because of his race, color, religion, or national origin. What constitutes unequal treatment? Section 601 and section 602 of Title VI do not say. They leave the determination of that question to the executive department or agencies administering each program, without any guideline whatever to point out what is the congressional intent."

42. We should remind ourselves here of the Wittfogel thesis that technological bureaucracies become political despotisms. The more the bureaucracy grows and is assigned the task of interpreting and implementing the law, the more the Wittfogel thesis applies. Liberalism as a social ideology encourages the view that even legal issues are mere technical problems.

CHAPTER 3

1. The classic study is Laurence R. Veysey, *The Emergence of the American University* (Chicago: University of Chicago Press, 1965).

2. U.S. Commission on Education, *Report,* 1889-90, II, p. 114.

3. H. Münsterberg (1913), *American Patriotism and Other Social Studies* (New York, Books for Libraries Press, 1968), pp. 49-51.

4. W. Wilson, *Princeton for the Nation's Service* (1902), pp. 721, 729-30.

5. T. Veblen, *Higher Learning in America* (Stanford, California: Academic Reports, 1954), p. 15.

6. Ibid., p. 21.

7. Ibid., p. 187.

8. Ibid.

9. Saul K. Padover, *The Complete Jefferson* (New York: Harper, 1943), pp. 425-26.

10. James D. Richardson, *A Compilation of the Messages and Papers of the Presidents* (1897; New York, Johnson Reprint Corp., 1968), Vol. 7, p. 3078.

11. Eli Ginzberg and Douglas W. Bray, *The Uneducated,* New York: Columbia University Press, 1953), p. xv.

12. Stoke, *Vital Speeches of the Day,* May 15, 1959.

13. Hannah in "Education: Instrument of National Policy," *Congressional Record,* July 28, 1959.

14. Clark Kerr, *The Uses of the University* (New York: Harper & Row, 1963), p. 87.

15. J. B. Conant, *Education and Liberty: The Role of the Schools in a Modern Democracy* (Cambridge: Harvard University Press, 1953).

16. Veblen, op.cit., p. 146.

17. A. MacLeish, *The Next Harvard* (Cambridge: Harvard University Press), p. 4.

18. Carnegie Council, Policy Studies in Higher Education, *Making Affirmative Action Work in Higher Education* (1975), p. 2.

19. For the debate on the level of primary and secondary education, see Virgil M. Rogers, "Non-Public School Students: Shall Public Funds Be Used to Aid Them?" in *Better Schools,* June 1958.

20. Clark Kerr, op.cit., p. 121.

21. Ibid., p. 130.

22. Kenneth J. Arrow, *The Limits of Organization,* (New York: Norton & Co., 1974), p. 16.

23. One important exception to this dominant view is the work of Herbert Blumer. I am indebted to Stanford Lyman for calling Blumer to my attention. See

the forthcoming book by Lyman and Arthur J. Vidich, *American Sociology: Worldly Rejections of Religion and Their Directions* (New Haven: Yale University Press).

24. Talcott Parsons, "Full Citizenship for the Negro' American? A Sociological Problem," in Talcott Parsons and Kenneth B. Clark, eds., *The Negro American* (Boston: Houghton Mifflin, 1966), pp. 709-754.

25. For a recent Marxist perspective see Michael Reich, *Racial Inequality: A Political-Economic Analysis* (Princeton: University Press, 1981).

26. Everett C. Ladd, Jr. and Seymour Martin Lipset in *Chronicle of Higher Education*, January 16, 1979.

27. Lekachman is referred to by Walter Goodman in his article on Irving Kristol in the *New York Times Magazine*, December 5, 1981.

28. Nisbet's remark was made in an interview in the *Chronicle of Higher Education*, November 10, 1982.

29. The transcript of the program is available from Columbia University, Media and Society Seminars. In order the quotations are from pp. 7-8, 11, 31, 33, 42-43, 22, 37, and 19.

CHAPTER 4

1. A. E. Bayer, *College and University Faculty: A Statistical Description*. ACE Research Reports, vol. 5, no. 5. (Washington, D.C.: American Council on Education, 1970), p. 17.

2. A. E. Bayer, *Teaching Faculty in Academe: 1972-1973*. ACE Research Reports, vol. 8, no. 2. (Washington, D.C.: American Council on Education, 1973), p. 30.

3. Carnegie Council, Policy Studies in Higher Education, *Making Affirmative Action Work in Higher Education* (1975), pp. xii, 2. This report originally appeared in the AAUP Bulletin, Summer, 1973.

4. Ibid., p. 3.

5. Ibid., p. 8.

6. Ibid., p. 2.

7. Ibid., p. 1.

8. Ibid., p. 12.

9. Clark Kerr, op. cit., p. 6. See also William V. Shannon, member of the *New York Times* Editorial Board, "End of an Era," February 26, 1974: "Most probably, 'affirmative action' is an interim phenomena, a strategy for the next ten or twenty years but not for longer."

10. R. A. Lester, *Antibias Regulation of Universities: Faculty Problems and Their Solutions*. (New York: McGraw-Hill, 1974), p. 13.

11. Ibid., p. 65.

12. J. S. Mill, *Liberty*, chapter one.

13. See, for example, the statement by C. V. Hamilton in Robert M. O'Neil, *Discriminating Against Discrimination* (Bloomington: Indiana University Press, 1975), p. 97.

14. Carnegie Council, op.cit., p. 45.

15. "Women candidates were not invisible in the major universities which granted them doctorates but denied them faculty appointments." Gertrude Ezorsky, "Hiring Women Faculty," *Philosophy & Public Affairs* 7, no. 1 (1977), p. 82.

16. Quoted in Sidney Hook "The Road to a University 'Quota System'," *Freedom at Issue*, no. 12 (March-April 1972), p. 2.

17. "Members of a cultural group share basic values . . . and they interact

intellectually by . . . clarifying, criticizing, and extending them (values). . . . In this way they come better to understand themselves. . . . the intellectually most active and advanced of a cultural group play a crucial role in the above-mentioned process of self clarification. . . . W. E. B. Dubois makes this point about the talented tenth of every group. . . ." B. Boxill, "The Morality of Preferential Hiring," *Philosophy & Public Affairs* 7, no. 3 (1978), p. 256.

18. Lester, op. cit., p. 115. Role models are supposed to increase the aspirations of minority students. However, the evidence seems to indicate that such students frequently have higher aspirations already, See, e.g., Armor, "The Evidence on Busing" in *Public Interest* 90 (1972), pp. 101-02.

19. Lester, op. cit., p. 15.

20. For how this affected the U.S. Census recently see Robert Reinhold, *New York Times*, May 14, 1978, pp. 1, 14.

21. Ernest Gellhorn and Barry B. Boyer, "The Academy as a Regulated Industry." in *Government Regulation of Higher Education*, ed. Walter C. Hobbs (Cambridge: Ballinger, 1978).

22. Lenore J. Weitzman, "Affirmative Action Plans for Eliminating Sex Discrimination in Academe," in Rossi and Calderwood, eds., *Academic Women on the Move* (New York: Russell Sage Foundation, 1973). see pp. 500-01.

23. See Jenne K. Britell "The Dangers of Suppressed Research" in the *New York Times* Jan. 4, 1981, Education section, p. 29.

24. Ezorsky, op. cit.

CHAPTER 5

1. William V. Shannon, member of the editorial board of the *New York Times*, "End of an Era" (February 26, 1974): "Universities have traditionally applied other admission standards than proven intellectual merit. They have given preference to athletes, to sons of alumni and to that mythic figure—'the well-rounded boy.' Why cannot universities now give an edge to blacks?"

2. R. Wasserstrom, "A Defense of Programs of Preferential Treatment," in *Phi Kappa Phi Journal* (Winter 1978), pp, 16-17.

3. O'Neil, *Discriminating Against Discrimination*, p. 104.

4. James S. Coleman, et. al., *Equality of Educational Opportunity*, Department of Health, Education, and Welfare, 1966.

5. Christopher Jencks, et. al., *Inequality: A Reassessment of the Effect of Family and Schooling in America* (New York: Basic Books, 1972).

6. This is confirmed by David K. Cohen, Thomas F. Pettigrew, and Robert S. Riley, "Race and the Outcome of Schooling," in Frederick Mostellet and Daniel P. Moynihan, eds., *On Equality of Educational Opportunity* (New York: Random House, 1972): "school racial composition . . . its significance for educational policy seems slight." This statement applies to grade school, not colleges.

7. "Equalitative affirmative action recognizes that there currently exist solid psychometric techniques whereby qualifications and characteristics presumably related to job performance can be equitably and reasonably quantified." Letter to the editor of the *New York Times* (November 28, 1977) by Alberto Pedro Simon Montare, Assistant Professor of Education, Rutgers University.

8. ". . . any setting of statewide minimum competency standards for awarding the high school diploma . . . is basically unworkable, exeeds the present measurement arts of the teaching profession and will create more social

problems than it can conceivably solve." Panel established by the National Academy of Education, chaired by Stephen K. Bailey of Harvard's Graduate School of Education, asked to report to HEW Secretary Califano. Reported in the *New York Times* (March 3, 1978) in an article by Gene I. Maeroff.

9. "We know . . . that the (LSAT) is not racially biased. Five separate studies have indicated that the test does not underpredict the law school performance of blacks and Mexican Americans." Brief Amicus Curiae for the Association of American Law Schools in support of petitioner at 13, Regents of the University of California v. Bakke.

10. David Kirp and Mark Yudoof in O'Neil, op.cit., p. 102.

11. Ibid., p. 102.

12. Ibid., p. 111.

13. Ibid., pp. 93, 109.

14. Ibid., p. 160.

15. For a devastating and brilliant critique of affirmative action with regard to law schools read Lino A. Graglia, *Disaster by Decree: The Supreme Court Decisions on Race and the Schools* (Ithaca, N.Y.: Cornell University Press, 1976); and "Racially Discriminatory Admission to Public Institutions of Higher Education," *Southwestern University Law Review*, vol. 9 (1977), no. 3, pp. 583-96.

16. In support of his contention, O'Neil, op.cit., pp. 97-98, cites Supreme Court Justice Brennan, the ACLU, and a Chicano governor of New Mexico. First, these references are not experts but advocates of a cause. Second, in the first two instances the authors cited were referring to black attorneys who had both gone through regular admissions and who had passed the bar exam. It is highly improper for any of the parties to generalize from this to special admissions candidates.

17. The number of students who are trained by foreign schools and pass the National Board Examinations is very low.

18. "But there was the underlying assumption that Allan Bakke had to be the unfortunate victim of temporary measures that were probably less than just. Few of the foxes in the defense could make the leap of faith to a concept that minority students with lower grades and test scores could possess human qualities growing out of their individual racial experiences that made them better qualified than some whites who wanted to be physicians." Dreyfuss and Lawrence, *The Bakke Case: The Politics of Inequality* (New York: Harcourt, Brace Jovanovich, 1979).

There are two rebuttals worth noting. "I know of no studies showing that minority status *per se* confers upon the physician some special healing potency." —Ronald Pies, letter to the editor, *New York Times*, September 28, 1977. Second, Professor Bernard Davis of Harvard Medical School reported on the poor performance of special minority students in the *New England Journal of Medicine* (1976).

CHAPTER 6

1. See chapter two, note 14.

2. The argument for affirmative action may be schematized as follows:
   * 1. *If* you are black, *then* you have been discriminated against.
   * 2. *If* you have been discriminated against, *then* you have not been allowed to develop your full potential. (*Revised:* you develop your full potential *if and only if* you have *not* been discriminated against.)
   * 3. *If* you have not been allowed to develop your full potential, *then* you

were not able to acquire maximum merit. (*Revised:* you have full merit *if and only if* you have developed your full potential.)
* 4. *If* a society aspires to be just *then* it allows for the full development of potential, *and* it sees to it that social roles are equivalent to merit.
* 5. Our society does aspire to be just.
6. *Therefore,* our society seeks to develop everyone's full potential (from 4 and 5).
7. *Therefore,* our society seeks to equate social roles and merit (from 4 and 5).
8. *If* anyone had maximum merit, *then* he would have his rightful role (from 7).
9. *If* anyone develops his full potential, *then* he acquires maximum merit (from 3 only as revised).
10. *Therefore, if* anyone develops his full potential, *then* he acquires his rightful role (from 8 and 9).
* 11. The innate potential of blacks is roughly proportionately equal to that of whites.
12. *If* the potential of blacks is equivalent to the potential of whites, *then* the potential merit of blacks is equivalent to the potential merit of whites (from 11 and 9).
13. *If* the potential merit of blacks is equivalent to the potential merit of whites, *then* the roles of blacks should be proportionately equivalent to the roles of whites (from 12, 11, and 8).
14. *If* a society is just, *then* it seeks to develop full potential (from 4).
15. *If* a society is just, *then* it will also seek to eliminate discrimination (from 14, and 2 only as revised).
* 16. But *if* it is not always possible for a just society to eradicate totally all of the effects of discrimination, *then* in those cases it should give compensation.
* 17. One way of granting compensation is to treat the victim of discrimination as if he had full merit.
* 18. *If* we treat a person *as if* he had his full merit, *then* we give him the role he would have had.
19. *If* we grant compensation, *then* we give people their rightful role (from 15, 16, 5, 17, and 18).
20. Since the roles blacks should have is equivalent to the roles whites should have, to grant compensation is at present to adopt affirmative action, that is, to equate the roles (from 10, 11, 13, and 19).

MAKING THE ARGUMENT VALID

The argument as stated and schematized is not quite a valid argument. For example, step 9 is not entailed by step 3. In its initial formulation it would involve the *fallacy of denying the antecedent.* If, however, we equate potential and merit, step 9 follows. The move from step 2 to step 15 presents us with the same problem. It is only by revising step 2 that we again avoid the fallacy of denying the antecedent. It is only by equating potential and lack of discrimination that the argument becomes valid. As we shall see below, this revised premise is crucial because it allows that if you are not a victim of discrimination you automatically develop your full potential. This revised premise also permits us to conclude that if you have not developed your full potential, then we may conclude that you have been discriminated against without having to provide additional empirical evidence of the discrimination.

IS THE ARGUMENT SOUND?

In order to assess the soundness of the argument we must isolate the underived premises and examine each in turn. The underived premises are: 1, 2, 3, 4, 5, 11, 16, 17, and 18. These premises may be examined under five convenient headings. The first two premises concern the concept of discrimination. The second premise, in addition, involves questions of a fundamental nature about mankind such as potential, freedom, and responsibility. Premises 3, 4, and 5 invoke the norms of what I shall call the liberal-utilitarian paradigm. Premise 11 is by far the most important. Logically it will help to elucidate the first two premises, and it will serve as the explanatory link between the norms and the application of the policy of affirmative action. Put another way, it connects the diagnosis with the prescription. Philosophically it raises profound issues about the methodology of the social sciences. Finally, premises 16, 17, and 18 concern the concept of compensation.

(1) $B \rightarrow D$
(2) $D \rightarrow -P$ *(revised:* $P \equiv -D) \equiv [(P \rightarrow -D) \cdot (-D \rightarrow P)]$
(3) $-P \rightarrow -M$ *(revised:* $P \equiv M)$
(4) $J \rightarrow [P \cdot (M \equiv R)]$
(5) J
(6) $\therefore P$ *(from* steps 4 and 5)
(7) $\therefore (M \equiv R)$ *(from* steps 4, 5, and 6)
(8) $\therefore M \rightarrow R$ *(from* step 7)
(9) $\therefore P \rightarrow M$ *(from* step 3 as revised)
(10) $\therefore P \rightarrow R$ *(from* steps 9 and 8)
(11) $P_b \equiv P_w$
(12) $\therefore (P_b \equiv P_w) \rightarrow (M_b \equiv M_w)$ *(from* steps 11 and 9)
(13) $\therefore (M_b \equiv M_w) \rightarrow (R_b \equiv R_w)$ *(from* steps 11, 12, and 8)
(14) $\therefore J \rightarrow P$ *(from* steps 4 and 5)
(15) $\therefore J \rightarrow -D$ *(from* steps 14 and 2 as revised)
(16) $-D \rightarrow C$
(17) $C \rightarrow$ as-if M
(18) as-if $M \rightarrow R$
(19) $\therefore C \rightarrow R$ *(from* steps 15, 16, and 5, 17 and 18)
(20) $C \rightarrow (R_b \equiv R_w)$ *(from* steps 19 and 11, 12, and 13)

All of the premises are expressed by Bernard R. Boxill, "The Morality of Preferential Hiring," *Philosophy & Public Affairs* 7, no. 3, 1978, pp. 246-68.
    3. "But among younger generation blacks and whites, by the late 1960s, individuals with similar home backgrounds and the same education had the same income—regardless of race. Gross black-white differences had not disappeared, but the reasons for the remaining differences between young whites and blacks were factors at work before they ever set foot in an employer's office." Thomas Sowell, *Inquiry*, August 21, 1978, p. 11.
    4. "No reasonable person doubts that past immoral and illegal discrimination is largely responsible for the present underrepresentation of blacks and American Indians in desired positions." Kent Greenawalt, *Discrimination and Reverse Discrimination* (New York: Knopf, 1983), p. 54.
    5. Joe R. Feagin and Clairece Booker Feagin, *Discrimination American Style: Institutional Racism and Sexism* (Englewood, N.J.: Prentice-Hall, 1978).

6. Advocates of affirmative action do not want compensation in the form of remediation but in the form of realignment. See Boxill, op.cit.

7. (revised 2) $P \equiv -D$
   (3) $P \equiv M$
   (3a) $\therefore M \equiv -D$ (*from* 2 and 3)
   (3b) $\therefore -D \rightarrow M$ (*from* 3a)
   (15) $J \rightarrow -D$
   (15a) $J \rightarrow M$ (*from* 15 and 3b)
   (8) $M \rightarrow R$
   (15b) $\therefore J \rightarrow R$ (i.e., reassign everyone to his rightful role)

8. Participation as a goal was first suggested in the nineteenth century by T. H. Green. Green, however, was concerned with the individual. Participation for the group, even in the form of proxies, is a recent doctrinaire liberal development.

9. "No one deserves his greater natural capacity nor merits a more favorable starting place in society." John Rawls, *A Theory of Justice* (1971), p. 102.

"Most of what are regarded as the decisive circumstances for higher education have a great deal to do with things over which the individual has neither control nor responsibility: such things as home environment, socio-economic class of parents, and, of course, the quality of primary and secondary schools attended. Since individuals do not deserve having had any of these things vis-á-vis other individuals, they do not, for the most part, deserve their qualifications. And since they do not deserve their abilities they do not in any strong sense deserve to be admitted because of their abilities." Richard Wasserstrom, "Racism, Sexism and Preferential Treatment: An Approach to the Topics," *U.C.L.A. Law Review* 24, no. 2 (February 1877), p. 620.

"The Chancellor has identified the wrong offender. Failure to learn is the result of the failure of the teaching process. The system encourages the protection— sometimes deliberately, sometimes unwittingly—of teachers who don't teach and supervisors who don't supervise. . . . Perhaps if the chancellor proposed a plan to eliminate underachievers among the professional staff, he would eliminate the need for a plan to hold back underachieving students." Clinton Howze, Jr., Community Superintendent, District 3, N.Y.C. Letter to the editor of the *New York Times,* (November 21, 1979).

10. See Wasserstrom, op.cit.

11. B. Boxill, op.cit., p. 253. The same point is explicitly made by Sara Ann Ketchum, "Evidence, Statistics, and Rights: A Reply to Simon," *Analysis* 39 (1979), pp. 150-51. See also a statement by the U.S. Department of Labor (1965): "Intelligence potential is distributed among Negro infants in the same proportion and pattern as among Icelanders or Chinese, or any other group. . . ."

12. "Decades of discrimination by public bodies and private persons may have far reaching effects that make it difficult for minority applicants to compete . . . on an equal basis. The consequences of discrimination are too complex to dissect case-by-case; the effects on aspirations alone may raise for minority applicants a hurdle that does not face white applicants . . . and a (school or employer) dealing with imponderables of this sort ought not to be confined to the choice of either ignoring the problem or attempting the Sisyphean task of discerning its importance on an individual basis." Brief for the United States (Justice Department) as *amicus curiae* at 56, Regents of the University of California v. Bakke, No. 76-811.

13. "Blacks are viewed as a group; they view themselves as a group; their identity is in large part determined by membership in the group; their social status is linked to the status of the group; and much of our action, institutional and personal, is based on these perspectives." Owen Fiss, "Groups and the Equal

Protection Clause," *Philosophy & Public Affairs* (1976), p. 148.

"In my judgment, there is in the United States enough mobility and inter-dependence so that it is proper to take a national view." Greenawalt, op.cit., p. 56.

14. "While it may give minorities a little edge in some instances, and you may run into a danger of what we now commonly call reverse discrimination, I think the educational system needs this. Society needs this as much as the people we are trying to help. . . . a society working toward affirmative action and inclusiveness is going to be a stronger and more relevant society than one that accepts the limited concepts of objectivity. . . . I would admit that it is perhaps an individual injustice. But it might be necessary in order to overcome a historic group injustice or series of group injustices." Andrew Young, *Atlanta Journal and Constitution,* September 22, 1974.

15. " . . . by refusing to allow him [white male applicant] to get the job because of an unfair advantage, preferential hiring makes the competition fairer." B. Boxill, op.cit., p. 266.

"The use of minimum racial, ethnic, religious and sexual quotas as a technique for correcting a serious discrimination in employment is a justifiable means of offsetting past wrongs by temporarily recruiting people from a group which has been discriminated against. . . . the alleged discrimination experienced by the individual white applicant under a system of compensatory treatment is not the same as the discrimination previously suffered by blacks. The white applicant is not being barred from employment because of his race; rather his claim to a particular job is being deferred while a remedy is applied." Memorandum of the Equality Commisison of the *American Civil Liberties Union,* November 29, 1972.

16. Lois Tuckerman Weinberg, "An Answer to the 'Liberal' Objection to Special Admissions," in *Educational Theory* 29 (1979), p. 28.

17. "With adequate education and training, most people might competently perform almost any job, or at least a very large range of jobs." Norman Daniels, "Merit and Meritocracy," *Philosophy & Public Affairs* (1978), p. 219.

18. "The idea of merit must today be broadened to include a variety of other measures of individual potential and ability. . . . it is time to modify our screening practices in employment so as to give greater attention to the capabilities and experience of minorities and women." Feagin and Feagin, op.cit., pp. 172-74.

A similar point is made by R. Wasserstrom, "The University and the Case for Preferential Treatment," *American Philosophical Quarterly* (April 1976), p. 165.

19. It is interesting to note that in two studies it was a concern for potential discrimination, or discrimination against a third party, rather than actual discrimination against the person reporting which the researchers found.

One survey of female employees finds that only 8.1 percent of all working women report discrimination on their job. Of that 8.1 percent, one-half indicated that they felt the discrimination to be slight. "Sex Differences in Compensation," *Journal of Human Resources* (Fall 1971), pp. 434-47.

In the case of blacks, it has been noted: "Despite the fact that a relatively high proportion of (black) men felt that their progress had been equal to or greater than that of comparable whites, the majority of the respondents . . . thought that they did not have equal opportunity with whites in their firm." U.S. Department of Labor, "A Study of Black Male Professionals in Industry," *Manpower Res. Monograph* No. 26 (1973).

CHAPTER 7

1. H. H. Humphrey, *Beyond Civil Rights* (New York: Random House, 1968), pp. 181-82.

2. Ibid., p. 140.

3. Ibid., p. 144.

4. Ibid., p. 120.

5. Casper W. Weinberger, "Regulating the Universities," in *Bureaucrats and Brainpower*, ed. Paul Seabury (San Francisco: Institute for Contemporary Studies, 1979), p. 64.

6. President J. Carter, quoted in the *New York Times*, August 24, 1977.

7. Original draft language (September 12, 1977): "We doubt that it is ever proper to use race to close any portion of the class from competition by members of all races."

8. Nathan Glazer, *Affirmative Discrimination*, p. 71, n. 35.

9. A poll conducted in 1983 by B'nai B'rith found: "73 percent of all respondents . . . disapproved of giving members of minorities special advantages to rectify past discrimination. . . . a majority of the poll's non-white respondents, 52 percent, said that companies should hire the most qualified applicants . . . and should not be required by law to hire a fixed percentage of members of minorities. . . ." An earlier poll by the Harris Organization found that "69 percent of the respondents favored affirmative action provided there were no quotas." Reported in the *New York Times*, September 25, 1983.

10. From 1971 to 1974, 252 students were admitted to Davis Medical School in the regular program. Of these students, 41, or 16 percent, were Asian-Americans, though they are much less than 16 percent of the population either of the U.S. or even of California. Yet, Asian-Americans are officially designated as oppressed.

11. Most of the leadership of the British Labor party consists of middle-class academics. Such leaders are painfully aware of the fact that there is no chance at all of a majority of British voters voting for socialism. Hayward, the national secretary, was quoted as follows: "Proportional representation means coalition government at Westminster on the lines of our European partners, and it would be goodbye then to any dreams or aspirations for a democratic socialist Britain."

12. See Jude P. Dougherty, "The Finding of Law" in *Proceedings of the American Catholic Philosophical Association* (1975), pp. 1-12.

13. Justice Blackmun's opinion in *Bakke* specifically cites Cardoza as well as Woodrow Wilson.

14. For an explicit statement of the view that law is an extension of social science, that legal problems are technical social problems, not moral problems or conflicts or grievances needing adjudication, and the liberal teleological assumption that individuals fulfill themselves in society because of a harmony of interests, see Carlin, Howard, and Messenger, "Civil Justice and the Poor: Issues for Sociological Research" in *Law and the Behavioral Sciences*, ed. Friedman and Macaulay (Indianapolis: Bobbs-Merrill, 1969), p. 192.

15. "Compensation to individuals could not be administered without a racial code and a large-scale procedure for the racial classification of individuals; and that group reparations . . . embrace the equally grave hazards of selecting, with no satisfactory guideposts, the black organizations to participate in the program or creating an official body of black 'representatives' to make these decisions." B. Bittker, *The Case for Black Reparations*, (New York: Random House, 1973), p. 104.

16. For an authoritative and comprehensive analysis of fascism, including

194   Nicholas Capaldi

the alternative explanations for it, see A. James Gregor, *The Ideology of Fascism* (New York: Free Press, 1969) and *The Fascist Persuasion in Radical Politics* (Princeton: Princeton University Press, 1974).

17. Mussolini, "*Che cosa vuole l'America?*" in *Opera* XXVI, 300-02.

18. James Burnham, *The Managerial Revolution* (New York: John Day, 1941), chapter 13.

19. Arthur Schlesinger, Jr., conveniently overlooks all of this in his article, "Sources of the New Deal," in *Paths of American Thought*, ed. Morton White (Boston: Houghton Mifflin, 1963).

20. American intellectuals and liberals impressed by Il Duce included: Lincoln Steffens, *Autobiography* (New York: Harcourt, Brace, 1931), II, 812-20; Herbert W. Schneider, *Making the Fascist State* (New York: H. Fertig, 1928); Charles Beard, review of Schneider, *New Republic*, January 23, 1929; Horace Kallen, "An Apology for Fascism," *New Republic*, January 12, 1927.

For the typical modern liberal position of that period see T. V. Smith, *The Democratic Way of Life* (Chicago: University of Chicago Press, 1926). Herbert Crowley of the *New Republic* saw fascism as a "temporary" stage.

21. An insightful exception to all this is Karl Radek: "Fascism is middle-class socialism. . . . " "Communism and Fascism," *Living Age* (September 29, 1923), pp. 585-87.

22. An interesting case is Franco. Franco did represent the conservative right, but he used the Falange, which was ultimately absorbed and eliminated.

Baran and Sweezy recognize that the "ruling capitalist oligarchy" are not the perpetrators of fascism; rather, it is individuals who feel "excluded" from the establishment. Paul Baran and Paul Sweezy, *Monopoly Capital* (New York: *Monthly Review*, 1966). See also L. Huberman and Sweezy, "Goldwaterism" in *Monthly Review* (1964), pp. 273-283.

23. Recent liberal analyses of fascism have tended to identify it as an ideology of delayed industrialization. The most influential such work is W. W. Rostow, *The Stages of Economic Growth* (1960). A. F. K. Organsky has a similar thesis. The idea seems to be that fascism delays full development in order to serve the old elites. Not only is this false—Italy experienced remarkable growth under fascism—but fascists replaced the old establishment and exercised a form of control over the economy and the political system far greater than any traditional regime ever had. The really major objection to this kind of liberal interpretation is that in the case of Nazi Germany, the Nazis took power in an industrially mature (fully developed) economy, not in a developing country. The appearance of fascism subsequent to the failure of the Weimar Republic requires liberal theoreticians to argue that Nazism is not fascism but an aberration.

24. Recent scholarship has finally begun to locate fascism on the left and to see it as the descendent of totalitarian democracy. In the classic study of that title, Talmon pointed out that revolutionary democrats of the eighteenth century saw their task as creating a new kind of man, with a new mentality and values and sensitiveness. Renzo DeFelice, Italy's leading historian of fascism, has argued that it was precisely fascism's intent to create a new man. In another study, Ledeen has pointed out how Mussolini was the heir to the followers of D'Annunzio, and it was D'Annunzio who argued for the liberation of oppressed peoples and for the creation of new unalienated man.

25. Mussolini, "*L'uono e la divinità,*" *Opera* XXXIII, 22. Gentile, *Genesi e struttura della società* (Florence, 1946), quoted in Gregor, op.cit., p. 209.

26. Gentile, *Origini e dottorina del fascismo* (Rome, 1929), p. 59. quoted in Gregor, op.cit., pp. 222-23.

27. Ubaldi, "*Per una realistica filosofia del fascismo,*" *Gerarchia* XVIII

(September,1938), pp. 620-21.
28. B. Bittker, op.cit., p. 131.
29. In 1979, AT&T published in its employee magazine a debate on affirmative action between Sidney Hook and Daniel C. Maguire, professor of theology at Marquette University. Maguire's remarks appear on pp. 22-23, and p. 26.
30. Ibid.
31. Ibid.
32. Ibid.
33. Ibid.
34. Ibid.
35. Ibid.
36. B. Boxill, op.cit., p. 256.
37. Derrick Bell, Harvard Law School's first black professor: "Assuring numerical minorities adequate participation in governing bodies is a well-recognized, accepted practice used by our political parties (and by the new Zimbabwe Government, where whites are represented in disproportionate numbers). Blacks must be guaranteed proportionate representation in our government on all policy-making levels whether appointed or elected." Op-ed, "Reagan and Black Rights," *New York Times,* November 25, 1980).
38. One of the few people to recognize the dangers in the ethnic revival is Orlando Patterson, professor of sociology at Harvard and author of *Ethnic Chauvinsim: The Reactionary Impulse* (New York: Stein and Day, 1977). The following is a quote from Patterson: "Thus the call for a diversity of cohesive, tightly knit groups actually amounts to an assault on the deeply entrenched principle of individualism." Moreover, "The fact that the ethnic revival is largely ideological should not lead us to underestimate it. We know from the history of ethnic movements that ideology, under the right circumstances, can transform reality. European fascism was first and foremost an ideological movement, and, in a disturbing parallel with modern America, fascist ideology had its roots in the romantic revolt against the Enlightenment—a revolt that, in its early phases, was generally liberal, very concerned with the social and human costs of 'progress,' and espoused the principle of ethnic pluralism."
39. Derrick Bell, "The Referendum: Democracy's Barrier to Racial Equality," *Washington Law Review* 54 (1978-79), pp. 1-29.
40. Consider the alternative interpretation by Nathan Glazer, *Affirmative Discrimination,* pp. 192-94.

The differences between the Italian and East European neighborhoods and the black neighborhoods expanding into them cannot be wished away: the first emphasize strongly a neighborhood-centered, family-centered, job-centered life, respect for authority, close attachment to local institutions. Most intrusions would in any case be seen as a threat. . . . It may well be true that black styles of life respond to black experience, that is, oppression and discrimination, but that will not ease matters. . . .
   There is a second factor that introduces a special tension between the later white ethnic groups and blacks: the comparison of experience. From the point of view of the white ethnics, they entered a society in which they were scorned; they nevertheless worked hard, they received little or no support from government or public agencies, their children received no special attention in school or special opportunity to attend college, they received no special consideration from courts and legal defenders. They contrast their situation with that of blacks and other minority groups today and see substantial differences in treatment. They consider themselves patriotic and appreciative of the United States even though they received no special benefit. They look at the minority groups and find them abusive of the state though

they do receive special benefit. This may be crude and unfair comparison. . . . But the perception cannot be dismissed as false. . . .

41. Bell, op.cit., p. 10.
42. Ibid., p. 11.
43. Ibid., p. 25.
44. O'Neil, op.cit., p. 158. It should be added that there are institutional factors in perpetuating quotas: the need for affirmative action bureaucrats to justify their job, potential law suits and damage claims, the pressure to replace minority failures with other minority candidates which makes it economically more attractive to keep the first person in whom so much has already been invested.
45. William T. Coleman, Jr. "Equality—Not Yet," op-ed in the *New York Times,* July 13, 1981. Mr. Coleman was secretary of transportation, 1975-77, and is currently chairman of the NAACP Legal Defense and Education Fund.

CHAPTER 8

1. In the original plan and draft of the book I included a chapter on the historical development of the philosophy of liberalism from Hobbes, Locke, and Smith to the present. When that chapter began to exceed a hundred pages it became clear that it would have to be a subject for another book. Reluctantly I had to eliminate it. I say reluctantly because the dialectic of that development strikingly illustrated many of the elements of the issues that emerged in the debate over affirmative action.

In the meantime, I can suggest the following books to the interested reader. The best description of liberalism as an ideology and a state of mind is Kenneth Minogue's *The Liberal Mind;* the best accounts of its development in the nineteenth century are Elie Halevy, *The Growth of Philosophic Radicalism* and V. C. Dicey, *Law and Public Opinion in England in the Nineteenth Century;* for the important transition from classical to modern liberalism see Stefan Collini, *Liberalism and Sociology: L. T. Hobhouse and Political Argument in England 1880-1914.* For an insightful look at how the notion of a perfect system was bequeathed from classical liberals to modern liberals see James Buchanan and Gordon Tullock, *The Calculus of Consent.*

2. The defeat of Lord Asquith's government led to the Tory vs. socialist split and the end of classical liberalism in Britain. Asquith had been T. H. Green's student.

3. Leonard Hobhouse, *Metaphysical Theory of the State* (1918), p. 133.

4. R. O'Neil, op.cit., p. 149.

5. The recent controversy stirred up by the publication of Derek Freeman's book, *Margaret Mead and Samoa: The Making and Unmasking of an Anthropological Myth* (Cambridge, Mass.: Harvard University Press, 1983) is an example of what happens when someone challenges the ideology of modern liberalism in social science.

INDEX

Goodman, Ellen, 74
Goodman, Walter, 186
Graglia, Lino A., 188
Green, T. H., 170-71, 191, 196
Greenawalt, Kent, 190, 192
Greene, Graham, 1
Gregor, A. James, 194
Griggs v. *Duke Power Company*, 33, 37, 39, 96, 142
group entitlement, 4, 5, 22, 24, 25, 142, 146, 152, 156, 158, 164, 165
Gulag Archipelago, 27

Halevy, Elie, 196
Hamilton, C. V., 186
Hannah, John A., 61, 185
Harlan, John Marshall, 8, 31
Harper, William Rainey, 61
Harris, Patricia Roberts, 47
Harvard Law Review, 82
Harvard University, 45, 62, 82, 87
Hatch Act of 1887, 59-60
Hatch, Orrin, 49, 183-84
The Heart of the Matter, 1
Hegel, G. W. F., 128, 170-71, 173
HEW, 4, 14, 16, 41, 44, 45, 47, 77, 78, 79, 80, 82, 85-87, 94, 96, 98, 99. 101, 150, 161
hidden variable argument, 11, 13, 18, 66, 69, 87, 126, 130
Higher Learning in America, 54
historicism, 21, 32
Hobbes, Thomas, 170, 173, 182
Hobhouse, L. T., 170-71, 172, 196
Holmes, Peter, 95
Hook, Sidney, 13, 14-16, 195
Hufstedler, Shirley M., 74
Humphrey, Hubert H., 28, 46, 141-43, 146, 183, 193

ideally integrated school, 11-12
ideally integrated society, 30-31, 32, 48, 117
The Idea of a University, 54
International Brotherhood of Teamsters v. *United States*, 39, 43
interventionism. *See* state activism

Jefferson, Thomas, 60
Jeffries, Leonard, 93
Jencks, Christopher, 107, 187
Jensen, Arthur, 182-83
Jim Crow laws, 4, 7, 8, 9, 11, 16, 121, 184

Johnson, Lyndon B., 29, 141, 143, 146
Jones, Nathaniel R., 13, 182
judicial review, 35, 184

Kaiser Aluminum, 48
Kennedy, John F., 29, 141, 144
Kerner Commission, 11, 12, 144
Kerr, Clark, 53, 61, 62, 64-65, 79, 182, 185, 186
Ketchum, Sara Ann, 191
Khomeni, Ayatollah, 122
King, Martin Luther, 10
Kirkpatrick, Jeane, 110
Kristol, Irving, 70, 186
Ku Klux Klan, 7

Land Grant Act of 1862, 59
law school, 111-14
Lekachman, Robert, 70, 186
Lesser, Gerald, 95
Lester, Richard A., 89, 186, 187
Lewis, Anthony, 74
liberal culture (and the university), 53, 54, 55, 57, 59, 69, 73, 168
liberalism, 17, 18, 29, 32, 35, 41, 42, 46, 48, 58, 65, 67, 68, 75, 78, 80, 81, 83, 88, 89, 90, 92, 94, 98, 107, 109, 110, 112, 116, 124, 139, 149, 150, 156, 182, 190; alternative versions of, 125-26; history of, 167-78; bibliography on, 196; and cultural relativism, 86-87; and freedom, 126; and higher education, 70-74; and prejudice, 90-91; and totalitarianism, 128, 162. *See also* social science
liberalism, classical, 80, 99, 137, 139, 154, 155, 157; defined 170. *See also* meritocracy
liberalism, doctrinaire, 2, 3, 4, 5, 6, 13, 19, 61, 62, 70, 82, 93, 104, 117, 121, 133, 140, 146, 153, 154, 159, 168-69, 175, 179, 191; working definition, 19-21
liberalism, modern, 7, 59, 64, 80, 81, 82, 84, 86, 99, 132, 140, 144, 150, 151, 156, 168, 174, 196; defined 170. *See also* elitism, egalitarianism, doctrinaire liberalism
Lincoln, Abraham, 60
Lipset, Seymour Martin and Ladd, Everett C., 70, 186
Locke, John, 126
Los Angeles Times, 45
Luther, Martin, 52

www.ingramcontent.com/pod-product-compliance
Lightning Source LLC
Chambersburg PA
CBHW051725260326
41914CB00031B/1750/J